A Postmodern Theology
of Ritual Action

A Postmodern Theology of Ritual Action

An Exploration of Foot Washing among
the Original Free Will Baptist Community

By JONATHAN L. BEST

PICKWICK *Publications* · Eugene, Oregon

A POSTMODERN THEOLOGY OF RITUAL ACTION
An Exploration of Foot Washing among the Original Free Will Baptist
Community

Pickwick Publications
An Imprint of Wipf and Stock Publishers
199 W. 8th Ave., Suite 3
Eugene, OR 97401

www.wipfandstock.com

PAPERBACK ISBN: 978-1-5326-4953-0
HARDCOVER ISBN: 978-1-5326-4954-7
EBOOK ISBN: 978-1-5326-4955-4

Cataloging-in-Publication data:

Names: Best, Jonathan L, author.

Title: A postmodern theology of ritual action: an exploration of foot washing among the Original Free Will Baptist community / by Jonathan L. Best.

Description: Eugene, OR : Pickwick Publications, 2019 | Includes bibliographical references.

Identifiers: ISBN 978-1-5326-4953-0 (paperback) | ISBN 978-1-5326-4954-7 (hardcover) | ISBN 978-1-5326-4955-4 (ebook)

Subjects: LCSH: Free Will Baptists (1727–1935). | Foot washing (Rite). | Ritual.

Classification: LCC BX6367 B3 2019 (print) | LCC BX6367 (ebook)

Manufactured in the U.S.A.   02/25/19

To my wife and daughter

Contents

Acknowledgments

I WANT TO EXTEND a general thank you to the people of the Original Free Will Baptist denomination. I am forever indebted to love and support. It is my hope and prayer that my work brings to light your humble spirit, service, and love. I also want to extend a special thank you to the people at Free Union OFWB, Pinetown, NC. You helped to raise me into the man I am today.

To my mother and father, Carney and Peggy Best, words cannot express how much you mean to me. I am very blessed to have such loving and supportive parents. In your own gentle and loving way, you have always encouraged me to do my very best. You have always given me the confidence I need to succeed, yet more importantly, you taught me how to live and love others. This work belongs to you as much as it does to me.

Finally, I wish to thank my dear and wonderful wife Rebekah Whitley Best. Reading and writing is often a lonesome and burdensome task, even more so for one's spouse. I hope that this victory will pave the way for a bright and happy future shared together. My success is our success, and this work is yours as well as mine. You, more than any philosopher or theologian, have taught me the value of being-with. Being, existence itself, is best shared. I look forward to a continued future of being-with you. All my love, passion, and strength I give to you as your husband.

Introduction

RITUAL ACTION AS A PROBLEM

IN THIS WORK, I explore ritual action[1] as a complex philosophical, theological, and social problem. I consider this complexity and its connection to human activity. Deciphering human behavior is difficult enough, but even further difficulties arise when we consider the relationship between action and religion. Therefore, ritual action confronts us with a multitude of social and theological questions. Sociological questions converge with questions of metaphysics, semiotics, theology, God, and many more. Religion complicates action, which leads us toward a dizzying array of approaches and positions. For theologians, this movement between these conflicting and polarizing positions is akin to navigating a difficult maze. Walls, both old and new, continue to block our way. Along the way, several approaches promise us a way forward toward clarity: metaphysics, theology, mathematics, aesthetics, and even psychoanalysis.

Tragically, religious practitioners suffer the most from the theologian's maze. As theologians navigate this maze, they continually offer the promise and claim to know what religious practitioners believe and understand. Without consideration or humility, the *experts* claim to speak for religious communities and congregations. Thus, religious communities must endure experts who claim to know what *their* ritual actions mean and why they do them.

It matters little if the expert is a theologian, philosopher, or social theorist. Ultimately, he or she is an outsider. Yet, these experts fail to deliver the

---

1. *Ritual action* supports the connection between ritual and action. Catherin Bell defines this term as a ritual that "involves interaction with its immediate world, often drawing it into the very activity of the rite in multiple ways." She divides ritual action into six categories where "action is primarily communal, traditional (that is, understood as carrying on ways of acting established in the past), and rooted in beliefs in divine beings of some sort." Bell, *Ritual*, 94, 266.

1

clarity they promised. Instead, experts ignore the religious community as he or she confidently plunges us all into their carefully constructed mazes. Ironically, the religious practitioners should be leading the experts, and yet their voices are missing. Experts miss what these ritual actions mean to practitioners. Consequently, the key to the maze is in ritual action itself because religious practitioners already know what their actions mean. Religious communities already possess profound theological and social clarity about their ritual actions. The practitioners of action understand the maze, and they should be leading the experts. Ritual action is already meaningful with rich theological and religious significance.[2] The experts do not impart meaning, people do.

Previous ways of interpreting action only provide a partial view for understanding the role of action in Christian practice. Other ways to interpret ritual action, such as metaphysics, semiotics, and ritual studies, fail to bridge the gap between theory and practice in the lives of Christian communities.[3] Therefore, I consider meaning and its expression as a theological problem. Thus, I seek to answer two important questions. Where is meaning found in ritual action? How do Christian communities express this meaning?

Like Wittgenstein's search for meaning in language, there is a need to do the same for ritual action. Wittgenstein offers us a model for approaching ritual action. He suggests that our task is to "bring words back from their metaphysical to their everyday use,"[4] which moves us away from the speculative and theoretical. It eliminates the temptation to give or find meaning from the outside. Meaning has been present all along in the lived expressions of human interaction and activity.[5]

2. Vasquez, *More than Belief*, 117.

3. Swinton and Mowat, *Practical Theology*, 26.

4. Wittgenstein, *Philosophical Investigations*, 48.

5. According to Wittgenstein, "Philosophy simply puts everything before us, and neither explains nor deduces anything. —Since everything lies open to view there is nothing to explain. For what is hidden, for example, is of no interest to us. . . . The aspects of things that are most important for us are hidden because of their simplicity and familiarity. (One is unable to notice something—because it is always before one's eyes.) The real foundations of his [or her] enquiry do not strike a man [or woman] at all. Unless *that* fact has at some time struck him.—And this means: we fail to be struck by what, once seen, is most striking and most powerful." Wittgenstein, *Philosophical Investigations*, 50.

Problematizing Ritual Theory

Ritual action poses difficult interdisciplinary challenges for theologians, philosophers, and social theorists. This is the challenge of how we approach, converse, and interpret ritual action given the complexities of human behavior. At the root of this complexity is the question of the origin of meaning. Does meaning come from an outside source, such as a doctrine or theory, or does it arise within action itself? My work explores and advocates for the idea that ritual action is already meaningful within itself. Ritual action is meaningful by virtue of the behaviors, stories, and relationships of the community.

A practical theological lens offers us a means to explore ritual action through the values stories, behaviors, and overall experiences of religious practitioners in community.[6] Practical theology helps us move away from speculative theology and philosophy, and instead focus on concrete action. Therefore, I suggest that the basis for interpretation is that meaning is found in action itself and not from an external source.[7]

This is not how some scholarship approaches how ritual action. Catherine Bell notes that ritual action may become separated from the conceptual aspects of religion, and hence treated as something secondary or arbitrary.[8] In this perspective, rituals act out concepts and beliefs, doing little to shape religious belief. Another approach separates ritual and action, thus making ritual action "a mechanism for integrating thought and action."[9] Ritual bridges the enormous gap that exists between beliefs and action. Ritual becomes the way "individual perception and behavior are socially appropriated or conditioned."[10] Such approaches treat ritual as a secondary object, separated from thought and belief.

---

6. In Swinton and Mowat's words, "Practical Theology is critical, theological reflection on the practices of the Church as they interact with the practices of the world, with a view to ensuring and enabling faithful participation in God's redemptive practices in, to and for the world." Swinton and Mowat, *Practical Theology*, 6.

7. Ritual action is the lived language of its participants. The search for meaning outside action itself is a about a dead rather than a living language. Wittgenstein states, "Every sign *by itself* seems dead. *What* gives it life? In use it is alive." Wittgenstein, *Philosophical Investigations*, 128.

8. Catherine Bell is especially critical of theoretical descriptions that treat ritual in this way. Beliefs are given priority over ritual turning it into "thoughtless action—routinized, habitual, obsessive, or mimetic—and therefore the purely formal, secondary, and mere physical expression of logically prior ideas." Bell, *Ritual Theory*, 19.

9. Bell, *Ritual Theory*, 20.

10. Bell cites Durkheim as an example of this kind of approach. Bell, *Ritual Theory*, 20.

Historically, Mircea Eliade represents these approaches. For him, myths and symbols provide a better picture of the religious experience than ritual. Ritual functions on a different level than symbols and myths. According to Eliade, ritual is arbitrary and bound to change, while the original symbol or myth stays the same.[11] Sacred myths are the ultimate foundation for *homo religiosus*[12] so the "one becomes truly a [human] only by conforming to the teaching of the myths, that is, by imitating the gods."[13] For Eliade, the acting out of myths is a sacred activity that brings us closer to the divine. The rituals are replaceable, but the foundational myths are not. Action is imitation and remembering, so that the "whole religious life is a commemoration, a remembering."[14] Life is sacred because of its connection to a sacred origin, and this sacred origin is re-enacted repeatedly to connect us to the transcendental realm. Consequently, action only has value to the extent that it manifests the transcendental realm.[15] Ritual and reality are completely dependent on the myth, the conceptual, for its content. Beliefs reign supreme, and religion becomes a "secondary expression of these very beliefs, symbols, and ideas."[16] Ritual as reenactment presents a top down model of religious experience. This view considers ritual action as inconsequential to meaning and the practice of religion.

Clifford Geertz, sometimes considered a precursor to postmodernism,[17] breaks us away from Eliade by incorporating "semiotics, hermeneutics, and practice into the study of religion."[18] Geertz moves away from ritual as reenactment. Instead, he focuses on the way religious practices make meaning. Ritual practices requires us to make a "thick description"[19] in order

---

11. This is not only characteristic of Eliade, but of phenomenologists generally. As Bell notes, Phenomenologists saw "more stability, even eternality, in the structures underlying myth." Bell, *Ritual*, 10.

12. Eliade frequently uses this term to describe the religious person.

13. Eliade, *Sacred and Profane*, 100.

14. Eliade, *Sacred and Profane*, 101.

15. For Eliade, everything connects to the time of origins. The task of ritual action is to overcome and subdue the present moment. Meaning does not occur in the present moment or with the religious participants. Rather, meaning occurs in the past. Thus, we access the divine by ignoring the present to manifest the past. According to Eliade, the task is "reactualizing sacred history, by imitating the divine behavior, [one] puts and keeps [oneself] close to the gods—that is the real and the significant." Eliade, *Sacred and Profane*, 202.

16. Bell, *Ritual*, 11.

17. Vasquez, *More than Belief*, 212.

18. Vasquez, *More than Belief*, 211.

19. Clifford Geertz makes the case that a good interpretation of "anything—a poem, a person, a history, a ritual, an institution, a society—takes us into the heart of that of

to delve deeper into their meaning. He focuses exclusively on a semiotic analysis of ritual actions that "understands all human practices through the prism of representation and signification."[20] He reduces religion to an act of communicating and sharing meaningful information through its symbols. Consequently, interpretation of any ritual action becomes a manner of decoding its symbols. The practices and experiences that make these symbols are considered secondary.[21]

Geertz describes symbols as areas where meaning is stored. Therefore, ritual activity does not contain meaning in itself. Rituals dramatize the meaning contained within religious symbols.[22] Religious symbols create a system of meaning, which "seems to mediate genuine knowledge, knowledge of the essential conditions in terms of which life must, of necessity, be lived."[23] Thus, religious symbols form the social worldview, thereby creating ways in which these values are lived. The force of these religious symbols is strong enough to eliminate human interpretation and preference in ritual. We sacrifice the subjective using an imposed structure.[24] In this view, symbols define religion.[25] Symbols define meaningful action rather than practice, resulting in a "one-dimensional view of religion."[26] Geetz's approach ultimately results in an excessive amount of textualism that understands religious practices through a social-scientific language.[27]

---

which it is the interpretation. When it does not do that, but leads us instead somewhere else—into admiration of its own elegance, of its author's cleverness. . .it is something else than what the task at hand . . . calls for." Geertz, *Interpretation of Cultures*, 18.

20. Vasquez, *More than Belief*, 212.

21. Vasquez states, "Geertz reduces religion to signification, to its semiotic function, which becomes a precondition for meaningful practice. For Geertz, the power of religion is not in the situated practices that authorize it as an autonomous and efficacious field of human activity." Vasquez, *More than Belief*, 214.

22. Geertz, *Interpretation of Cultures*, 127.

23. Geertz, *Interpretation of Cultures*, 129.

24. Geertz values religious symbols at the expense of human action and imagination. The meanings stored in symbols provide an objective, or universal, guideline for behavior. He suggests that all cultures desire the need for some factual basis in its religious commitments. Geertz, *Interpretation of Cultures*, 131.

25. Geertz defines religion as "(1) a system of symbols which acts to (2) establish powerful, pervasive, and long-lasting moods and motivations in [humans] by (3) formulating conceptions of a general order of existence and (4) clothing these conceptions with such an aura of factuality that (5) the moods and motivations seem uniquely realistic." Geertz, *Interpretation of Cultures*, 90.

26. Vasquez, *More than Belief*, 220.

27. Vasquez criticizes Geertz for treating all religious activity as a text. The textuality of religious practices is Geertz's interpretative framework. As texts, their symbolic systems are decoded to discover their meaning. While Vasquez is critical of Geertz's

Geertz is not alone in his emphasis on symbols at the expense of action. Other well-known ritual theorists share the same perspective.[28] Such an approach gives little thought "to how rituals themselves change or to why a community's sense of appropriate ritual changes."[29] Ritual is a way of acting and doing certain activities, which distinguishes it from other behaviors. Ritual action is therefore a practice and "must be taken as a non-synthetic and irreducible term for human activity."[30] Ritual action is above all the practice of participants. As a practice, ritual action is comprised of certain defining characteristics.[31] These characteristics form a way of behavior, called ritualization,[32] which differentiates it from other actions. Ritual action, as ritualization, involves "nuanced contrasts and the evocation of strategic, value-laden distinctions."[33]

The way actions are deployed matter as much as the actions themselves. Symbolic heavy approaches miss this. When symbols are treated as systems of belief, analysis misses the strategic and nuanced nature of ritual action. Boundaries are blurred by the actions of everyday ritual actors. Ritual actors have a voice in how symbols and myths are employed. Ritualization does not merely act out a program. It involves complex interactions and exchanges with a multitude of behaviors.[34]

Ritual marks out a difference between the ordinary and extraordinary in daily life, highlighting the way things could or should be.[35] It is an assertion of difference between the conflicting spheres of the everyday and the

textual approach, he is not saying that we cannot consider how action acts as a text. Vasquez is criticizing approaches that ground all action and behavior as a text, becoming "the alpha and omega of practices." Vasquez, *More than Belief*, 219.

28. Catherine Bell describes two general approaches toward ritual since the start of the twentieth century. The first approach examines the role of ritual in maintaining social groups. The second approach, which Geertz represents, examines the role ritual plays in adapting ideals and traditions to changing social conditions. See Bell "Ritual, Change, Changing Rituals," 168.

29. Bell "Ritual, Change, Changing Rituals," 168.

30. Bell, *Ritual Theory*, 81.

31. Bell helpfully names the four features of practice as 1) situational, 2) strategic, 3) embedded in misrecognition, and 4) the will to act. Bell, *Ritual Theory*, 80.

32. Bell defines ritualization as production of differentiation. It is a "way of acting that specifically establishes a privileged contrast, differentiating itself as more important or powerful." Bell, *Ritual Theory*, 89.

33. Bell, *Ritual Theory*, 89.

34. Bell strongly advocates, "Ritual should not be analyzed by being lifted out of the context formed by other ways of acting in a cultural situation. Acting ritual is first and foremost a matter of nuanced contrasts and the evocation of strategic, value-laden distinctions." Bell, *Ritual Theory*, 89.

35. Smith, *To Take Place*, 109.

ritual. Ritual action is not a mechanical process, instead its improvisation and innovation uses the ordinary in extraordinary ways.[36] Ritual action is produced and characterized by this differentiation.[37]

Ritual action is more than a "negative by product or, one might say, waste product, immediately discarded, of the construction of the systems of objective relations."[38] Practice is never accidental or reducible as structuralism and other objectivistic approaches would have it. The practice of action is the key to its meaning.[39]

The search for universally acceptable definitions distorts and undercuts the meanings already visible in ritual actions. Such a search for universals only confuses and creates a need for further categories "to account for all the data that do not fit neatly into the domain of the original term."[40] As a result, the search for meaning turns from ritual action and instead looks at everything besides the ritual itself. As the search moves further away from ritual action, we must take greater leaps of logic and rational thinking to account for anomalies.[41]

AIM AND SCOPE

This work is an in-depth theological and philosophical conversation that seeks a better approach toward meaning within ritual action. Using the interdisciplinary approach of practical theology, this work incorporates

36. Smith makes the case that ritual thrives in difference and improvisation. He states, "Ritual precises ambiguities; it neither overcomes nor relaxes them. Ritual, concerned primarily with difference, is, necessarily, an affair of the relative. . . . In ritual, the differences can be extreme, or they can be reduced to microdistinctions—but they can never be overthrown. The system can never come to rest." Smith, *To Take Place*, 110.

37. According to Bell, ritualization "involves the very drawing, in and through activity itself, of a privileged distinction between way of acting, specifically between those acts being performed and those being contrasted, mimed, or implicated somehow . . . ritualization is a way of acting that specifically establishes a privileged contrast, differentiating itself as more important or powerful." Bell, *Ritual Theory*, 90.

38. Bourdieu, *Outline of a Theory*, 24.

39. Bourdieu is very candid about the limits of semiotics, linguistics, and other structuralist approaches. He claims that "Saussurian linguistics privileges the *structure* of signs, that is, the relations between them, at the expense of the *practical functions*, which are never reducible, as structuralism tacitly assumes, to functions of communication or knowledge. Bourdieu, *Outline of a Theory*, 24.

40. Bell, *Ritual Theory*, 70.

41. Thus, Bell claims, "a good deal of writing about ritual involves extensive exercise in cleaning up all the data and terms that are not included in the main definition." Bell, *Ritual Theory*, 69. Theology, in particular, seems to thrive on cleaning up data and terms that do not fit in neat categories.

hermeneutics and postmodern philosophy. I give particular focus to both deconstruction and social theory. Postmodern in tone and approach, my work is an effort to show how we might open a dialogue between scholars and religious communities. As an interdisciplinary work of practical theology, I suggest that meaning belongs to the community, and communal actions are meaningful through the behaviors, stories, and relationships of the community. I demonstrate this by engaging the Original Free Will Baptists (OFWB), a small denomination in Eastern North Carolina, and their practice of foot washing.

There is little work or research on either the Original Free Will Baptists or foot washing. In terms of theology, very little has been published on the Original Free Will Baptists, a group active in North Carolina since the sixteenth century. Combine this with the gap that exists in foot washing scholarship, and my research addresses an important need in theology and philosophy. The combination makes this a completely new and original work in aim and scope.

Using qualitative research, along with hermeneutical and postmodern tools, I converse with the OFWB narrative. I hope to provide a new lens for viewing ritual action, one that offers a new perspective on the problem of meaning, its place in communities, and how the community shares that meaning with others.

OUTLINE AND CHAPTER SUMMARIES

In chapter 1, "Hermeneutics and Ritual Action," I propose that ritual action requires that we investigate the various issues and difficulties involved in interpreting action. This investigation includes an awareness of the general difficulties in interpretation and a better sense of the hermeneutical scope. Hermeneutics refocuses our attention back toward action itself. Thus, it makes an outside theory, theology, or philosophy unnecessary for approaching action. Hans-Georg Gadamer and Paul Ricoeur are particularly important for understanding interpretation, including parallels between text and actions. I argue that hermeneutics is a gateway toward a better position for observing and conversing with ritual action. Most importantly, hermeneutical tools help to demonstrate that ritual action is a language, one that speaks through participant gestures and experiences. In this chapter, I suggest that the interpreter does not need to speak for ritual action. Instead, the interpreter must listen. However, hermeneutics alone is not enough for this listening. Going further requires us to move toward deconstruction.

Chapter 2, "Learning to Listen," widens the conversation. Here I develop a premise that theologians should cultivate skills for listening to ritual action. Listening requires us to use deconstruction, which continues the process begun by hermeneutics. Deconstruction represents a positive endeavor helping to open interpretation into new fields and places within conversation. Because meaning is instable and continual adapts, greater openness toward this instability provides us with a means to engage ritual action at an ethnographic level. Here I use both Jacques Derrida and John Caputo as promoters of *weak thought*. Weak thought represents an important counter to strong concepts and ideas such as structuralism. Weakness places the interpreter on the side of the interpreted, and this includes a willingness to meet practitioners in their lived experience. Weakness connects to the event of ritual action, which consists of the indescribable and unpredictable in action. Having prepared the way, deconstruction moves us toward a conversation with the Original Free Will Baptists and their practice of foot washing.

Chapter 3, "A Conversation with the Original Free Will Baptists," presents the Original Free Baptist narrative. Pivoting between methodology and practice, the Original Free Will Baptist narrative is a guide for encountering and conversing with ritual action. This narrative provides the pathway for further listening and conversation. The Original Free Will Baptist have little in the way of a written theology on foot washing. This, combined with their small size, relative obscurity, and lack of previous studies, make this community a perfect candidate for listening and conversation. These factors highlight the need to engage the lived experience of the Original Free Will Baptists. I used qualitative approaches to gather their narrative into a written from. Through interviews, focus groups, and observation, I present the Original Free Will Baptist narrative using the participants. Foot washing represents the Original Free Will Baptist identity, an identity built on humility, service, and love. This identity becomes the catalyst for theological reflection.

In chapter 4, "Relation, Space, Story, and Action," I go deeper by engaging and exploring how foot washing has shaped the Christian experience of Original Free Will Baptists. Using postmodern philosophy and social theory as guides, my focus shifts toward understanding how their narrative speaks today.[42] I amplify their narrative of foot washing as a model for contemporary Christian practice. I partner postmodern thinkers such as Jean-Luc Nancy, Pierre Bourdieu, and Henri Lefebvre with the Original Free Will

---

42. I use postmodern philosophy and social theory as guides to help me listen to the Original Free Will Baptist story. Neither approaches are prerequisites to conversation. Instead both help to foster and encourage uninhibited dialogue.

Baptist story. Thus, I demonstrate how the Original Free Will Baptist story models, exemplifies, and expands the ideas of these thinkers.[43] For example, I suggest that Original Free Will Baptists live both Bourdieu's *habitus* and Nancy's *being-with* in ways that go beyond both. Foot washing establishes relationship, prescribes action, contains networks of relationship, and lives in the everyday lives of participants. So much so that it becomes the Original Free Will Baptist identity. As identity, its interpretation is secondary to its practice. Therefore, this chapter shifts our conversation from analysis and toward understanding how this story speaks today.

Chapter 5, "Love and Community," moves our conversation toward love and grace. This is an important and critical shift for establishing a relational practical theology. Foot washing's theology points to an overcoming of estrangement, acceptance for the other, and the reunion of the estranged. Foot washing correlates with much of the theology of Paul Tillich, Karl Barth, and Dietrich Bonhoeffer. It illustrates Christian life, love, and community. I propose that foot washing, as practiced by Original Free Will Baptists, accepts the other and proclaims the message of Jesus Christ. Therefore, they show us how to create a new community. This is the community where the singular *I* is brought into a communion of *being-with*, where love and grace is a living expression of Nancy's *being-singular-plural*. The narrative reveals the possibility of a community that unequivocally accepts the other. Foot washing is an acceptance of the other. In opening the self for the other, we are by implication opening ourselves toward Christ. The Original Free Will Baptist narrative offers a new ecclesiology built upon a new Christ-reality, a reality of love.

Chapter 6, "Toward a Relational Practical Theology," concludes this conversation with the reality of love. Love, as modeled by foot washing, offers interesting possibilities for the future. The most important possibility is the necessity of relationality in ritual action. Martin Buber's seminal work, *I and Thou*, severs as our basis for a future theological, philosophical, and social engagement with ritual action. This relationality critiques theological methods that are detached from lived experience and contemporary context. Here I suggest instead that theology is a relationship. Furthermore, it is an encounter with the *Thou*, making theology an encounter rather than a discipline. In this view, theology is a matter of acting, working, and being-with the other. Ritual action models this encounter, drawing our gaze toward the other. Ritual action holds the key for encounter, positioning us toward the

---

43. In many ways, the Original Free Will Baptists are already living out the ideas and concepts of many philosophers and theologians. Remarkably, they do not do this by reading and applying a theory. Their practices go beyond theory and into a lived praxis.

eternal *thou*. Foot washing demonstrates why ritual action should speak on its own terms. The Original Free Will Baptist experience is a model of this openness and is necessary for a relational practical theology.

THE GOAL OF THE CONVERSATION

This work is a practical theology that considers the practices of people as essential, relevant, and necessary for understanding how God works in community. As a practical theology, I anticipate that my research will intersect and influence several fields outside of practical theology. Thus, I endeavor to show how practical theology can provide deep theological and philosophical engagement with contemporary culture.

As Wittgenstein moved the search for meaning back to the usage of words, my work seeks to do the same for ritual action. I share his conviction that "What we do is to bring words back from their metaphysical to their everyday use."[44] This focus on ritual action, which eliminates our temptation to find meaning from the outside, shows us that meaning was neither missing nor hidden. Instead, meaning was present all along in the lived expressions that comprise human interaction and activity. What should be of interest to theology and is people. This is what this work contributes. It acknowledges that people ought to be our source of theological reflection. It is with people that new discoveries and possibilities await.

44. Wittgenstein, *Philosophical Investigations*, 48.

CHAPTER ONE

Hermeneutics and Ritual Action

THE DIFFICULTY OF INTERPRETATION

INTERPRETATION IS NEVER AN easy task. It is a complex process of exploring people and their actions. Meaning is not self-evident. Instead, meaning may appear as self-contradictory or completely absent in certain situations. The complexities of human action and behavior do not always lend themselves to clear and apparent meanings. This is especially so for religious meaning. It is a truism to say that religious texts and actions are difficult to discern. There is a need for interpretation that delves into the heart of practice and respects the integrity of such practices. Interpretation that seriously considers the interpreted, without recourse to something outside action itself.

All narrative or literary objects are estranged from their author and context. It is futile to attempt a reconstruction of the original world or its author.[1] Consequently, this estrangement functions on many levels and is a major barrier in interpretation. Historical distancing is an ongoing process that makes the job of interpretation ongoing.[2] Once born, history affects

1. Ricoeur suggests, "What the text signifies no longer coincides with what the author meant; henceforth, textual meaning and psychological meaning have different destinies." Ricoeur, "Hermeneutical Function," 139.

2. Historical distancing affects all finite objects of interpretation. Since we cannot overcome historical distancing, interpretation is an ongoing process. Gadamer writes that "the true meaning of a text or a work of art is never finished; it is in fact an infinite process. Not only are fresh sources of error constantly excluded, so that all kinds of things are filtered out that obscure the true meaning; but new sources of understanding are continually merging that reveal unsuspected elements of meaning." Gadamer, *Truth and Method*, 298.

all objects of interpretation. The written word, the delivered speech, and the enacted ritual are immediately subjected to distanciation.[3]

As interpreters, we are not immune to this distancing effect. History affects us all, and separation with our historical situation is impossible.[4] The interpretative situation is much like standing on the precipice of an ever-growing chasm. The ability to accurately interpret the original work, and the author behind that work, retreats further in the distance with each passing generation. Interpretation becomes guesswork. Moreover, it becomes difficult to determine the meaning of the original situation and its application to the present. Recognition of our situation and horizon are thus immensely important in interpretation. Finitude is a continual barrier in interpretation. No one has the luxury of seeing all the factors involved in interpretation.[5] The act of interpretation is one of continually coming up short. This limit is what is what Hans-Georg Gadamer meant by the *situation*.[6] Varying factors limits how we can interpret and view our world. These include obvious factors such as race, gender, culture, and creed. The situation is also comprised of less obvious elements such as stories, life decisions, and the experiences that make each of us unique. Personal history limits our own vision.[7]

3. "Distance, then is not simply a fact, a given, just the actual spatial and temporal gap between us and the appearance of such and such work of art or discourse. It is a dialectical trait, the principle of a struggle between the otherness that transforms all spatial and temporal distance into cultural estrangement and the ownness by which all understanding aims at the extension of self-understanding." Ricoeur, *Interpretation Theory*, 43.

4. Historical and contemporary circumstances affect individuals in ways that are not often discernible. Gadamer writes that "[t]he very idea of a situation means that we are not standing outside it and hence are unable to have any objective knowledge of it. We always find ourselves within a situation, and throwing light on it is a task that is never entirely finished. . . . *To be historically means that knowledge of oneself can never be complete.*" Gadamer, *Truth and Method*, 301 (emphasis original).

5. Gadamer is against the idea that one can objectively stand out of one's environment. He writes, "The very idea of a situation means that we are not standing outside it and hence are unable to have any objective knowledge of it. We always find ourselves within a situation, and throwing light on it is a task that is never entirely finished." Gadamer, *Truth and Method*, 301.

6. Gadamer defines situation as a concept that "represents a standpoint that limits the possibility of vision." Gadamer, *Truth and Method*, 301.

7. We are always bound to history. According to Gadamer, "Long before we understand ourselves through the process of self-examination, we understand ourselves in a self-evident way in the family, society, and state in which we live. The focus of subjectivity is a distorting mirror. The self-awareness of the individual is only a flickering in the closed circuits of historical life. *That is why the prejudices of the individual, far more than* [one's] *judgments, constitute the historical reality of* [one's] *being.*" Gadamer, *Truth and Method*, 278 (emphasis original).

Interpretation and Horizon

Interpretation connects to our situations and experiences. Situation sets the limits of interpretation, while the horizon has the potential for opening that interpretation. Thus, the horizon encompasses the whole scope of our vision. This vision includes its possible expansion into the future. Though bound by a situation, our horizon is the element of potential in interpretation. The horizon opens new paths of interpretative engagement. Thus, horizon is a position of remaining open to the object of interpretation.[8] General openness requires us to be attentive to important claims texts, objects, and actions place on our lives. Things such as texts, musical performances, and rituals possess powerful ways of garnering our attention. They challenge and redefine what was previously known, but on the condition that we remain open to its claims. Furthermore, the horizon is not a blank slate, rather it represents an anthology of experiences that all of us bring into conversation.[9] Texts, performances, and rituals are conversation starters. They make claims that we as interpreters can adopt, argue, or reject.[10] In fact, argument is important in interpretation. Arguments and conflicting viewpoints can be important for expanding and moving the conversation forward. To interpret is to make a claim, therefore argument and defense offer the possibility to go deeper into conversation. When conflicts arise, interpretation uses that as an opportunity to go further.[11] Interpreting ritual action may bring conflicts when encountering unfamiliar, and even familiar, rituals. Arguments are a chance for going beyond the superficial

8. Horizon is not a fixed category like situation. Gadamer describes horizon as the "range of vision that includes everything that can be seen from a particular vantage point. Applying this to the thinking mind, we speak of narrowness of horizon, of the possible expansion of horizon, of the opening up of new horizons. . . . A person who has no horizon does not see far enough and hence over-values what is nearest to him." Gadamer, *Truth and Method*, 301.

9. Gadamer defines conversation as a "process of coming to an understanding." Gadamer, *Truth and Method*, 387.

10. Tracy describes these works as classics. He writes, "Classics [important authoritative works of a given community] arrive with powerful claims to attention, yet their claim is, after all, a claim to our attention and a challenge to our usual expectations. . . . Any contemporary interpreter enters the process of interpretation with some preunderstanding of the questions addressed by a classic text. The good interpreter is willing to put that preunderstanding at risk by allowing the classic to question the interpreter's present expectations and standards." Tracy, *Plurality and Ambiguity*, 16.

11. Tracy suggests, "Arguments, at their best, are moments within the wider conversation. Both topical and formal arguments are needed to adjudicate the counterclaims emerging in the wider conversation. Topical arguments analyze all substantive claims, Formal arguments analyze all claims to consistency. Both are helpful whenever conflicts of interpretation emerge. And conflicts do emerge." Tracy, *Plurality and Ambiguity*, 25.

All interpretation begins from an initial situation and possible horizon. The limit and scope of that horizon depends on our openness in interpretation. The horizon can be narrow or even completely absent if we remain closed in the interpretative task. As such, the horizon lies in our own hands. The goal is not to escape from the horizon, but to embrace our own situation as necessary for interpretation.[12] Estrangement is thus beneficial in the interpretative process. Acknowledging estrangement avoids the illusion of objectivity, which allows us to go further in interpretation. A closed interpretation, one that seeks an objective path to knowledge and understanding, attempts interpretation from the outside. It escapes real engagement with the object, text, or action in interpretation.

Further Problems in Interpretation: Action as a Text

The problems of interpretation are vast, especially for texts. Texts provide an excellent example of the problems we face in interpretation. For example, texts suffer a semantic distancing between the author and the contemporary reader. As time goes by, understanding the author's mind becomes an arduous and increasingly difficult task. The author is no longer available for questioning once the text is written down. There is no longer a direct one-to-one correspondence between the author's meaning and the interpreted meaning. The text no longer depends on the author. Consequently, the text acquires semantic autonomy.[13] The text leaves the author and his or her world behind. Interpretation is not an attempt to decipher a single fixed meaning. The text expands its public to a potentially unlimited number of interpreters. Meaning is open to an infinite array of readers across various times and spaces.[14] The interpretive focus does not center on the author

12. Gadamer describes this as one's prejudice. Though today it may have negative connotations, for Gadamer it is the inescapable element of oneself. Prejudice is one's own self-awareness. Thus, Gadamer states, "Reason exists for us only in concrete, historical terms—i.e., it is not its own master but remains constantly dependent on the given circumstances in which it operates." Gadamer, *Truth and Method*, 277.

13. Semantic autonomy of the text is a key concern for Ricoeur. For him, when a discourse is inscribed, the "author's intention and the meaning of the text cease to coincide. This dissociation of the verbal meaning of the text and the mental intention of the author gives to the concept of inscription its decisive significance. . . . Inscription becomes synonymous with the semantic autonomy of the text, which results from the disconnection of the mental intention of the author from the verbal meaning of the text, of what the author meant and what the text means. The text's career escapes the finite horizon lived by its author." Ricoeur, *Interpretation Theory*, 29–30.

14. Ricoeur suggests that "a written text is addressed to an unknown reader and potentially to whoever knows how to read. . . . In other words, reading is a social

and his or her world. As such, understanding is a process of questioning the things in themselves. All the while, we remain open to surprises in interpretation.

Problems of interpretation go beyond texts. These problems move into other aspects of action and behavior. Textual interpretation is but one example of a larger problem of meaning. Consider the action of speaking. There are considerable problems of interpretation present in speaking. Like a text, speaking creates a semantic distance between what was said and the speaker. Semantic distance is a continual problem since the experience of the speaker is not directly transferable to the listener.[15] There is a distance between the discourse, the situation of speaking, and the audience. The experience of the speaker, like the writer, is a private experience. However, the meaning is a public event of interpretation.[16]

Ritual action brings problems like interpreting text or speech. The principles of textual interpretation provide important first steps toward encountering ritual action's meanings. Thinking of action as a text suggests ways that we can encounter and interpret ritual action. In Paul Ricoeur's words, "the notion of a text is a good *paradigm* for human action . . . human action is in many ways a quasi-text."[17] Like a text, action has a propositional content, is detached from its author or agent, has an importance that goes beyond the initial situation, and can be addressed to an unlimited array of possible readers.[18] Action's propositional content allows for the detachment of meaning, similar to a text's detachment from its author.

The interpretative task goes beyond the text and the speech act. Interpretation is necessary for a variety of actions. Estrangement affects anything situated in the world, thus a thing is no longer immediately accessible.[19] This

---

phenomenon, which obeys certain patterns and therefore suffers from specific limitations. . . . A work also creates its public." Ricoeur, *Interpretation Theory*, 31.

15. Ricoeur describes semantic distancing as an immediate event where "what is said is already at a distance from the very act or even of saying. But a similar primary distance may be noticed between the discourse and its speaker, the inner structure and the outer referent, the discourse and its initial situation, and the discourse and its first audience. The problem of interpretation is already started." Paul Ricoeur, "Philosophy and Religious Language," in *Figuring the Sacred*, 37.

16. According to Ricoeur, "Experience by one person cannot be transferred whole as such and such experience to someone else. . . . The experience as experience, as lived, remains private, but its meaning, becomes public." Ricoeur, *Interpretation Theory*, 15–16.

17. Ricoeur, "Explanation and Understanding," 160.

18. Ricoeur, "Model of Text," 203–8.

19. Hans-George Gadamer opens interpretation beyond the written text. For Gadamer all tradition requires interpretation. He states, "It is not only the written tradition

is more obvious for art and written texts, as the object no longer connects to its original world. No one can reconstruct the work's original world. No finite work cannot overcome the estrangement between it and its original situation and audience.[20]

Like texts and speech, ritual action is not limited to its original social situation and audience. Instead, it can be interpreted and applied to new social contexts. Visually, ritual action allows for an infinite array of possible *readers*. Like texts, ritual actions go beyond their initial circumstances through their continual re-enactment in new circumstances and times. Though a ritual's original context can give clues to its meanings, ultimately ritual action creates a special world whereby action "exceeds, overcomes, transcends, the social conditions of its production and may be re-enacted in new social contexts."[21] The meanings of the ritual action can emerge from their social conditions. As a result, ritual actions present new possibilities and meanings for their readers.

THE ELEMENTS OF HERMENEUTICS

Interpretation can help us overcome the remoteness between us and the object of interpretation. The goal of interpretation is to make the remote familiar. Hermeneutics is a process of understanding that takes place between the interpreter and the interpreted.[22] Hermeneutics is typically a theory of

---

that is estranged and in need of new and more vital assimilation; everything that is no longer immediately situated in a world—that is, all tradition, whether art or the other spiritual creations of the past: law, religion, philosophy, and so forth—is estranged from its original meaning and depends on the unlocking and mediating spirit that we, like the Greeks, name after Hermes." Gadamer, *Truth and Method*, 157.

20. Reconstructing is like decoding a ritual in terms of its symbols. Decoding and reconstructing ignore the contemporary meaning of the work or action. Gadamer is especially critical of hermeneutical methods that attempt to reconstruct the past. We cannot reconstruct the past with the object of interpretation. According to Gadamer, "Reconstructing original circumstances, like all restoration is a futile undertaking in view of the historicity of our being. What is reconstructed, a life brought back from the lost past, is not the original. . . . A hermeneutics that regarded understanding as reconstructing the original world be no more than handing on a dead meaning." Gadamer, *Truth and Method*, 159–60.

21. Ricoeur, "Model of Text," 208.

22. Ricoeur describes interpretation as a way to overcome semantic distance. He suggests that the "purpose of all interpretation is to conquer a remoteness, a distance between the past cultural epoch to which the text belongs and the interpreter himself [or herself]. By overcoming this distance, by making himself [or herself] contemporary with the text, the exegete can appropriate its meaning to himself [or herself]: foreign, he [or she] makes it familiar, that is, he [or she] make it his own," Ricoeur, "Existence

interpreting texts.[23] However, hermeneutics also has important implications for exploring the meaning of other experiences and activities. Hermeneutics is a process of conversation with anything that conveys a message.

The hermeneutical process depends on remaining open in interpretation. Openness in interpretation is dependent on continual engagement with the object of interpretation. This process cannot move forward if we block ourselves from the other. After all, a conversation is not possible when only one person is participating. Dialogue is fundamentally important in interpretation. Therefore, hermeneutics is a process of asking questions of and investigating the object in its current form, rather than its historical shadow.[24] As an authentic dialogue, the priority is the question rather than the answer. The question expands our horizon. It is necessary for the "logical structure of openness that characterizes hermeneutical consciousness."[25] Hermeneutics uses questioning as a manner of opening the object of interpretation.[26] Opening an object moves it from an estranged condition to one of familiarity. This opening makes it possible for us to hear it in the contemporary situation.[27] Dialogue rescues the hermeneutical horizon from fixation and stagnation.

As a dialogue, the interpreter can work with two different horizons, his or her own and the other. Hermeneutics is a process of transposing ourselves into the contemporary situation of the other. It works at the contemporary situation of the other, becoming aware of the shared otherness between oneself and the other. This dialogue and transposition goes beyond a mere empathy for the other. We incorporate the other into our own horizon. This enables us to see the other within a larger context. It is a balance between shaping interpretation to our own expectations,[28] while avoiding interpreta-

---

and Hermeneutics," 101.

23. Ricoeur defines hermeneutics as "the theory of the operations of understanding in their relation to the interpretation of texts." Ricoeur, "Task of Hermeneutics," 43.

24. The search for a past truth sacrifices contemporary understanding and application. Gadamer states, "The text that is understood historically is forced to abandon its claim to be saying something true. We think we understand when we see the past from a historical standpoint. . . . In fact, however, we have given up the claim to find in the past any truth that is valid and intelligible for ourselves." Gadamer, *Truth and Method*, 302–3.

25. Gadamer, *Truth and Method*, 356.

26. In interpretation, questioning is an attempt to move past the superficial and into the heart of the other. Gadamer writes, "When a question arises, it breaks open the being of the object." Gadamer, *Truth and Method*, 356.

27. Gadamer describes questioning as the way texts enter "the living present of conversation." Gadamer, *Truth and Method*, 362.

28. In interpretation it is "necessary to guard against overhastily assimilating the

tion that remains blind to the larger context of the other.[29] Hermeneutics and understanding is a fusion of horizons between us and the other. Here, in this space, between past and present understandings and contemporary prejudices, a new relationship emerges.[30] We seek others for understanding instead of mastery. In this relationship, the interpreter and the other complement one another. The goal of hermeneutics is not technical control but better understanding of ourselves and the other.[31]

Relationship, Conversation, and Classic

Hermeneutics is process of building relationships rather than a semiotic decoding or metaphysical enforcement. The other of interpretation can speak without its own history or symbols superseding it. As a relationship, the interpreter and other are continually interpreting each other. This back and forth interpretive movement has no end. The interpreter grows alongside the other through time and experience. Texts, art, music, and ritual are not static entities, sentenced to dwell forever in the obscure vacuum of academic scholarship. They live through conversation and argument. They stand ready to challenge traditional norms and contemporary theories. Their essence comes in conversation, never confined to any one point in time and history. When one conversation ends, a new conversation awaits the next scholar or student. One does not discard the past. Rather, each new conversation builds on the past. In conversation, a new level of understanding emerges. Gadamer writes that the goal is "not merely a matter of putting

---

past to our own expectations of meaning." Gadamer, *Truth and Method*, 304.

29. Our horizon is a process to "look beyond what is close at hand—not in order to look away from it but to see it better, within a larger whole and in truer proportion." Gadamer, *Truth and Method*, 304.

30. We are not meant to interpret in isolation. The risk of objectification is too great when we attempt to interpret and understand from the outside. Rather interpretation is a coming together of horizons. Gadamer suggests, "There is no more an isolated horizon of the present in itself that here are historical horizons which have to be acquired. *Rather, understanding is always the fusion of these horizons supposedly existing by themselves*. . . . Old and new are always combining into something of living value, without either being explicitly foregrounded from the other." Gadamer, *Truth and Method*, 305 (emphasis original).

31. Westphal thus maintains that the "goal is not increased technological control of our environment, natural and social, but increased self-understanding. . . . The work is not so much a completed object or a thing to be mastered by methods of some science but rather an *event*, an unfinished event that is brought toward (but not to) completion in the process of interpretation." Westphal, *Whose Community?*, 102 (emphasis original).

oneself forward and successfully asserting one's own point of view but being transformed into a communion in which we do not remain what we
were."[32] The intent of conversation is coming to understand the truth claim
addressed by the other.[33]

Special forms of conversation acquire the status of a *classic*. Classics[34]
disclose a reality, a certain way of being-in-the-world, which never fail to
challenge and provoke us. Thus, classics push the conversation forward.[35]
Their effect is haunting, and their claims continue to linger in our conscious
and subconscious. Classics draw our gaze and attention to them.[36] They
have no need to force the conversation. As a movement built on relationship
and dialogue, the conversation with a classic has "a spirit of its own."[37]

Texts are not the only candidates for classics. In fact, classics can be
any expression of the human condition.[38] Ritual action can also have the
status of classic. Rituals can move, provoke, and challenge both participants
and observers. Every movement has meaning and purpose, nothing is arbitrary. Each gesture, from the position of the hands to the movement of the
feet, has a mysterious way to move and inspire. Ritual action seeks attention,
it needs participants. Its life is expressed through the body. It has a special
ability to unite and remind its participants. Its lives through repetition,

32. Gadamer, *Truth and Method*, 371.

33. Westphal, *Whose Community?*, 117.

34. Tracy later goes on to develop the idea of theological "fragments" rather than
classics. See Tracy, "Fragments," 170–84.

35. Tracy especially stresses the need to understand interpretation as a never evolving conversation. He suggests that "text and reader are never static realities but realities-
in-process demanding the interaction of genuine conversation to actualize questions
and responses (the subject matter). The principal identity which both text or reader
possess is the identity-in-difference of ever new and ongoing interpretation. Every classic text, moreover, comes to any reader through the history of its effects (conscious and
unconscious, enriching and ambiguous, emancipatory and distorted) upon the present
horizon of the reader." Tracy, *Analogical Imagination*, 105.

36. Tracy claims that classics are able to draw our attention to them. Tracy writes
"that certain expressions of the human spirit so disclose a compelling truth about our
lives that we cannot deny them some kind of normative status. Thus do we name these
expressions and these alone, 'classics'. . . The presence of classics in every culture is
undeniable. Their memory haunts us. Their actual effects in our lives endure and await
ever new appropriations, constantly new interpretations." Tracy, *Analogical Imagination*, 108–9.

37. Gadamer, *Truth and Method*, 385.

38. Tracy definition of classic includes several different forms. Classics are the
expression of the human condition; as such they belong to the people. They are not
obscure texts to lock away and protect. He writes, "Classics exist. To agree with this, one
need not limit the candidates for classical status by elitist criteria of the classicist." Tracy,
Analogical Imagination, 107–8.

and each repetition is a reminder. As classics, we do not easily forget ritual actions.[39]

Application

Application is the central problem of hermeneutics. It is essential to the hermeneutical process. As a fusion of horizons, the conversation continually moves forward to application. Conversation is never for the sake of itself, as if it were a self-contained thing. Conversation never stands still as merely interesting; it moves forward toward a goal or application. Classics demand it. Therefore, hermeneutics a continual process of understanding, interpretation, and application.[40] The result of hermeneutics is not a repetition of what the author has already said. Hermeneutics is not a scholarly parrot. It is a process that moves the conversation toward a concrete application. Consequently, the practical implications of hermeneutics outweigh the theoretical aspects. It is a way of re-imagining the interpreted text, object, or action so that it can return to the life of the community.[41] Hermeneutics is a never-ending process of conversation, resulting in a fusion of horizons, which moves toward understanding and interpreting for here and now. Since the present is never stagnant, the hermeneutical process cannot end.[42]

39. Classics continual provoke both the mind and heart. They are not easily forgotten or dismissed. According to Tracy, "Most of us can recall, for example, recalling a novel, poem or essay that had great impact on our lives. Years later we reread it. If it is a candidate for classic status, it will still have that power. Now however, it will bear a new interpretation for our later, either more mature or less authentic lives. Yet the text will still compel and concentrate our attention with the same kind of power of recognition of an essential truth about ourselves and our lives." Tracy, *Analogical Imagination*, 116.

40. Hermeneutics goes beyond the mere decoding of symbols one might typically find in ritual studies (see introduction), instead is a process that seeks the practical implications of interpretation. Gadamer writes, "Understanding always involves something like applying the text to be understood to the interpreter's present situation. Thus we are forced to go one step beyond romantic hermeneutics [Schleiermacher], as it were, by regarding not only understanding and interpretation, but also application as comprising on unified process. . . . We consider application to be just as integral a part of the hermeneutical process as are understanding and interpretation." Gadamer, *Truth and Method*, 307.

41. "The texts that concern Gadamer do not merely give rise to theories of various sorts; they found and nourish communities in their life together, partly by describing how things are but especially by prescribing how they can and should be." Westphal, *Whose Community?*, 109.

42. "The text, whether law or gospel, if it is to be understood properly . . . must be understood at every moment, in every concrete situation, in a new and different way. Understanding here is always application." Gadamer, *Truth and Method*, 307–8.

Hermeneutical conversation involves more than the interpreter and the other. From beginning to new beginning,[43] the entire process is a communal endeavor. Hermeneutics is not a private activity. It resists a solely private conversation.[44] It is not a conversation for the scholarly elite who decode the signs so that the non-scholar can understand. The scholar contributes to the conversation but does not own it. Conversation is a communal activity. Therefore, any conversation that does incorporate the larger community invites suspicion. How can any interpretation have an authentic claim to truth if it does not include the community?[45]

Experience

Experience opens us toward hermeneutical conversation. Our past enters into conversation with the unknown experience of the other. Our experience, or world view, shatters at the encounter of the other. In a genuine conversation the other informs, challenges, and defies our expectations. Experiences, both old and new, make change possible. Embracing our own experience provides us with a better understanding of the new and ourselves. Experience is a gauge for encountering the unexpected. Thus, it provides us with a gateway to the other. As such, knowing our own experience gives us a better sense of seeking out that which is new and different.[46]

43. The conversation never ends. The hermeneutical conversation may repeatedly renew itself as times and situations change, but hermeneutics does not have a definite end.

44. The conversation with a classic text, work of art, or action belongs to the entire community. We are not entering in a one-on-one conversation, instead it is a conversation involving both the past and present. In the case of ritual action, it quite obviously belongs to the community. The community gives it visible form. We do not interpret as if the community does not exist. Instead, we enter into conversation with them, the wider community, and the past expressions of this ritual. Tracy makes this clear when writing, "Any conversation with a classic is always interactive. Once the result of that conversation is communicated to others, it enters yet another dialogue, in principle, with the whole community of competent readers. . . . We belong to history and language; they do not belong to us. If we would belong to them well, we must question them and question ourselves through them. Through that questioning we participate in the conversation of all humankind, living and dead." Tracy, *Plurality and Ambiguity*, 29.

45. Dialogue with the wider community is essential for Tracy. He writes that the "larger dialogue with the entire community of capable readers is a major need for any claim to relative adequacy in interpretation." Tracy, *Analogical Imagination*, 121.

46. Experience has two different senses, new and old. New experience corrects the old. The previous experience is not wrong; rather it enters a dialogue with the new. We can never have the same experience twice; therefore, new experience is always dialoguing with the old. These are the "experiences that conform to our expectation and confirm it and the new experiences that occur to us. This later 'experience'—in the

Rituals and actions can be strange and unfamiliar to the interpreter. Ritual movements may involve unusual gestures, curious vestments, and corporal invocations. Our own past experiences may not line up neatly with the new. However, it does provide the opportunity to explore how these new experiences can change the ways in which we view our own practices. This is because experience directs us towards the new. Past experiences allow us to better absorb new ones. Thus, in the hermeneutical conversation, experience builds upon experience. Experience teaches us what we can gain from the new. In addition, it adds rather than erases the old. Experience builds a spirit of openness, rather than dogmatism.[47]

Hermeneutics draws on our experiences to further understand the other. It is a manner of entering the hermeneutical conversation. As a result, this requires an embrace of our own limitations and finitude. Experience shows us what we have left to learn and the never-ending project of knowledge. The result is a value for the unexpected nature of interpretation, and an appreciation of the real limits in interpretation. Finitude moves us toward the unknown, as opposed to shunning it.[48]

Performance

Interpretation is like a musical performance. When performing, it is not enough to simply reproduce the original as faithfully as possible. There is always an interpretive element in music.[49] The greatest musicians go beyond

---

genuine sense—is always negative. If a new experience of an object occurs to us, this means that hitherto we have not seen correctly and now know it better. . . . We acquire a comprehensive knowledge. We cannot, therefore, have a new experience of any object at random, but it must be of such a nature that we gain better knowledge through it, not only of itself, but of what we thought we knew before—i.e., of a universal." Gadamer, *Truth and Method*, 347–48.

47. Gadamer proposes that "experience always implies an orientation toward new experience. That is why a person who is called experienced has become so not only *through* experiences but is also open *to* new experiences. The consummation of [one's] experience, the perfection that we call 'being experienced,' does not consist in the fact that someone already knows everything and knows better than anyone else. Rather, the experienced person proves to be, on the contrary, someone who is radically undogmatic." Gadamer, *Truth and Method*, 350.

48. Finitude is not an obstacle to overcome. Instead, Gadamer contends that "experience is experience of human finitude. The truly experienced person is one who has taken this to heart, who know that he [or she] is master neither of time nor the future." Gadamer, *Truth and Method*, 351.

49. We cannot "stage a play, read a poem, or perform a piece of music without understanding the original meaning of the text and presenting it in his [or her] reproduction and interpretation. But, similarly, no one will be able to make a performative

the technical mastery of a musical piece.[50] Rather than merely rehearsing the notes correctly, they bring new life into a piece. Variations in tone, pitch, and time all contribute to a unique performance of the musical piece. The performance changes even though the notes have not.[51] The musician's interpretative style brings unique performances to musical pieces. There is a fusion of horizon between the musician and the musical piece rather than the musician and the composer.

The performance of hermeneutics is an event.[52] This event brings interpreted objects and situations to life. Hermeneutics is not a matter of subordinating the other to a foreign past, author, or symbol. It is not a matter of subordinating the other to the interpreter. Hermeneutics bridges multiple views together. Hermeneutics helps the other speak in new and ever-changing scenarios. Without the interpreter, the other remains mute behind a veil of alienation. A symphony remains silent without the work of musicians to perform it. A play is lifeless without the actors who give it life and existence. In this sense, hermeneutics is a way of performing texts, situations, and actions so that we can hear their voices across the temporal distance.[53] Performance is more than just an analogy, instead "all performance is interpretation and all interpretation is performance."[54]

Hermeneutics makes it possible for ritual actions to reach new audiences and situations. A cycle of understanding, interpretation, and application perform and re-perform the text. When the ritual ends, the task of hermeneutics begins. Through hermeneutics, ritual action acquires the

---

interpretation without taking account of that other normative element—the stylistic values of one's own day." Gadamer, *Truth and Method*, 309.

50. Performance needs to go beyond technical mastery; if this were not so, computers would be the greatest musicians. The fictional character Data, a sentient android from the television show *Star Trek: The Next Generation*, laments that though he can play the violin flawlessly, he has no interpretive style of his own. His work lacks *soul*. See Scheerer, "Inheritance."

51. Glenn Gould, arguably one of the greatest pianists of the twentieth century, perfectly demonstrates the hermeneutical process. His interpretative genius was not due to his faithful reproduction of the musical pieces, but in the way he was able to continually reinterpret music, most notably the works of J. S. Bach. The difference between the 1955 and 1981 *Goldberg Variations* highlights how different conversations lead to new and exciting applications of the original. See Gould, "Bonus Track."

52. Gadamer writes, "*Understanding proves to be an event.*" Gadamer, *Truth and Method*, 308 (emphasis original).

53. Hermeneutics "has a task of application to perform, because it too serves applicable meaning, in that it explicitly and consciously bridges the temporal distance that separates the interpreter from the text and overcomes the alienation of meaning that the text has undergone." Gadamer, *Truth and Method*, 310.

54. Westphal, *Whose Community?*, 102.

opportunity to be heard. This is not to say that ritual action was mute prior to hermeneutics. In conversation the interpreter seeks the right language with the other. Interpretation is matter of finding the best way of conversing with the other, so that the other is better able to be understood given varying contemporary situations. As such, there can be no single universal way of interpreting a ritual action, text, or work of art.[55] Even if a ritual action does not change, the interpreter does not. Performance not only varies from person to person, but it even varies across the course of one's life.[56] Therefore, we are having a different conversation whenever we engage with the object of interpretation. Ultimately interpretation "is not at means through which understanding is achieved; rather it enters into the content of what is understood."[57]

The interpreter's job is thus complex and deeply engaging. The interpreter has more in common with the musician or actor than the detached scholar.[58] We do not expect a musician to be completely objective toward the work he or she is performing. If a pianist performed Beethoven's *Moonlight Sonata* without feeling, we might consider it an "uninspired performance." Scholarly production and performance are not natural enemies.[59]

---

55. Any interpretation is part of an evolving process. Since interpreters do not live in a vacuum, neither do the objects of interpretation. Gadamer writes that "interpretation must find the right language if it really wants to make the text speak. There cannot, therefore, be any single interpretation that is correct, 'in itself,' precisely because every interpretation concerned with the text itself. . . . Every interpretation has to adapt itself to the hermeneutical situation to which it belongs." Gadamer, *Truth and Method*, 398.

56. Life experiences and age are going to continually change the hermeneutical conversation and one's own self-understanding. Westphal writes, "We understand [identify and interpretation] in terms of the person we ourselves are. I am the *same* person I was at fifteen and at fifty, but at the same time I am significantly *different*." Westphal, *Whose Community?*, 103 (emphasis original).

57. Gadamer, *Truth and Method*, 399.

58. Both the scholar and performer are understanding and interpreting the original musical piece, play, or text to bring it to life. Interpretation if a life-giving process and thus drastically different from objectivity typically associated with scholarship. Gadamer writes that "the concept of interpretation can be applied not only to scholarly interpretation but to artistic *reproduction*—e.g., musical or dramatic performance." Gadamer, *Truth and Method*, 400 (emphasis original).

59. Gadamer does not see scholarship and performance as natural enemies. He suggests that "there is no essential difference between the interpretation that a work undergoes in being performed and that which the scholar produces." Gadamer, *Truth and Method*, 400–401.

LANGUAGE

Expression is a necessary element for all things. Things seek to overcome the natural estrangement in finite existence, thus everything seeks communication.[60] Everything, *being*, has an expressive nature. Expression is a reaching out toward the other. Things need some manner of expressing their existence to those on the outside.[61] All things express messages intended to give information. They continually convey a message of some kind. The intent and purpose of any work of art, text, or ritual action is to move away from itself. As such, there is a movement away from things-in-themselves. Things are not satisfied with remaining mute. Their existence depends on creating an audience for themselves.[62] Communication and language are essential for existence. Things of interpretation, such as art and music, actually speak. They validate their existence, and are most alive, in this reaching

60. Rahner maintains that the nature of all things is expression. He states that "all beings are by their nature symbolic, because they necessarily 'express' themselves in order to attain their own nature." Rahner, *Theological Investigations*, 224.

61. Finitude seeks to overcome its own limitations. Art, music, texts, actions, and so on cannot directly speak their experience. History obscures the author. This does not mean that the work itself is silent. It has a meaning, several in fact that it seeks to express. Ricoeur describes this as a wonder. He writes that "for an existential investigation communication is an enigma, even a wonder. Why? Because being-together, as the existential condition for the possibility of any dialogical structure of discourse, appears as a way of trespassing or overcoming the fundamental solitude of each human being. . . . What is experienced by one person cannot be transferred whole as such and such experience to someone else. My experience cannot directly become your experience. . . . Here is the miracle. The experience as experienced, as lived, remains private, but its sense, its meaning, becomes public." Ricoeur, *Interpretation Theory*, 16.

62. Ricoeur describes this process for texts. Though Ricoeur is discussing the written text, the implications go well beyond that. As mentioned above, action is a quasi-text for Ricoeur. Therefore, Ricoeur's arguments on the written texts has implications for action and other modes of communication. Gadamer frames much of hermeneutical thought around art and performance. He suggests that a work "creates its public. In this way it enlarges the circle of communication and properly initiates new modes of communication. To that extent, the recognition of the work by the audience created by the work is an unpredictable event. . . . It is the semantic autonomy of the text which opens up the range of potential readers and so, to speak, creates the audience of the text. On the other hand, it is the response of the audience which makes the text important and therefore significant." Ricoeur, *Interpretation Theory*, 31.

out. Expression does not hold back, instead it gives itself so that it can com-municate itself.[63] It is a manner of projecting into the life of another.[64]

All things project themselves toward others with language. Art, music, action, texts, and so on exteriorize their meanings and intentions through language.[65] Things create their own public through language. If the thing has a message or meaning to share, it will express that meaning through language. The absence of the spoken word does mean that things have noth-ing to say. It may make it difficult to determine meaning, but meaning is not absent. Rather meaning is not immediately apparent.[66]

Language is not a fixed medium consisting of only words, sentenc-es, and paragraphs.[67] It is a fluid concept incorporating many different forms.[68] Art, music, or action communicate through their own special sort of language. Pictures, actions, events, and music are all capable of transmit-ting a message or experience through their very own language game.[69]

63. Things find fulfillment in communicating themselves. Rahner describes this as their symbolic nature. A thing "expresses itself and possess itself by doing so. It gives it-self away from itself into the 'other', and there finds itself in knowledge and love, because it is by constituting the inward 'other' that it comes to (or: from) its self-fulfillment, which is the presupposition or the act of being present to itself in knowledge and love." Rahner, *Theological Investigations*, 230.

64. Projection is communication. It is a way of expression into the life of another. Rahner suggests that a being "does so by really projecting its visible figure outside itself as its—symbol, its appearance, which allows it to be there, which brings it out to exis-tence in the world." Rahner, *Theological Investigations*, 231.

65. Ricoeur defines language as the "exteriorization thanks to which an impression is transcended and becomes an ex-pression, or, in other words, the transformation of the psychic into the noetic. Exteriorization and communicability are one and the same thing for they are nothing other than this elevation of a part of our life into the *logos* of discourse." Ricoeur, *Interpretation Theory*, 19.

66. Merleau-Ponty describes the expressive qualities of art and music. If a thing has something to say, it will be able to convey a message through language. He suggests that "every language conveys its own teaching and carries its meaning into the listener's mind. A school of music or painting which is at first not understood, eventually, by its own action creates its own public, if it really says something; that is, it does so by secret-ing its own meaning." Merleau-Ponty, *Phenomenology of Perception*, 179.

67. Schleiermacher describes language as "what mediates sensuously and exter-nally between utterer and listener." Schleiermacher, *Hermeneutics and Criticism*, 232.

68. The course of language is never set. According to Wittgenstein, "Language is a labyrinth of paths. You approach from *one* side and know your way about; you approach the same place from another side and no longer know your way about." Wittgenstein, *Philosophical Investigations*, 82.

69. Language can incorporate a variety of difference forms. According to Witt-genstein "There are *countless* different kinds of use of what we call 'symbols', 'words', 'sentences'. And this multiplicity is not something fixed, given once for all; but new types of language, new language-games, as we may say, come into existence, and others

The speaker does not need to visualize a word before speaking, saying, or expressing it. Speech and thought are not entirely separate concepts. To speak, we usually do not first consult the linguistic manual to find the right expression.[70] The expression is typically close at hand. We know what to say by saying it.[71] This principal is true for both the spoken word and ritual action. In the case of ritual action, the body does not require a retreat into the mind. We are not translating the mental word into a physical gesture, as if the mind and body were separate. The ritual action is already meaningful just by doing it.[72]

We do not find the key to language in syntax, instead, "*The essential being of language is Saying as Showing*."[73] To say is to show, meaning that saying is a way of letting things appear, be seen, and heard.[74] Saying is in an unveiling. The mystery of meaning no longer remains unspoken. This saying does not belong to human beings alone. All things participate in this saying through a self-showing.[75]

Language and Logos

Things reveal, or show themselves, through language. Language is not an end. Instead, it brings things into view. Language cooperates with human speech but is not bound to it.[76] It is the end result of this process of saying or revealing. Saying makes present and reveals the nature of things. It is thus an opening that clears the way toward communication and language. Saying

---

become obsolete and get forgotten." Wittgenstein, *Philosophical Investigations*, 11 (emphasis original).

70. At least in our native tongue or first language.

71. "To know a word or a language is, as we have said, not to be able to bring into play any pre-established nervous network . . . the near-presence of the words I know: they are behind me, like things behind my back, or like the city's horizon round my house, I reckon with them or rely on them, but without having any 'verbal image.'" Merleau-Ponty, *Phenomenology of Perception*, 180.

72. Merleau-Ponty describes the sensation of being pricked. When "the word as my hand reaches toward the part of my body which is being pricked; the word has a certain location in my linguistic world, and is part of my equipment. I have only one means of representing it, which is uttering it, just as the artist has only one means of representing the work on which he [or she] is engaged: by doing it. Merleau-Ponty, *Phenomenology of Perception*, 181.

73. Heidegger, *On the Way*, 123 (emphasis original).

74. Heidegger, *On the Way*, 122.

75. Heidegger describes self-showing as being "the mark of the presence and absence of everything that is present, of every king and rank." Heidegger, *On the Way*,123.

76. Heidegger, *On the Way*, 125.

is a drive and passion towards openness. Saying is the movement toward a thing's freedom to announce itself.[77]

Language does not need to be bound to conventional sentence structure. Words connect to the universal experience of the *logos*.[78] All forms of language express themselves through the *logos* by means of "gathering that, as a turning toward, pulls beings together into the gatheredness of their Being."[79] *Logos* is a manner of opening beings toward one another. The mystery of language is in its ability to open being.[80] Ritual action, music, art, and numerous other mediums all participate in the universal modes of expression, experience, and reason. They have an existence that *calls* toward the other. They affect and change the same lived reality in which all beings participate. Non-conventional forms are grounded in a language that seeks to gather being toward itself. Ritual action speaks because of its connection to the *logos*. It seeks to reveal itself to others in order to enter conversation with its participants and interpreters. As something that unites, expresses, and describe all experience, "language is the sole medium in which to express thought."[81] The *logos* makes this possible.

---

77. All things reveal themselves. It is part of this process of revealing and expression. As Heidegger describes it, "Saying is showing. In everything that speaks to us, in everything that touches us by being spoken and spoken about, in everything that gives itself to us in speaking, or waits for us unspoken, but also in the speaking that we do *ourselves*, there prevails Showing which causes to appear what is present, and to fade from appearance what is absent. Saying is in no way the linguistic expression added to the phenomena after they have appeared." Heidegger, *On the Way*, 126.

78. This refers to the universal *logos* rather than the Logos who is Christ, as described in the first chapter of John's gospel. Tillich describes *logos* as something that the all of reality participates in. It has philosophical roots meaning that "this *logos* is common; every reasonable being participates in it, uses it in asking questions and criticizing the answers received." Tillich, *Systematic Theology, Volume 1*, 23; Tillich elsewhere defines *logos* as "the word which grasps and shapes reality." Tillich, *Systematic Theology, Volume 1*, 75.

79. Heidegger defines the essence of logos as gathering. Heidegger, *An Introduction to Metaphysics*, 180.

80. Language is tied to expression and experience. It opens people and things toward the other, the one outside of oneself. A classic work is not silent, rather its connection to the *logos* means that it naturally moves toward gathering others into itself. It works towards opening itself up. Heidegger writes, "Language is the primal poetry in which a people poetizes Being. In turn, the great poetry by which a people steps into history begins the formation of its language. The Greeks created and experienced this poetry through Homer. Language was revealed to their *dasein* [existence] as a breakaway into Being, as the formation that opens beings up." Heidegger, *An Introduction to Metaphysics*, 183.

81. Power, *Sacrament*, 61.

Logos implies that language is more than the application and use of a system. Systems limit what may and may not qualify as a language and mode of expression. Language is more than a process of assignment, of making words into signs. Ritual action, along with art and music, is not void of meaning. It is not an empty vacuum waiting for theorists to give it meaning. The *words* already have meaning. The experiences and meanings of ritual action do not neatly conform to conventional language. Consequently, the job of interpretation is not finding the right words to make ritual action meaningful.[82] Ritual action is already meaningful. The interpreter's task is to observe, interpret, and understand. Interpreters assist ritual action by expressing those meanings through conventional words, but they do not create meaning.

Theses meanings are not subordinate to words. Ritual action and other forms of non-conventional language already have something to say. These meanings do not need the written or oral word to make them meaningful.[83] They are already meaningful. They affect us without even uttering or writing a single word. Meanings work together with words, taking form in a way that can be understood in particular times and circumstances.[84]

Language is more about the message conveyed than the form. Oral or verbal communication does not limit what we may call language. Therefore, language has more to do with the intent rather than the system employed. Human experience fuels the event of language. Language is thus any living exchange driven by the intent of meaning and communication.[85] Mediums like ritual action, being a language, refer to existence itself.

Ritual actions connect with the experiences of their audience. They express these messages through those that are participating with the action itself. Ritual action lives and delivers its message through life itself.

---

82. "A word is not a sign that one selects, nor is it a sign that one makes or gives to another; it is not an existent thing that one picks up and gives an ideality of meaning in order to make another being visible through it. This is mistaken on both counts. Rather, the ideality of the meaning lies in the word itself. It is meaningful already. . . . Experience is not wordless to begin with, subsequently becoming an object of reflection by being named, by being subsumed under the universality of the word. Rather, experience of itself seeks and find words that express it." Gadamer, *Truth and Method*, 416–17.

83. According to Mark Searle, "When ritual is subject to discursive analysis and theological evaluation, it is always more than words can tell." Searle, "Ritual," 57.

84. Power says that "thinking goes along with the speaking and writing; it is as it were a 'joint venture.'" Power, *Sacrament*, 62.

85. Language includes "all human media of encounter and exchange, bodily and ritual, as well as verbal. . . . The use of language is governed by intent. Intent is not here understood as a clearly formulated intention. It is rather a human drive, a search for the sense of being and for meanings by which to live." Power, *Sacrament*, 59–60.

No language has existence outside the lived experiences of its author or audience. If the right word cannot be found, either through the author's composition or the interpreter's interpretation, the expression never enters into lived existence. Ultimately "language itself brings itself to language."[86] Language is an expression of relation that goes beyond conventional definitions of language. Ritual action, art, and music all connect to a universal mode of expression built on word and experience.[87]

Language of Gesture

Ritual action is comparable to a language of gesture. Gesture is a non-verbal language where meaning occurs in the actions performed. It is a body language, "whether verbal or nonverbal, it is a way any community creates meaning."[88] Communities and groups use repetitive patterns and behaviors that help to form the community. Repeated gestures establish how members behave toward each other and those outside of the community.[89] It is an ingrained behavior that reveals the inner dynamic of the community. The defining characteristics of the community transfer to everyone.[90] Ritual action's gestures communicate their values to others. The group dynamic becomes the individual dynamic. As a result, the gestures of ritual action "transform the style and values of everyday action, thereby becoming the very ground of action itself."[91]

---

86. Language does not exist as something apart from being. Nor is the author in total control of language. Rather it is a cooperative effort of the author working with language to find the word that best fits. Without language the thought remains unspoken. Heidegger uses the example of a poet who puts into language the experience he or she encounters in language. Heidegger, *On the Way*, 59.

87. Language is more than a tool. Gadamer views "the misunderstanding in the question of the linguisticality of our understanding is really one about language—i.e., seeing language as a stock of words and phrases, of concepts, viewpoints and opinions. In fact, language is the single word, whose virtuality opens for us the infinity of discourse." Gadamer, *Truth and Method*, 553.

88. Uzukwu, *Worship as Body Language*, 5.

89. Uzukwu writes that "gestural behavior is repetitive; it establishes a way of doing; it is above all a pattern of communication that ensures group identity." Uzukwu, *Worship as Body Language*, 5.

90. Uzukwu describes this as "a programmed way of acting that characterizes an ethnic group so that participants express their being part of the group through the ritual gesture." Uzukwu, *Worship as Body Language*, 41.

91. Grimes, *Beginnings in Ritual Studies*, 66–67.

A gesture's meaning is inseparable from the action itself. The action is necessary to understand its meaning.[92] The gesture belongs to its own world, its context. The language of gesture is never a free agent in terms of its meaning. Gesture does not belong to something outside its own world. Neither can gesture be entirely individualistic. Instead, a gesture's nature reflects the community that performs it.[93]

Things can be meaningful without ever saying a word.[94] As a speechless language, the language of gesture does not depend on symbols or our knowledge of the symbols. Symbols do not speak what would otherwise be incomprehensible. This language does not depend on experts to make it accessible for a wider audience. Consequently, the language of gesture is unrestricted in revealing itself. Gesture shows or self-presents itself.

The gesture embodies the values that it communicates. The gesture does not refer to a value or emotion, as if it is a sign. Instead it communicates its value by becoming the very value or message itself.[95] It provokes an intimate relationship between the gesture and observer. Gesture presents itself to the observer, not as an arbitrary illustration, but as an invitation or beckoning. It reaches toward the observer with a desire to be incorporated into the very being of the observer.[96] It fuses itself and its qualities into the participant's being.[97] Therefore, the gesture communicates its meaning through a real presence. Its language is one of intimacy and connection.

92. Here the context is the visual arts, but what he argues is equally valid for physical movements and ritual. Gadamer attests that "gesture reveals no inner meaning behind itself. The whole being of the gesture lies in what it says." Gadamer "Image and Gesture," 79.

93. All "gesture is human, but not every gesture is exclusively the gesture of a human being. Indeed, no gesture is merely the expression of an individual person. Like language, the gesture always reflects a world of meaning to which it belongs." Gadamer "Image and Gesture," 79.

94. Ritual action does not speak in the verbal sense, though it can use spoken words, but like artwork there is a unique eloquence that we encounter. Speaking of classical art work, Gadamer states, "If we consider the rich, colorful, and resplendent eloquence that speaks to us so clearly and fluently from the classical periods of painting represented in our museums, and compare it with the creative art of our own time, we certainly have the impression of speechlessness." Gadamer, "The Speechless Image," 83.

95. Merleau-Ponty uses the example of an angry gesture. The one receiving the gesture does not need to recall previous feelings or search for meanings outside the gesture to understand it. He writes, "I do not see anger or a threatening attitude as a psychic fact hidden behind the gesture, I read anger in it. The gesture *does not make me think* of anger, it is anger itself." Merleau-Ponty, *Phenomenology of Perception*, 184.

96. "It is as if the other person's intention inhabited my body." Merleau-Ponty, *Phenomenology of Perception*, 185.

97. Rappaport suggests "that in ritual, transmitter, receiver and canonical messages become one—are fused—in the participant." Rappaport, *Ritual and Religion*, 145.

Understanding the language of gesture is less about intellect and more about intimacy.[98]

Ritual action defines the self, and gestures form the body into its own image. It molds the body into specific postures to bring its message into existence. When words do not suffice, the body becomes a conduit for meaning. Some experiences and messages are so overwhelming that words lack the depth necessary to convey it. Words do not have the same level of possession or captivation of the physical. Speaking or writing about commitment is not the same as expressing it in a physical way. For example, ritual actions such as baptism and communion continue to exist because these physical actions communicate a unique message. Even in a literate society, these ritual actions continue to exist because something would be missing without the physical displays. Part of the message would be missing.[99]

Physical gestures actualize the abstract. It molds abstract messages such as humility, service, and love into forms that we can see and feel. The abstract becomes immediately available for both the observer and participants. Kneeling, praying, and touching sculpts the body to convey a specific emotion or message. These physical displays mark the body, thus leaving a lasting impression on its participants.[100] Over time, these physical displays continue to modify our behavior. Participating in ritual action changes our being, not just once, but at every performance of the action. The act of performing is an act of accepting. Through enactment, we accept the message and in turn, we become a living metaphor. The ritual action, in both its visible and invisible characteristics, lives in us.[101]

98. "I do not understand the gestures of others by some act of intellectual interpretation; communication between consciousness is not based on the common meaning of their respective experiences, for it is equally the basis of the meaning. . . . I join it in a kind of blind recognition which precedes the intellectual working out and clarification of the meaning." Merleau-Ponty, *Phenomenology of Perception*, 185.

99. Rappaport makes this point. He writes that the body "communicates both to the self and to others not only what could be conveyed by an apparently corresponding set of words (e.g., 'I accept Allah'), but also a commitment of the living self to that message. Such physical acts seem to be more than 'mere talk.' It is the visible, present, living substance—bone, blood, gut and muscle—that is being 'put on the line,' that is 'standing up [or kneeling down] to be counted,' that is 'putting its money where its mouth is,' that constitutes the accepting agent." Rappaport, *Ritual and Religion*, 146.

100. The body puts theory into practice. Ritual action expresses a knowledge of lived practice. According to Rappaport, when a "sign is carved on the body the abstract is not only made substantial but immediate: nothing can be experienced more immediately than the sensations of one's own body. . . . As the abstract is made alive and concrete by the living substance of men and women, so are men and women predicated by the abstractions which they themselves realize." Rappaport, *Ritual and Religion*, 149.

101. "The performer lives both the order and his acceptance of it in the formal

As this is occurring, ritual action collectively uses the language of gesture to bring together the religious community. Through this language, it speaks to create relationship between individuals. The gesture forms individuals into community, making it possible to act and behave corporately.[102] Ritual action brings individual presences together through the sharing and speaking of the gesture. Ritual action speaks, individuals listen, and community is formed.

Ritual action forms community because behavior creates meaning.[103] It creates this meaning through the world it manifests. Its meaning is not one of association or one-to-one correspondence. It is not bound to any fixed meaning. Gestures do not always have to mean the same thing. They continually push and transcend these boundaries. Ritual action pushes outward to "transform (renew, create, re-create) society and thus to ensure the well-being of humans through the ritual action itself."[104] Through a pattern of behavior, the language of gesture opens new ways of understanding ritual action.[105] The gesture can be both this and that. Clasping our hands can express the act of prayer, humility, mediation, or all three. Therefore, gesture allows us to reach out to others in a variety of ways.[106] The explicit goal is connection with the other, by becoming a "living relation with oneself or with one's fellows, language is no longer an instrument, no longer a means; it is a manifestation, a revelation of intimate being and of the psychic link which unites us to the world and our fellow men [and women]."[107]

---

posture or gesture. A living metaphor of the union of form and substance is generated as the self-referential and the canonical come together in the ritual act." Rappaport, *Ritual and Religion*, 153.

102. Uzukwu emphasizes that "the rite is a gesture (body movement), it seeks its meaning within a social body. This fundamental reference of ritual to the community indicates how interdependent humans are: humans express by acting together their belonging to a social body." Uzukwu, *Worship as Body Language*, 43.

103. Merleau-Ponty describes behavior as a power force. He states, "Behaviour creates meanings which are transcendent in relation to the anatomical apparatus, and yet immanent to the behaviour as such, since it communicates itself and is understood." Merleau-Ponty, *Phenomenology of Perception*, 189.

104. Uzukwu, *Worship as Body Language*, 46.

105. Merleau-Ponty describes the human body as having "an indefinite series of discontinuous acts, significant cores which transcend and transfigure its natural powers. This act of transcendence is first encountered in the acquisition of a pattern of behaviour, then in the mute communication of gesture." Merleau-Ponty, *Phenomenology of Perception*, 193.

106. According to Merleau-Ponty, [a human] transcends [oneself] towards a new form of behaviour, or towards other people, or towards one's own thought, through one's body and one's speech." Merleau-Ponty, *Phenomenology of Perception*, 194.

107. Merleau-Ponty, *Phenomenology of Perception*, 196.

Ritual action speaks, and its voice is the gesture. The language of gesture involves the whole body. Ritual action communicates a message that others can read and interpret. It is not so different from other types of communication as to make it incompatible with hermeneutics. Instead of the written and spoken word, it uses the body. Bodily action is the means through which ritual action speaks. Using the language of gesture, the body takes on the meaning it expresses.[108] Like words on a page, the body acts as a page for ritual action. Yet unlike a page, the body is never a passive recipient. This does not mean that the spoken and written word are unimportant. The physical does not replace other language forms. Instead, the physical creates a relationship with the written and spoken word. The body works with the word to create a richer and fuller experience. Speech, writing, and the body each bring varying characteristics that interpreters need to consider.[109] A hermeneutics of ritual requires varied approaches so as to not focus on one aspect at the expense of others.

The body has an active role in forming and presenting the meaning of ritual action. Therefore, hermeneutics focuses on the actions of the body. Interpreting and understanding ritual action means changing our perspective on language. The interpreter enters conversation with the ritual action itself, which includes gestures and those who perform the gestures. That is where interpretation begins. The body is not the result of meanings formulated outside of it. The body is where meaning begins. To understand ritual action is to engage the body, entailing all physical aspects of ritual action. Hermeneutics can contribute toward understanding ritual action but only if it takes the physical seriously. Interpretation and understanding cannot take place from a distance.[110] The most important aspect of hermeneutics is that we enter a conversation with ritual action by engaging both the action itself and those who perform it. The role of hermeneutics is to show "that existence arrives at expression, at meaning, and at reflection."[111]

108. The body is a powerful form of expression. Merleau-Ponty states that "the body . . . must become the thought or intention that it signifies for us. It is the body which points out, and which speaks." Merleau-Ponty, *Phenomenology of Perception*, 197.

109. "The relationship between the physical and the spoken in ritual is, rather, complementary, each class claiming virtues the other lacks." Rappaport, *Ritual and Religion*, 152.

110. "Whether it is a question of another's body or my own, I have no means of knowing the human body other than that of living it, which means taking up on my own account the drama which is being played out in it, and losing myself in it." Merleau-Ponty, *Phenomenology of Perception*, 198.

111. Ricoeur, "Existence and Hermeneutics," 106.

The Language of Ritual Action and Its Implications

Ritual action communicates by transmitting knowledge and announcing itself to others. Its self-showing is not unintelligible, instead it is "one of many ways in which human beings construe and construct their world."[112] The saying of ritual action is an act of discovery and knowledge. Ritual action is a dynamic activity of revealing the unknown to its participants and audience. It teaches its participants and transforms the world around it. It does so through the body.[113] Ritual action teaches and communicates a ritual knowledge gained through action. Thus, ritual action informs and transforms its participants in the action itself. Ritual action, therefore, lives very much in the moment. What it expresses and communicates is neither merely illustrative nor translatable.[114] In order to understand ritual action, we must engage with ritual action in the act of doing it. It teaches "not through detachment but through engagement."[115]

Ritual action creates a world. It gives meaning to the actions performed and the objects used in the ritual.[116] It creates a way of behaving and doing in the world. Ritual teaches through action, using pattern and repetition to show how we are supposed to act. It does not argue its point of view through lengthy speeches or written treatises. Ritual action suggests through performing the ritual.[117] It shows us how to act in the world using

112. See Jennings, "On Ritual Knowledge," 111–27.

113. Jennings is avoiding the Cartesian split between the mind and body. It is not that the mind acts and the body follows. Instead, the body and mind work together to perform the appropriate gesture in ritual action. Jennings's argument is that ritual action has an active effect on its participants. It can teach and transform those involved. He suggests, "Ritual knowledge is gained by and through the body. We might speak here of the 'incarnate' character of ritual knowledge or say that it is gained through 'embodiment.' This would be somewhat misleading, however. It is not so much that the mind 'embodies' itself in ritual action, but rather that the body 'minds' itself or attends through itself in ritual action." Jennings, "On Ritual Knowledge," 115.

114. Jennings states, "Ritual knowledge is gained, not in advance of it, nor after it. If ritual knowledge were prior to action, then we would be reduced once again to understanding the ritual as an illustration or demonstration of what is already known in some other way. If ritual knowledge were gained primarily after the action, then an unwarranted priority would be given to the re-cognitive as opposed to the cognitive, to the reflective-critical rather than to the active." Jennings, "On Ritual Knowledge," 116.

115. Jennings, "On Ritual Knowledge," 116.

116. "Ritual knowledge, then, is not so much descriptive as it is prescriptive and ascriptive in character. It prescribes and ascribes action." Jennings, "On Ritual Knowledge," 116.

117. To describe this, Jennings using the example of the Eucharist. He believes that that the Eucharist teaches us how to do it. The Eucharist provokes and encourages imitation. We must do it to understand and know it. Jennings describes ritual as "a doing,

gestures and objects. Performance enables ritual action to *speak*. It conveys its message by grafting itself into the lives of participants. As such, ritual action is never arbitrary. These gestures and objects are critical. Variation matters, as changes can create different meanings within the same ritual.[118] Furthermore, ritual action delivers a unique message that we cannot find anywhere else.[119]

Physical display is a language of lived expression. It shows meanings instead of reporting them. Thus, not everything is *translatable*. We need to experience the original to get the full meaning.[120] A description of ritual is not the same as witnessing or performing it. The qualities and meanings do not fully translate. However, having a translated text is certainly better than no text, but it can never be the same as the original. We sometimes miss the way ritual action brings certain qualities into existence. For example, ritual action brings qualities like humility into physical existence. It does so to express and teach it to others.[121] Ritual action delivers its message to the whole person with an importance that goes beyond a single moment.[122]

---

a praxis, and above all a bodily doing, acting, performing. It is precisely this doing which is 'communicated' or 'transmitted' or taught by ritual action. On one level we can say that the doing of the ritual teaches us to do the ritual." Jennings, "On Ritual Knowledge," 117.

118. "If there were no variation in the ritual performance, we would have to conclude that there is here neither search nor discovery but only transmission and illustration of knowledge gained elsewhere and otherwise." Jennings, "On Ritual Knowledge," 114.

119. Rappaport asks this very same question. He writes, "Why is it that humans, who can communicate with ease, efficiency and subtlety through language should also employ such an awkward, limited and expensive mode of communication as physical display? An obvious answer, of course, is that physical display indicates more, more clearly or other than, what words are able to communicate." Rappaport, *Ritual and Religion*, 140.

120. Rappaport makes the case that "more ambiguity veils the informative force of a speech than it does such physical acts a bowing or saluting. If a man [or woman] only voices subordination he [or she] may seem to be doing no more than stating, reporting or asserting it (since stating, describing, reporting and asserting are almost never done through posture or gesture) by performing an act taken to be in itself subordinating. This is to say that the performative nature of physical acts is likely to be clearer than the equivalent utterance, which could possibly be taken for a mere report of statement." Rappaport, *Ritual and Religion*, 143.

121. Rappaport explains, "Through kneeling, bowing, saluting, tugging the forelock, uncovering the head or covering it, subordination, piety, devotion (or whatever the gestures represent), are 'realized,' that is, made into *res*, and as such achieve an apparent naturalness equal to that of flowers or wind, if not rock." Rappaport, *Ritual and Religion*, 143.

122. Jennings writes that ritual "teaches one not only how to conduct the ritual itself, but how to conduct oneself outside the ritual space—in the world epitomized by or

Ritual action's communication is inviting. It seeks to both reveal itself and invite the other to join in its activity. Ritual action needs participants to "complete it, or continue it, or perfect it."[123] Therefore, ritual action does not convey a secret knowledge. It seeks observers to respond to its call. It is public act that is open to all observers.[124]

The idea of language has important implications for interpreting ritual action. The meaning and intent of ritual action is a projection of meaning. Ritual action seeks to communicate meaning through saying, or showing, itself. It does not seek to withhold itself. Ritual action desires connection. It involves participants who outwardly project the meanings of the ritual action itself. Ritual action's communication is neither unintelligible nor irrational.[125] Its connection to language opens a pathway towards hermeneutics. Like a speech or text, ritual action is a projection for communication. It makes no difference that much of ritual action is non-verbal. The intent is communication.

RITUAL ACTION AS DISCOURSE: ENTERING THE CONVERSATION

Ritual action's communication is neither senseless nor unintelligible. Through the language of gesture, ritual action communicates a message that a receiver can interpret and understand. It is a meaning that we can interact and converse with it. Ritual action can do this because it is a living language. Its importance is not in structure, but rather in its use. Ritual action's connection to the *logos* allows it to reveal itself towards others. Ritual action reveals itself through the language of gesture. Moreover, discourse is the moment of this reveal. Discourse is the lived expression and usage of language. When entering conversation with ritual action, we are engaging in its discourse. Language is never the final product of expression. Expression is a means to overcome language by moving beyond it. Language, the means

---

founded or renewed in and through the ritual itself." Jennings, "On Ritual Knowledge," 119.

123. Jennings, "On Ritual Knowledge," 123.

124. "Ritual action not only permits but invites, and even directs, attention to itself. It does this in order to evoke a response to itself on the part of the observer." Jennings, "On Ritual Knowledge," 125.

125. Jennings believes that ritual action is an intelligent action equal to other forms of communication. As he puts it, "Ritual action is intelligent action which is different in kind, though not in degree, from such other forms of intelligent action as toolmaking, theoretical formulation, or painting." Jennings, "On Ritual Knowledge," 124.

and the how of expression, lives in the shadow of discourse.[126] Language births the event of discourse.

Therefore, ritual action is a mode of discourse. Discourse "is *the* event of language."[127] Discourse is the expression of being-in-the-world, a living language of everyday life. It connects us with the everyday experience.[128] Discourse is the existential factor of language. Consequently, the absence of discourse would leave us with only a dictionary. Discourse drives our usage of language. It is the state of disclosure.[129]

Discourse is the way we interact in the world. It consists of the everyday conversations that comprise daily life. From mundane talk about the weather to late night conversations about the pressing issues of existence, discourse is necessary for bringing us into a state of "Being-with-one-another."[130] Communication occurs in discourse "whenever one wishes, asks, or expresses oneself about something. In this 'something said', discourse communicates."[131] Likewise, ritual action interacts with the world through discourse. The sights, sounds, and physical movements all contribute in the expression and sharing of ritual action's being. Ritual action comes alive through discourse. Ritual action shares its being, its Dasein,[132] through situation and experience. As such, ritual action brings life to language.[133]

126. Ricoeur states that language is the "means of which, we express ourselves and express things. To speak is the act by which the speaker overcomes the closure of the universe of signs. . . . To speak is the act by which language moves beyond itself as sign toward its reference and toward its opposite. Language seeks to disappear; it seeks to die as an object." Ricoeur, "Structure, Word, Event," 112.

127. Ricoeur, *Interpretation Theory*, 9 (emphasis original).

128. Heidegger claims that "if disclosedness is primarily constituted by Being-in-the-world, then discourse too must have essentially a kind of Being which is specifically *worldly*. The intelligibility of Being-in-the-world—an intelligibility which goes with a state-of-mind—*expresses itself as discourse*." Heidegger, *Being and Time*, 204 (emphasis original).

129. While language may be comprised of words, or a system, discourse is the ability to express and disclose. Heidegger writes that "discourse is existentially language, because that entity whose disclosedness it articulates according to significations, has, as its kind of Being, Being-in-the-world." Heidegger, *Being and Time*, 204.

130. Being-in-the-world moves toward being-with through discourse. Heidegger, *Being and Time*, 204.

131. Heidegger, *Being and Time*, 205.

132. Heidegger's term for an existence. More specifically an existence concerned with one's own Being and its relationship and understanding of Being. *Dasein* is orientated towards the ontological. *Dasein* is referring to both the singular and corporate nature of ritual action. Ritual action is one activity, yet its existence also includes the participants who enact the ritual action. It is both corporate and singular. Heidegger, *Being and Time*, 32.

133. "Language is not a world of its own. It is not even a world. But because we are

Ritual action speaks through discourse because of the experiences of its participants.

Ritual action is a form of discourse. Whether in the form of texts, symbols, or gestures, ritual action is not senseless. It is saying something to someone. Thus, religious expression conveys a specific meaning in the form of discourse. Ritual action is an event that actualizes itself through the actions and activities of people, and discourse is the way religious communities express what is important. Religious experience connects to language, not in the sense of structure, but in meaning.[134] Discourse is not bound to academic scholarship or theological tomes. Instead the most important source of discourse is the religious community.[135]

Ritual action is a discourse. Therefore, hermeneutics requires us to "identify these originary modes of discourse through which the religious faith of a community comes to language."[136] The mode of communication matters. Ritual action is a unique form of communication. Meaning that it requires a unique hermeneutical approach sensitive to its form. All "religious experience comes to language through specific modes of discourse,"[137] therefore all interpretation must work with the given form.[138]

The discourse of ritual action is more than a systematic structure. Discourse conveys a message that only exists in the performance of language. Therefore, discourse "has an *act*, as its mode of presence. . . . To speak is a present event."[139] The event of discourse has a temporary existence, the giving and receiving of its message occurs when language is enacted.[140]

---

in the world, because we are affected by situations, and because we orient ourselves comprehensively in those situations, we have something to say, we have experience to bring to language." Ricoeur, *Interpretation Theory*, 21.

134. Ricoeur states that "a religious faith may be identified through its language, or, to speak more accurately, as a kind of discourse. . . . Whatever may be the nature of the so-called religious experience, it comes to language, it is articulated in a language, and the most appropriate place to interpret it on its own terms is to inquire into its linguistic expression." Ricoeur, "Philosophy and Religious Language," 35.

135. Academics do not have a monopoly on religious discourse. For Ricoeur religious communication occurs in the "expressions embedded in such modes of discourse as narratives, prophecies, legislative texts, proverbs and wisdom sayings, hymns, prayers, and liturgical formulas" Ricoeur, "Philosophy and Religious Language," 37.

136. Ricoeur, "Philosophy and Religious Language," 37.

137. Ricoeur, "Philosophy and Religious Language," 39.

138. For Ricoeur, this means that "its meanings are ruled and guided by the modes of articulation specific to each mode of discourse." Ricoeur, "Philosophy and Religious Language," 39.

139. Ricoeur, "Philosophy and Religious Language," 114

140. The system only has an existence within the system. It does not actualize or

This means that discourse only occurs in the present moment. The event of discourse vanishes immediately after it occurs. However, a trace remains. Discourse leaves its propositional content behind. The performed content comes and goes; limited to the experience of the present moment. What is said, however, lingers on.[141] In the strictest sense, the event is indescribable. This does not mean that only silence remains. Significant events, in the act of actualization, make themselves visible to their audience or reader.[142] The event of discourse, while fleeting, reveals itself through its meaning. Meaning is the goal of discourse, so that "if all discourse is actualized as an event, it is understood as meaning."[143]

Discourse can occur with a great degree of freedom. Discourse is comprised of a variety of different choices, including and excluding differing actions. These choices unleash unique combinations that create new actions.[144] Discourse is the creative force in communication that makes it possible to create and enact an infinite number of actions. Discourse is not bound to one way of engaging audiences. It has the freedom to change its approach, including the position of the hands, the order within the ritual, who performs it, and so on. It has a polysemic nature, meaning that ritual action can have more than one meaning. Ritual action, like all discourse, can vary its approach based on context.[145] Ritual action remains a communal activity, and its discursive function overcomes it owns structure to adapt

bring to life any part of language. Discourse, the performance of language, brings to life language. Ricoeur explains that the language "system in fact does not exist. It only has a virtual existence. Only the message gives actuality to language, and discourse grounds the very existence of language since only the discrete and each time unique acts of discourse actualize the code." Ricoeur, *Interpretation Theory*, 9.

141. Ricoeur clarifies the distinction between system and discourse. He describes how a "system in fact does not exist. It only has a virtual existence." Next, Ricoeur makes the case that "discourse is not merely transitory and vanishing. . . . It may be identified and re-identified as the same so that we may say it again or in other words." Ricoeur, *Interpretation Theory*, 9.

142. "Every apology for speech as an event, therefore is significant if, and only if, it makes visible the relation of actualization, thanks to which our linguistic competence actualizes itself in performance." Ricoeur, *Interpretation Theory*, 11.

143. Ricoeur, *Interpretation Theory*, 12.

144. Here Ricoeur is specifically talking about the act of speaking and writing. Though there is nothing here that we cannot apply to ritual action. The premise of action as a text allows us to make this connection. Ricoeur describes discourse as a "series of choices by which certain meaning are selected and others excluded." Ricoeur, "Structure, Word, Event," 114.

145. Ricoeur notes that words have more than one meaning. He argues that "our words are polysemic; they have more than one meaning. But it is the contextual function of discourse to screen, so to speak, the polysemy four words and to reduce the plurality of possible interpretation." Ricoeur, *Interpretation Theory*, 17.

to new times and circumstances. True discourse is not ignorant of its world and audience.

Discourse has a reference, "To speak is to say something about something."[146] Discourse moves beyond itself, as language, toward its intended meaning. We move away from discursive systems, by going toward the lived expressions of language. Through reference, the language or system goes toward its intended goal of speaking to someone.[147] Reference is only available in the use of language. It is the moment when language comes to life, using language to speak to specific times and circumstances. This movement from theory to practice is known as the speech event.[148]

Ritual action as a discourse transcends itself as a system.[149] The language of gesture cannot move beyond itself as it is. It needs to refer to something or to someone to reach its intended purpose. Ritual action comes alive in its use.

YES, AND . . .

Ritual action pushes beyond itself to create a new world.[150] It redefines the world around it to propose a new way of being-in-the-world. Ritual action redefines the present, looking for new ways of being or experience in both participants and observers. Ritual action reshapes the everyday into its own image. It reshapes the present into an undefined image, open to interpretation, but substantially different than what was before. Ritual action communicates, makes itself known, so that it might make a new future in the present. This present future embodies the qualities it teaches and transmits. This is not the distant future, but a future of the here and now.[151] This fu-

146. Ricoeur, "Structure, Word, Event," 114.

147. Ricoeur suggests that the "reference expresses the movement in which language transcends itself." Ricoeur, *Interpretation Theory*, 20.

148. Reference "is what the sentence does in a certain situation and according to a certain use. It is also what the speaker does when he [or she] applies his words to reality. That someone refers to something at a certain time is an event, a speech event." Ricoeur, *Interpretation Theory*, 20.

149. As a discourse, ritual action only speaks in the moment of reference. It needs to say something to someone. Or as Ricoeur puts it, "Words refer to other words in the round without end of the dictionary. Only discourse, we say, intends things, is applied to reality, expresses the world. Ricoeur, "Philosophy and Religious Language," 43.

150. "A world that I might inhabit and wherein I might project my ownmost possibilities. This is what I call the world of the text, the world probably belonging to this unique text." Ricoeur, "Philosophy and Religious Language," 43.

151. Theological speaking, Ricoeur compares this new world to a "new covenant, the kingdom of God, a new birth." Ricoeur, "Philosophy and Religious Language," 44.

ture continually reshapes the present one individual at a time. The event of discourse is present in every person, creating an individual and collective phenomenon. Thus, it is and is not an individual event. The discourse event happens simultaneously in both the individual and the community, and the goal is to reshape communities. Therefore, discourse creates a new world, yet this can only begin at the individual level. Ritual action's beauty is found in its simplicity. It needs neither eloquent speech nor moving prose, all ritual action needs is the body. It moves us at the most basic and primal level. Ritual action moves us toward a level of gesture, touch, and love.

Hermeneutics is a helpful starting point for engaging ritual action. It provides a gateway for entering the world of ritual action, a world where the fusion of horizons occurs between the interpreter and ritual action. It moves us beyond a language of speaking and writing. Hermeneutics gives special attention to the unique nature of ritual action. It gives attention to the body, thus recognizing it as neither incidental nor illustrative. Consequently, the body becomes necessary for meaning. The value of hermeneutics is not in structuralism, semiotics, or metaphysics. Hermeneutics is important because it helps us to see and understand ritual action. The world of ritual action is the domain of hermeneutics.[152] We must enter, live, and experience this world. Furthermore, hermeneutics brings us into this rupture, the breach created by the world of ritual action. It positions us toward understanding. This does not mean that there are no more barriers in interpretation. Like other forms of language, ritual action is not immune to the distancing effect between author and observer. Entrance into this world requires a hermeneutics that takes seriously the physicality of ritual action. The interpreter must bridge together hermeneutics and the language of gesture. The concept of language needs expansion to fully understand how ritual action uses the body in communication. Ritual action's connection to language and the body opens us to new ways of interpreting how ritual action conveys meaning to the outside world.

Hermeneutics represents a beginning rather than an end. It opens the door toward meaning but going further requires the openness of deconstruction. We must go further into the various and often contradictory aspects of meaning. Deconstruction offers a new approach toward ritual action that includes radical openness in interpretation and meaning.

152. According to Ricoeur, "General hermeneutics invites us to say that the necessary stage between structural explanation and self-understanding is the unfolding of the world of the text." Ricoeur, "Philosophy and Religious Language," 44.

Chapter Two

Learning to Listen
Deconstruction and Ritual Action

OPENING THE CONVERSATION

LEARNING TO LISTEN IS easier said than done. Speaking is neither remarkable nor surprising for many people. It is not unusual to compliment someone as a good speaker. Those who speak or write well are often applauded and admired. Talking comes naturally to human beings. We often express our feelings, desires, beliefs, and concerns through talking. Talking is a way to announce our existence. Not doing so runs counter to social norms. Talking is not a bad thing. Progress requires speaking and communication with one another.

The other side of talking is listening. The act of communication is incomplete without it. Talking means very little if no one receives what is communicated. Without someone to listen, there is no communication. Even talking to oneself requires listening. Words are lost, thoughts remain mute, and expression goes silent at the absence of listening. Good listening is essential for conversation, understanding, and interpretation.

Learning to Listen

Ritual action revolves around having something to say. The major problem is a lack of listening. Often there is so much to say that we neglect the act of listening. When there is so much to say, listening often feels like an afterthought. Listening is the most important act when engaging with ritual action. Before writing or speaking, there needs to be listening. This requires a shift in perspective beginning with the current situation, practice, or ritual action at hand. This approach takes seriously the voice of the interpreted. Hermeneutics prepares one to listen. The actual act of listening requires both attentiveness to the situation and a spirit of openness.

However, hermeneutics alone is not enough for listening to ritual action. We must change how we listen to hear ritual action. Achieving this level of listening requires a movement and reorientation in perception. This requires an engagement with absolutes and grounds of understanding, meaning that that we need to *let go* or deconstruct what we already know. This is not a stripping away of our prejudices, but rather a removal of imposed expectations. Listening requires us to let go of what we expect to hear or find. Deconstruction offers an approach that brings radical openness toward interpreting ritual action. Deconstruction leaves meaning open and avoids absolutes. Difficult and risky, such a movement toward the unexpected requires further explanation.

WHY DECONSTRUCTION?

Deconstruction is not easy to define and is perhaps undefinable. We cannot label it as a method or system.[1] It has no rules, no doctrines, and no how-to manual.[2] No one is a master or an expert of deconstruction. It is not a tool to use, as if deconstruction were a thing we can control.[3] Deconstruction is something already happening within things themselves.[4] It comes from the natural desire for things, texts, situations, and so on to be as clear as possible. Deconstruction is less about doing and more about listening without interrupting the other.

We can point to certain traits that characterize deconstruction. As the name implies, deconstruction challenges the structuralist belief in principle or signifying essences.[5] Namely the idea that a prescribed structure

1. "To present 'deconstruction' as if it were a method, a system or a settled body of ideas would be to falsify its nature and lay oneself open to charges of reductive misunderstanding." Norris, *Deconstruction*, 1.

2. Smith, *Jacques Derrida*, 9.

3. Smith writes, "Deconstruction is not the effect of a master interpreter who comes and does something to a text, nor the result of bringing external tools or appliances to work 'on' a text." Smith, *Jacques Derrida*, 9.

4. In addition to texts, we can add ritual actions, situations, traditions, and so on. Smith suggests that "deconstruction happens within texts, from inside, out of their own resources." Smith, *Jacques Derrida*, 9.

5. Andrew Shepherd defines deconstruction as a theory that "declines the structuralist assumption that structuralist principles are essences. Eschewing any form of essentialism, 'deconstruction' seeks to reveal the way in which philosophical language, rather than signifying essences or givens, is itself historical, contingent and temporary."

is always present in a text, situation, or ritual action. A structuralist approach is the search for an assumed meaning that corresponds with "some deep-laid mental 'set' or pattern of response which determines the limits of intelligibility."[6] Instead of searching for systems of relationships that correspond to the mind or any other *a priori* truths, deconstruction argues against static or foundationalist definitions. It challenges theories that fail to take in account the dynamic nature of language and culture. Definitions are neither eternal nor correspond with anything outside of themselves. It challenges dualism, the division of being and language. This challenge includes hierarchical thought.[7]

Deconstruction can raise concerns among some. Some consider it as a direct challenge to the truth claims of scripture and Christianity. Mark Taylor suggests that "deconstruction is the 'hermeneutic' of the death of God."[8] Though God is not the direct topic here, this quote demonstrates the attitude many have toward deconstruction, namely that it promotes the death of absolutes and truth.[9] Opponents argue that deconstruction cannot speak constructively on ritual action. However, deconstruction's threat to religion, faith, and knowledge is severely overstated, based more on fear than reality.[10] A deconstructionist approach is one that seeks knowledge and the truth of things like any other manner of inquiry. In deconstruction, we hold a deep desire for truth and understanding. It is a willingness to sacrifice the illusionary and peripheral in order to find truth. Thus, it helps us see an inner truth and meaning in all things.[11] This truth desires to be heard. It

---

Shepherd, *The Gift*, 49.

6. Norris, *Deconstruction*, 3.

7. Shepherd suggests, "Philosophical discourse and language are disassembled by a rereading of the text, in which attention is paid to the way in which philosophical constructions depend on seemingly-fixed meanings and definitions, and clear-cut binary relationships which are often hierarchically-ordered." Shepherd, *The Gift*, 48.

8. Taylor, *Erring*, 6.

9. "Postmodernism has been thought by some to be profoundly anti-religious. . . . Postmodernism popularly invokes fears of relativism, nihilism, and linguistic idealism (there is nothing that is not the construct of language)." Ward, "Postmodern Theology," 335.

10. John Caputo addresses this fear. He writes, "Deconstruction is not out to undo God or deny faith, or to mock science or make nonsense out of literature, or to break the law, or generally, to ruin any of those hoary things at whose very mention all your muscles constrict. Deconstruction is not in the business of defaming good names but of saving them." Caputo, *Prayers and Tears*, 5.

11. Paul Tillich demonstrates some of the themes of deconstruction. In his words, "The surface must be penetrated, the appearance undercut, the 'depth' must be reached, namely the *ousia*, the 'essence' of things, that which gives them the power of being. This is their truth, the 'really real' in difference from the seemingly real." Tillich, *Systematic*

requires us to filter out the noise surrounding it to hear it.[12] Deconstruction makes no claims to be opposed to truth. Concerned with the truth, it is in fact a "theory of truth, in which truth spells trouble."[13]

As a theory of truth, deconstruction continues the hermeneutical process.[14] In its quest for truth, deconstruction accepts no substitutes or illusions.[15] Deconstruction's eagerness to do away with the superfluous may be quite shocking to some, especially when superfluous meanings and interpretations are long standing traditions. Deconstruction pushes hermeneutics forward and farther than it could ever go by itself. Yet its eagerness originates from a *desire* for truth. This desire requires deconstruction to listen intently. It suggests that we must break some things down and move aside what no longer works. For the conversation to continue, we must go deeper into the very heart of the matter.[16]

Deconstruction is a postmodern way of knowing that is best characterized as style, rather than a method. It does not draw from a strict doctrine of precepts nor does it employ complex systematic thinking.[17] Instead, its biggest strengths come from flexibility and adaptability.[18] It represents the best approach for communicating, interpreting, and exchanging ideas and

---

Theology, Volume 1, 101.

12. Deconstruction does nothing that things do not already do to themselves. Truth is never comfortable in the background. It will come to the surface, even if it must deconstruct its own self. Caputo explains that all things "tremble by their own inner impulse, by a force that will give them no rest, that keeps forcing itself to the surface, forcing itself out, making the thing restless. Deconstruction is organized around the idea that things contain a kind of uncontainable truth, that they contain what they cannot contain." Caputo, *What Would Jesus Deconstruct?*, 29.

13. Caputo, *What Would Jesus Deconstruct?*, 30.

14. "Deconstruction is at the same time a hermeneutics of truth." Caputo, *What Would Jesus Deconstruct?*, 30.

15. "The problem of the 'truly real' cannot be avoided. The seemingly real is not unreal, but it is deceptive if it is taken to be really real." Tillich, *Systematic Theology*, Volume 1, 101.

16. Caputo explains that the "point of deconstruction is to loosen and unlock structures, to let the shock of alterity set them in motion, to allow them to function more freely and inventively, to produce new forms, and above all to say yes, *oui, oui*, to something whose coming eye hath not seen nor ear heard. Deconstruction gives old texts new readings, old traditions new twists." Caputo, *Prayers and Tears*, 18.

17. Norris maintains that it is "a deliberate attempt to turn the resources of interpretative style against any too rigid protocols of method or language." Norris, *Deconstruction*, 17.

18. Caputo describes this as a "*style*, rather than as a body of doctrines; it is an inflection or alteration that continues the 'project' of modernity, but by other means. Where modernity thinks there are pure rules and a rigorous method—in ethics as well as in science—postmodernity advises flexibility and adaptability." Caputo, *Truth*, 5–6.

meanings in a postmodern age.[19] Under the influence of postmodernism, deconstruction works through exception and creativity.[20] It is a "constant reminder of the ways in which language deflects or complicates the philosopher's project."[21] As such this complication does not represent a barrier to interpretation. Instead, it enriches interpretation.

EMBRACING THE INSTABILITY OF MEANING

Deconstruction and postmodern thought work using the idea that meaning continually changes and adapts. Language and meaning are fluid concepts, continually under the influence of differing relationships. Language is a continual series of moves and countermoves. In this manner, language is strategic. It is based on both the experience of the sender and the receiver. Communication is a provoking endeavor, designed to move the receiver to react. The sender also reacts, anticipating any number of moves and countermoves.[22]

A game of tennis illustrates this process. The two players represent the sender and receiver of information. Each player prepares moves and countermoves to send the ball back to one another. As one hits the ball, the players are making moves in preparation for the ball's return. The ball, or in this case *meaning*, is never in a fixed location. Like conversation, the ball continually moves back and forth, never staying in any one location for too long. Of course, no analogy is perfect. The players in this game are not out to win and meaning eternally moves back and forth between them. But imagine more than one ball or a seemingly infinite amount of balls moving to and fro across the court. Thus, instead of one meaning, there are a multitude of meanings. The picture here is of a game that encourages an extreme degree of flexibility. Expectations do exist, but never to the detriment of

19. Knowledge and information have fundamentally changed, thus requiring new attitudes and relationship toward knowledge. It is the end of the era of metanarratives. Lyotard states, "The status of knowledge is altered as societies enter what is known as the postmodern age. This transition has been under way since at least the end of the 1950s." Lyotard, *Postmodern Condition*, 3.

20. Caputo, *Truth*, 6.

21. Norris, *Deconstruction*, 19.

22. Lyotard's theory is the "agonistic aspect of society." He states, "Each language partner, when a 'move' pertaining to him is made, undergoes a 'displacement,' an alteration of some kind that not only affects him in his capacity as addressee and referent, but also as sender. These 'moves' necessarily provoke 'countermoves'—and everyone knows that a countermove that is merely reactional is not a 'good' move." Lyotard, *Postmodern Condition*, 16.

creativity within the game itself.[23] Communication is responsive rather than a fixed idea outside of experience.

The instability of language can be a source of discomfort. It signals a lack of control, forcing some to do all they can to control language.[24] But control amounts to little more than an illusion, based more on fantasy than reality. We can never control words, nor can the meaning of words be predicted. The author is ultimately betrayed by his or her own words.[25] Meaning continues to evolve and change as time and circumstances change.

Language and meaning never sit outside the world. They are situated in a place and time. Language may even create a world of meaning, but it is not its own master. Creation does not equal control.[26] Instead language continues to grasp for meaning. As its creator, it seeks to bring meaning under its domain. Yet meaning is not a cooperative creation. It refuses to remain under the tight control of the other. In fact, the creator/created relationship between language and meaning may be built on an illusion. Language asserts control because it is certain that it is the first cause of meaning. What language fails to realize is that meaning goes much deeper. Meaning connects to a mystery that goes beyond time and space, past and future. It

---

23. Lyotard uses the example of two friends in conversation. "The interlocutors use any available ammunition, changing games from one utterance to the next: questions, requests, assertions, and narratives are launched pell-mell into battle. The war is not without rules, but the rules allow and encourage the greatest possible flexibility of utterance." Lyotard, *Postmodern Condition*, 17.

24. This complete control is of course impossible. Civilizations ancient and modern have attempted to control language and thought. The endeavor ultimately results in failure. People should be free, in language and in thought. According to Cupitt, "Undisciplined, wayward speech is frightening. We mustn't allow our tongues to run away with us: hence the traditionally popular sermon topic of 'the government of the tongue'. What is needed to keep language and the world in order is the rule of one original founding and commanding will that has complete control of language and therefore of all the world. Whereas inconsequential talkativeness equals lack of control, an untidy world." Cupitt, *Fountain*, 21.

25. "Words run, and meaning proliferates. I cannot hope fully to control the meaning of what I have said. There is no way of guarding it against any possibility of future misinterpretation. . . . Cultural conditions have changed, language itself has changed, and I have changed—and I do not know how it is that some people's texts have the capacity to keep renewing themselves by taking on interesting new meanings as the years go by, whereas other people's texts become stale and boring." Cupitt, *Fountain*, 21–22.

26. For language to be, it should first lose itself. Its meaning is not tied to any value within itself, rather its meaning is found in its own loss. Nancy puts it this way, "Language says the world; that is, it loses itself in it and exposes how 'in itself' it is a question of losing oneself in order to be of it, with it, to be its meaning—which is all meaning." Nancy, *Being Singular Plural*, 3.

abides in language but is not tied to it. Instead, meaning abides in all things without ever feeling the need to be restricted.[27]

Flexibility and circulation represent the spirit of deconstruction. Its mode of belief is one of continual movement and expression. Its only affirmation or creed is that meaning should remain in flux. Meaning circulates around and around, never remaining bound to any one form. It repeats itself moment after moment. It is a never-ending sequence of present moments. Therefore, deconstruction repeatedly affirms the here and now.[28] Circulation of meaning avoids linear thinking. Sometimes B does not necessarily follow A. It may need to move past Z first.[29]

Deconstruction releases meaning from the prison of reason. It recognizes that meaning and truth best function when they are free. Deconstruction struggles against the institutional prisons that seek to control meaning, using reason as a weapon.[30] Institutions can trap reason, as if meaning and truth require careful control. Power embeds reason and forces it to regulate meaning and truth.[31] Deconstruction is the fight against this institutionalization and power. Especially where knowledge is only considered legitimate when it serves the goals of the community in power.[32] So much so

27. Nancy describes meaning as circulation. He writes that "this circulation goes in all directions at once, in all the directions of all the space-times [*les espace-temps*] opened by presence to presence: all things, all beings, all entities, everything past and future, alive, dead, inanimate, stones, plants, nails, gods—and 'humans.'" Nancy, *Being Singular Plural*, 3.

28. Nancy writes, "Circulation goes in all directions: this is the Nietzschean thought of the 'eternal return,' the affirmation of meaning as the repetition of the instant, nothing but this repetition, and as a result, nothing (since it is a matter of the repetition of what essentially does not return)." Nancy, *Being Singular Plural*, 4.

29. There are no rules as to where meaning must go. For example, "Circulation— or eternity—goes in all directions, but it moves only insofar as it goes from one point to another; spacing is its absolute condition. From place to place, and from moment to moment, without any progression or linear path, bit by bit and case by case, essentially accidental, it is singular and plural in its very principle. It does not have a final fulfillment any more than it has a point of origin." Nancy, *Being Singular Plural*, 4–5.

30. Caputo affirms that reason "has been institutionalized. It is not allowed to roam the streets freely . . . today reason is housed within the framework of an institution, like the university, that it functions within an administrative setting." Caputo, *Radical Hermeneutics*, 228.

31. Caputo describes reason as "always embedded in systems of power. To a great extent what 'reason' means is a function of the system of power which is currently in place, and what is irrational is what is out of power. Indeed it is of the essence of the power which institutionalized reason exerts that it is able to define what is out of power as 'irrational.' Caputo, *Radical Hermeneutics*, 229.

32. Lyotard writes that "knowledge has no final legitimacy outside of serving the goals envisioned by the practical subject, the autonomous collectivity." Lyotard,

that "knowledge is no longer the subject, but in service of the subject."[33] The ultimate criterion for knowledge becomes "what is it worth?"[34] The meaningful is defined ahead of time.

Deconstruction renews individual freedom and the joy of genuine discovery. This means letting go traditional conceptions of the academic intellectual and replacing this with a role that serves the wider culture and community. Relinquishing of power allows intellectuals to serve the community instead of the other way around.[35] Deconstruction trades power for play to give the greatest possibility for freedom of thought. In deconstruction, we come to recognize that the best chance of discovery, of listening, occurs within the game of play.[36] This game uses questioning, exceptions, and creativity as its tools.[37] The goal is not to arrive at conclusions but to find further questions.

MOVING BEYOND THE CENTER

Deconstruction moves us toward thinking without foundations or centers so that the work of listening and interpretation can take place.[38] It helps us to let go of our supposed need for a metaphysical foundation.[39] This

---

Postmodern Condition, 36.

33. Lyotard, *Postmodern Condition*, 36.

34. Missing here is the exploration and discovery of knowledge. Freedom is sacrificed in the name of "usefulness." Lyotard, *Postmodern Condition*, 54.

35. Vattimo envisions a new role for intellectuals. This means that "philosophers no longer sovereign, no longer counselors of princes, certainly means imaging a new, as yet undefined, role for the intellectual: not a scientist, not a technician, something more like a priest or an artist—but a priest without a hierarchy, and an artist of the streets." Vattimo, *A Farewell to Truth*, 21.

36. Caputo asserts that deconstruction "speaks in the name of freedom—of speech and writing and action—and of keeping the game fair. It warns against a rationality which declares its other irrational and seeks exclusion, like the leper, or its confinement, like the mad." Caputo, *Radical Hermeneutics*, 234.

37. "Modernity favours the universal, postmodernists saviour the singular and idiosyncratic. Modernist do not welcome exceptions to their rules; postmodernists think that the exception is the engine of creativity and the occasion on which the system can reinvent itself. Where modernists seek certitude, postmodernists see the salutary effects of a healthy scepticism" Caputo, *Truth*, 6.

38. Vattimo suggests that "the end of metaphysics is not merely the discovery, by a philosopher or by a school of thought, that Being is not the objectivity to which science has reduced it. It is above all associated with a series of events that have transformed our existence, of which postmetaphysical philosophy gives an interpretation rather an objective description." Vattimo, *After Christianity*, 15.

39. "A way must be found past, or beyond, metaphysics, or at any rate metaphysics

means a reorientation toward action itself. Reorientation is eliminating an ultimate signified or center in interpretation. Traditionally, the center is thought of has an organizing principle or fixed point that limits the free play of interpretation.[40] Often understood as God or humanity, the center has taken many forms throughout history.[41] No matter the form, all points are oriented toward and respond to this center, yet the center sits outside the field of play.[42] Being untouchable, the center serves as a continual reference point. It provides stability and purpose to history, philosophy, texts, and actions. The center sets the rules for the game. However, it goes much further than this. In addition to setting the rules, the center is the game itself. Moreover, the center is not subject to the game's outcome. The outcome has already been determined by the center. The center, Derrida writes, has a "fundamental immobility and a reassuring certitude, which itself is beyond the reach of play."[43]

Is this center necessary for interpretation? Even if a center could be determined, how would we engage with it? How can it shape and determine the field of play when it is unknowable and outside the scope of structure and interpretation? Interpretation is like a whirlwind continually swirling around and around. Like a hurricane, the center is absent and void. The high winds are not in the center of the storm. The action takes place outside the center. The destructive force of the storm is in the outer bands of wind and rain, while the center remains tranquil and calm. If we were to focus solely on the center, the storm would be missed altogether.

The indeterminate nature of the center suggests that we can do away with it altogether. The nature, state, and purpose of the center cannot be

---

must be rejected, not because it fails to include the subject of the theory and is thus incomplete but because it legitimates, with its objectivism, a social and historical order from which the liberty and originality of human existence have been erased." Vattimo, *A Farewell to Truth*, 31.

40. According to Derrida, "The function of this center was not only to orient, balance and organize the structure—one cannot in fact conceive of an unorganized structure—but above all to make sure that the organizing principle of the structure would limit what we might call the *play* of the structure." Derrida, *Writing and Difference*, 278 (emphasis original).

41. Consequently, "the entire history of the concept of structure, before the rupture of which we are speaking, must be thought of as a series of substitutions of center for center. . . . Successively, and in a regulated fashion, the center receives different forms and names." Derrida, *Writing and Difference*, 279.

42. Derrida writes, "The center is at the center of the totality, and yet, since the center does not belong to the totality (is not part of the totality), the totality *has its center elsewhere*. The center is not the center." Derrida, *Writing and Difference*, 279 (emphasis original).

43. Derrida, *Writing and Difference*, 279.

agreed upon. As such there should not be so much effort to interpret around it.[44] It is like trying to play a game when no one can agree on what rules to follow.

To play the game, decentering works as a process of interpretation. Instead of substituting the center, we eliminate it, and in the place of the center is an exchange of signifiers without a signified.[45] Derrida makes the case that the signifier "must be abandoned as a metaphysical concept."[46] Instead, the signifier must be a concept of play. The removal of the metaphysical moves interpretation from reductionism to openness. Thus, this pushes the field of interpretative play wide open. Signifiers, unlike the center, cannot be exhausted.[47] Signifiers function as a supplementary, thus there is always something more.[48] The absence of a center adds to meaning. Therefore, meaning is the absence of meaning.[49] Deconstruction functions in this paradox.

Decentering is a manner of renewing interpretive play and play lives in the absence of presence. When we establish a center, play is pushed aside. For play to occur, it requires freedom and empty space.[50] Play requires freedom to explore without repercussions, and empty space is used to test and try out new interpretations. Due to its supplementary nature, play moves

44. Thus, "The substitute does not substitute itself for anything which has somehow existed before it. Henceforth, it was necessary to begin thinking that there was no center, that the center could not be thought in the form of a present-being, that the center had no natural site, that it was not a fixed locus but a function, a sort of nonlocus in which an infinite number of sign-substitutions came into play . . . everything became discourse." Derrida, *Writing and Difference*, 280.

45. Derrida, *Writing and Difference*, 279.

46. Derrida, *Writing and Difference*, 281.

47. Signification is never fixed because it is in flux. It is not a fixed concept, rather it is continually on the move. Because it is floating, there is never a lack of things that can be said about it. In other words, "The movement of signification adds something, which results in the fact that there is always more, but this addition is a floating one because it comes to perform a vicarious function, to supplement a lack on the part of the signified." Derrida, *Writing and Difference*, 289.

48. This more, Derrida maintains, is supplementarity. He suggests "that this movement of play, permitted by the lack or absence of a center or origin, is the movement of *supplementarity*. One cannot determine the center and exhaust totalization because the sign . . . occurs as a surplus, as a *supplement*." Derrida, *Writing and Difference*, 289 (emphasis original).

49. The *overabundance* of the signifier, its supplementary character, is thus the result of a finitude, that is to say, the result of a lack which must be *supplemented*." Derrida, *Writing and Difference*, 290 (emphasis original).

50. According to Francoise Dastur, "Play needs something like an empty space in order to be set free, that is, in order for it to have a field of infinite substitutions, where each signified is able to become in turn a signifier." Dastur, "Play and Messianicity," 191.

between presence and absence.[51] Play drives the movement between signifiers, creating an endless action of substitutions between terms.[52]

This is not a matter of introducing play into interpretation. Play makes interpretation possible. Derrida suggests that play is confirmed "before the alternative of presence and absence."[53] Embracing play means moving past talk of centers and foundations.[54] It means ending the quest to decipher the center, as if that is only where truth resides. Play is a risk and gamble for the unexpected in interpretation. It is much like walking a tight rope across a great chasm. We cannot count on there being a safety net in case of falling.[55] Getting to where we have never been requires letting go of the comfort and security of what is already know. In interpretation we are faced with two irreconcilable choices. We can choose to search for centers and metaphysical foundations, or we can choose play.[56]

Centers and foundations are rarely content with their given space. They have the tendency to gather more and more space until they become absolutes. As absolutes, they dominate the field, and consequently control all available space. They create an indomitable boundary that clouds all theoretical and interpretative judgments. Across all fields of knowledge,

51. "Play is the disruption of presence. The presence of an element is always a signifying and substitutive reference inscribed in a system of difference and the movement of a chain. Play is always play of absence and presence." Derrida, *Writing and Difference*, 292.

52. Dastur describes play as "always the interplay of presence and absence, because it is what allows the substitution of one term by another one, the supplement of one term by another one, the supplement of one term through another one." Dastur, "Play and Messianicity," 191.

53. Derrida, *Writing and Difference*, 292.

54. "Presence and absence are *functions* of play, as well as are subject, center, and origin, which, for Derrida, have nothing other than a functional value. Dastur, "Play and Messianicity," 191.

55. "[Interpretation] plays without security. For there is a *sure* play: that which is limited to the *substitution* of *given* and *existing, present,* pieces. In absolute chance, affirmation also surrenders itself to *genetic* indetermination, to the *seminal* adventure of the trace." Derrida, *Writing and Difference*, 292 (emphasis original).

56. Derrida suggests that there are "two interpretations of interpretation, of structure, of sign, of play. The one seeks to decipher, dreams of deciphering a truth or an origin which escapes play and the order of the sign, and which lives the necessity of interpretation as an exile. The other, which is no longer turned toward the origin, affirms play and tries to pass beyond man and humanism, the name of man being the name of that being who, throughout the history of metaphysics or of ontotheology—in other words, throughout his entire history—*has dreamed of full presence, the reassuring foundation, the origin and the end of play.*" Derrida, *Writing and Difference*, 292 (emphasis original).

centers and foundations grab more power.[57] In order for play to flourish, it needs room to meander and explore.

Difference

Play lives and thrives in difference, yet this difference is unexpected. It is not the limiting difference of structuralism. Structuralist difference, for example, is methodological. It is based on a system of differences. Identity distinguishes things from one another, which in turn are based on their difference to other identities.[58] Identity becomes a negative quality, having no substantial positive implications. As such, things are known by what they are not. A structuralist account is much like a dictionary, signs are only recognizable because of their difference to other signs. This reduces knowledge to a system of relations, and nothing can escape this structure.[59] It is like being caught in the horizon of a black hole. No idea, word, or concept can escape the differential causality. Truth suffers in this system because any positive assertion is based on a negative one.

Deconstruction does not advocate such a negative view.[60] Structuralist difference has no interest in truth. Structuralism abandons any truth beyond its system of relations.[61] We abandon play when everything becomes a system of differences. Terms, ideas, and actions become fixed and

57. From Aristotle to Newton, Hawking demonstrates how absolutes throughout history have generally proved to be incorrect. General relativity and quantum theory have both deconstructed the idea of space and time remaining fixed. Hawking, *A Brief History*, 18–34.

58. Claire Colebrook explains that for a structuralist, the "account of difference is primarily methodological: if we want to study a language or any other social structure it is more fruitful to look at the ways systems generate differences, rather than assume that various structures simply label the same common reality." Colebrook, "Difference," 59.

59. To explain this structure Colebrook explains, "We could only have the concept of 'cat' because we have a practice of differentiating among animals, and—in turn—of differentiating animals from humans and so on. Those differences between terms are negations, and we never arrive at anything positive, anything that simply *is*. Colebrook, "Difference," 61 (emphasis original).

60. "It is possible to note that some of the dismissive claims made about deconstruction—that it abandons truth, meaning, and reality to focus on the free play of difference—are far from accurate." Colebrook, "Difference," 60.

61. Colebrook explains that "Derrrida poses two objections to this acceptance of negative or relative difference. We cannot, without contradiction, abandon claims to truth and remain within a system of differences. The structuralist claim that we might look at systems in relation to each other, without any sense of what might be true above and beyond any system, is itself a truth claim." Colebrook, "Difference," 60.

therefore stagnate. Difference depends on the system, thus becoming a slave to the system.[62]

Abandoning truth and abandoning the center are not equal. Deconstruction is concerned with opening structures and systems. Deconstruction has something more mysterious in mind when referring to the endless play of signifiers, substitution, and reference. Colebrook explains that deconstruction's difference refers "to the difference from which systems of difference emerge."[63] In deconstruction, difference is the play that occurs before, between, and after concepts. Difference is a process of unraveling the systems of construction. It directs us toward what is happening in the presence and non-presence of things and events.[64]

Différance

Deconstruction's response to structuralism is not stronger concepts, but weaker ones. In fact, it offers something so weak that we cannot call it a concept at all, *différance*.[65] *Différance* is neither a word nor a concept, meaning it expresses a state between speaking and writing.[66] *Différance* comes before expression and has no form or being. Moreover, it has no existence, granting it the freedom to exceed all things as the least of all things.[67] The changing

---

62. Colebrook writes that "there can be a difference between two identities only if there is some system, network, or field of relations (such as language, consciousness, or even a space in which beings are distributed so that they might differ from each other)." Colebrook, "Difference," 57.

63. Colebrook, "Difference," 61.

64. Colebrook writes, "What Derrida is aiming to articulate is a non-identical or differing time that is not yet organized into before and after, and a space that does not have a centered point of view synthesized into a here and there." Colebrook, "Difference," 65.

65. "At the heart of Derridean deconstruction is the idea of *différance*, a word coined by Derrida, which is itself a pun of the French word *"différer."* In French, the word *différer* has two meanings: to *differ* and to *defer*, and thus, Derrida's invented word is illustrative of his understanding of language: that words have multiple meanings encapsulated within themselves, and that in each context one of these meanings must be deferred." Shepherd, *The Gift*, 48 (emphasis original).

66. Derrida explains that *différance* "belongs neither to the voice nor to writing in the usual sense, and which is located, as a strange space . . . *between* speech and writing, and beyond the tranquil familiarity which links us to one and the other, occasionally reassuring us in our illusion that they are two." Derrida, *Margins of Philosophy*, 5 (emphasis original).

67. Derrida claims that *différance* "does not exist, is not a present-being (*on*) in any form; and we will be led to delineate also everything *that* it *is not*, that is, *everything*; and consequently that it has neither existence nor essence. It derives from no category

of *e* to an *a*[68] is no mere linguistic trick,[69] it represents the anti-concept, the insensible, and the un-intelligble. It is the quintessential fuzzy term, bordering on being both utterly ridiculous and completely brilliant. As being both non-conceptual and non-categorical, it is perhaps both. Its realm is no realm at all, *Différance* lives in the in-between and far away spaces bordering on meaning and meaningless.[70]

This non-existent concept, being that which no weaker can be conceived, unsettles the settled. What *différance* does, or rather undoes, are foundationalist principles that attempt to view the world without interpretative lenses.[71] It challenges attempts that dismiss signs as arbitrary to a predefined center or its equivalent,[72] or bypasses signs to find the nature, cause, or source of things. As a result, signs become substitutes or place holders. The sign has nothing to say for itself, and thus defers its presence to another.[73] Instead, signs not only defer, but also differ. A sign's identity is in part built on its difference to other signs. Here structuralism is partially correct. Signs do differ, that is they distinguish themselves from other signs.

---

of being, whether present or absent." Derrida continues by stating that *différance* "is not only irreducible to any ontological or theological—ontotheological—reappropriation, but as the very opening of the space in which ontotheology—philosophy—produces its system and its history, it includes ontotheology,inscribing and exceeding it without return." Derrida, *Margins of Philosophy*, 6 (emphasis original).

68. For example, Derrida describes the *a* of *différance* as referring "to the generative movement in the play of differences. The latter are neither fallen from the sky nor inscribed once and for all in a closed system, a static structure that a synchronic ad taxonomic operation could exhaust." Derrida, *Positions*, 27.

69. Gary Gutting clarifies that "*différance* is not just an orthographical trick or joke. Derrida is now using it as a term that refers to linguistic differences that cannot be expressed in either speech or writing, so that it itself can be said to be somehow 'beyond' both speech and writing." Gutting, "Obscurity of 'Différance,'" 74.

70. "Derrida is blunt in letting us know that there will be no exposition, no explanation in familiar terms, of *différance*. All he is prepared to offer us is a vocabulary that walks the edge of contradiction or meaninglessness, precisely because it concerns what lies beyond consistency and meaning, beyond presence." Gutting, "Obscurity of 'Différance,'" 75.

71. Gutting argues that Derrida "is rejecting the idea of foundational experience that gives us the world just as it is in itself, free of any interpretation through concepts and/or language." Gutting, "Obscurity of 'Différance,'" 78.

72. "According to this classical semiology, the substitution of the sign for the thing itself is both *secondary* and *provisional*." Derrida, *Margins of Philosophy*, 9 (emphasis original).

73. Derrida writes, "The sign is usually said to be put in the place of the thing itself, the present thing, 'thing' here standing equally from meaning or referent. The sign represents the present in its absence. It takes the place of the present. . . . The sign, in this sense, is deferred presence." Derrida, *Margins of Philosophy*, 9.

Presence and Absence

Problems arise when we spend too much time on either side of defer and differ. Both defer and differ tend to lead us toward reductionism. Defer treats signs as arbitrary and illusions of the real. Differ traps signs in categorization. *Différance*, on the other hand, does something unique. Because the French verb *différer* can mean both *differ* and *defer*, *différance* represents the forgotten *middle voice*.[74] Philosophy has traditionally lived in the active or the passive.[75] Philosophy is active in its use of propositions and confident declarations. For philosophy, the active represents the idea of presence. Philosophy asserts truth, beauty, and goodness. The passive represents philosophy's negative aspects, such as *apophatic* or negative theology. The negative emphasizes what is not known or can never be known. Absence, rather than presence, becomes the dominate feature. *Différance*, with its distinctive middle voice, represents both and neither. It expresses what lives between presence and absence. The middle voice has elements of the active and passive but is neither. *Différance* is not an active agent. It does not do things to signs, actions, and words. *Différance* is not a presence now absent.[76]

   Différance is the condition or possibility of differential play. It suggests a space where differences interact.[77] However, *différance* is not the cause of these differences. It does not direct difference. *Différance* is the undefined play between the signs.[78] Caputo describes it as a "quasi-condition of possibility."[79] This demonstrates why *différance* cannot be a word or a concept. Descriptions are too strong for it. *Différance* suggests and allows instead of demanding and prescribing. Its traits are weak. *Différance* is an

74. According to Derrida, "We must consider that in the usage of our language the ending -*ance* remains undecided *between* the active and the passive. And we will see why that which lets itself be designated *différance* is neither simply active nor simply passive, announcing or rather recalling something like the middle voice." Derrida, *Margins of Philosophy*, 9 (emphasis original).

75. Derrida, *Margins of Philosophy*, 9.

76. Describing its middle voice, Derrida describes *différance* as "neither simply active nor simply passive, announcing or rather recalling something like the middle voice, saying an operation that is not an operation, an operation that cannot be conceived either as passion or as the action of a subject on an object." Derrida, *Margins of Philosophy*, 9.

77. *Différance* is "the systematic play of differences, of the traces of diffferences, of the *spacing* by means of which elements are related to each other." Derrida, *Positions*, 27.

78. This is described by Derrida as a "playing movement that 'produces'—by means of something that is not simply an activity—these difference, these effects of difference." Derrida, *Margins of Philosophy*, 11.

79. Caputo, *Deconstruction*, 102.

unsettling presence that upsets and questions structures, ideas, and traditions. Its intent is not to destroy, but to open these concepts toward truth.[80] *Différance* is far less like a bull in a china shop and more akin to a fleeting glimpse at the corner of one's eye. By the time we turn to look, it is already gone.

Différance does not provide easy answers. It is meant to be frustrating. Its game is one of disorder.[81] Thus, *différance* is not going to abide by the traditional rules. *Différance* pushes for continual play between ideas, things, and actions. It is the space that makes room for the unexpected to emerge. *Différance* allows for the breakdown of powerful thoughts, like metaphysics, so that we can be surprised.[82] If *différance* was only a method of destroying things, then it we could dismiss it. If its job was deconstruction for the sake of deconstruction, then there would be no reason to take it seriously. But *différance* has no such ambitions. Behind its perceived madness is a deep desire for truth and authenticity. It is the search for truth and authenticity underneath the many layers of power and authority. Thus, *différance* stands in opposition to power structures, traditions, and institutions that bury truth.[83] *Différance* provides the conditions for creating openness.[84]

80. *Différance* does not suggest that structures cannot exist. Instead it leads us toward transforming those structures, especially when those structures overpower other possibilities. To clarify, Derrida explains "that the production of difference, *différance*, is not astructural: it produces systematic and regulated transformations which are able, at a certain point, to leave room for a structural science." Derrida, *Positions*, 28.

81. *Différance* is meant to be difficult. As Caputo describes it, "*différance* imposes upon us all the necessity to work out meaning and reference by the work, sweat, and pain of the 'play' (some fun!) of differences." Caputo, *Deconstruction*, 103.

82. Gutting states, "*Différance, as Derrida* portrays it, seems to be that which undermines presence by introducing the contrary characteristics of negativity, incompleteness, complexity, dependence, and derivation, thereby compromising the 'integrity' of metaphysical and epistemological presence." Gutting, "Obscurity of Différance," 78.

83. *Différance* by its very nature is subversive, but subversive in the name of weakness. As Caputo explains that "the very idea of *différance*, if it is an idea, is the idea of no more reigning, no more sovereigns, no more kingdoms, not now, not ever. *Différance* is the very idea of instigating the subversion of kingdoms wherever they appear." Caputo, *Weakness of* God, 26.

84. There needs to be openness in order for the integrity of the game to be preserved. The job of *différance*, according to Caputo, is to "establish the conditions which make possible our beliefs and our practices, our traditions and our institutions, *and* no less to make them impossible, which means to see to it that they do not effect closure, to keep them open so that something new or different may happen." Caputo, *Prayers and Tears*, 12 (emphasis original).

Openness requires us to challenge those who may not be willing to give up their power.[85]

Différance does not make appearances. There is no visible evidence left behind in its wake. There is no such thing as a sighting of *différance*. It is much too elusive and too weak to see. *Différance* has no domain of its own. Thus, *différance* does not replace metaphysics. Its intent is not to replace one tyrant with another. Derrida describes *différance* as something without authority or control. He writes:

> It is not a present being, however excellent, unique, principal, or transcendent. It governs nothing, reigns over nothing, and no-where exercises any authority. It is not announced by any capital letter. Not only is there no kingdom of *différance*, but *différance* instigates the subversion of every kingdom. Which makes it obviously threatening, and infallibly dreaded by everything within us that desires a kingdom, the past or future presence of a kingdom. And it is always in the name of a kingdom that one may reproach *différance* with wishing to reign, believing that one sees it aggrandize itself with a capital letter.[86]

Différance suggests the possibility of hermeneutics without metaphys-ics. It eliminates the need to invoke some presence or absence to interpret.[87] Interpretation does not require a reference point outside the scope of the interpreted. Consequently, ritual action has no *ghost in the machine*, as if ritual action is empty until filled by an unknown essence.

---

85. *Différance* can be antagonistic. *Différance*, Caputo writes, "is neutral by be-ing uniformly nasty about letting vocabularies establish their credentials and get set in place, as if they really were making good in some strong sense on their claims. Its neutrality lies in its unremitting and unbiased antagonism, which does not single out theologians for particular abuse but which is equally hostile to all ontological claims, across the board." Caputo, *Prayers and Tears*, 14.

86. Derrida, *Margins of Philosophy*, 22.

87. Gutting follows with a critique with Derrida's use of *différance*. He makes the case that *différance* could easily become another metaphysic. *Différance* could become a language of ultimate truth as easily as it protects us from the illusion of ultimate truth. In Derrida, Gutting sees a tendency toward the former. It is therefore helpful to remember that we walk a fine line between both presence and absence. We always face the temptation of powerful concepts and ideas. *Différance* is no different. Used incorrectly *différance* could become a tyrant, yet the unnameable it represents resists such usage. Gutting explains that Derrida "is trying to develop a language to replace (or at least oppose) the traditional philosophical languages built around presence. This language flows from '*différance*' a term designed to escape from and undermine the allegedly fundamental distinctions of traditional philosophy." See Gutting, "Obscurity of 'Différance,'" 87.

Complicating Reference

Différance complicates reference. It complicates reference so that reference can remain open.[88] As such, *différance* does not escape the chain of difference and deferment.[89] It embraces both so that reference remains open and alive. Derrida famous statement, *"There is nothing outside of the text* [there is no outside-text; *il n'y pas hors-texte*],[90] is not meant to be limiting. It is not an endorsement of an extreme textuality such as biblical literalism. *Différance* is meant to be liberating. Derrida's statement affirms that nothing lives outside context. Reference cannot be limited to a dictionary, as if difference could be codified independent of context. Nothing can retreat into a world outside reference. We cannot bracket off terms and concepts so that they remain untouchable. This Platonic ideal presupposes a perfect realm where concepts reign free from the corrupting influence of context.[91] Actions, words, events, and ideas always remain bound to context, which is another way of saying relationship. Context and reference are a commitment to relationship, and everything remains connected to the other.[92] Nothing stands as if in a perfect state. This emphasis on context prevents metaphysical abuses that devalue activities such as ritual action.

Différance Toward Difference

Différance is hard to understand. It does not lend itself to easy explanations or unchanging principles. As a weak concept, *différance* is precisely not a transcendental puppet master. It does not command from above. *Différance* is content with allowing the repetition of difference to happen. It provides the fertile ground for keeping difference alive and healthy. *Différance* does not create difference because it lacks the power to do so. Though weak, it challenges the strong and powerful. It allows the *not* to challenge the *what is*.[93] In and of itself, *différance* points to something that is already hap-

88. "Deconstruction means to complicate reference, not to deny it; it insists that there is no reference without difference." Caputo, *Prayers and Tears*, 17.

89. Derrida, *Margins of Philosophy*, 26.

90. Derrida, *Of Grammatology*, 158.

91. "There is no 'access' to either the world *or ourselves* which is not subject to the differing and deferrings of differance; as such, the world and even consciousness are never simply of fully 'present.'" Smith, *Jacques Derrida*, 44–45.

92. According to Smith, "Derrida sketches a subject who is constituted by a relation to an exteriority—the alterity of the Other in the communal networks of signification." Smith, *Jacques Derrida*, 45.

93. This is the spirit of deconstruction. It makes room for the *not*. It chooses the

pening within things, actions, language, and ritual. According to Caputo, "Difference is not the external, the accidental, but a kind of a priori which inhabits things from the start."[94] *Différance* is not something imposed onto things. Instead, it is a part of our configuration. Therefore, *différance* is a constant movement back and forth as things continual refer to one another. It is a movement of repetition, and *différance* is within this repetition, constantly encouraging movement. *Différance* is the small voice urging us to play with terms and meanings. It is the continual *yes, and* in interpretation. *Différance* is life within the "flux."[95] Flux being the idea that things continually evolve and forever remaining unfinished.[96]

Différance is a commitment to openness. It abandons comfortable interpretations for hard ones. Its approach is one of continual anxiety.[97] The task of interpretation is burdensome because it never ends. There is always be more to discover as a small voice eternally whispers to us, "good, but not yet." Therefore, we need *différance* for approaching ritual action. It leads us toward an open and honest engagement with the actions. Hermeneutics initiates the conversation, but deconstruction leads us further into the conversation. Deconstruction rightly sees that the conversation cannot and should not end.[98] For ritual action this means a commitment to the conver-

---

not over the things that are. *Différance* opens us toward the *not*. Here we are reminded of the words of the Apostle Paul when he writes, "Consider your own call, brothers and sisters: *not* many of you were wise by human standards, *not* many were powerful, *not* many were of noble birth. But God chose what is foolish in the world to shame the wise; God chose what is weak in the world to shame the strong; God chose what is low and despised in the world, things that are *not*, to reduce to nothing things that are, so that no one might boast in the presence of God." 1 Cor. 1:26–29 (NRSV) (emphasis added).

94. Caputo, *Radical Hermeneutics*, 130.

95. Flux is a term Caputo uses to describe the undetermined nature of interpretation. Caputo writes that "this 'not' is built right in, that it is no merely temporary inconvenience which we hope to remove by the first of the month. It recognizes that we are caught up in the flux, breached by the 'not,' that the only honest thing to do, indeed the only thing to do at all, honest or not, is press forward." Caputo, *Radical Hermeneutics*, 130.

96. Caputo writes that "the thesis of de(con)structibility of the world means that whatever unities of meaning are constituted in natural languages, whatever normalized form experience assumes, whatever institutionalization our practices receive, all are alike vulnerable, alterable, contingent. They have not fallen from the sky; they are structurally, eidetically vulnerable, however much they have tended to gain acceptance." Caputo, *Radical Hermeneutics*, 144.

97. This state, Caputo describes, is the "readiness for this anxiety and solicitation, the readiness to be shaken, the openness for *différance*." Caputo, *Radical Hermeneutics*, 146.

98. "A hermeneutic comes to pass only in the element of movement and *kinesis*, and it requires ceaseless deconstructive vigilance to 'maintain' itself there, so that it will

sation of action. Deconstruction provides ways of listening to differences at play. It allows the conversation to live on its own without the heavy handedness of strong concepts like metaphysics, presence, and absence. Difference and *différance* suggest that weakness is the best approach to ritual action. Interpretation should begin from the bottom. It must be a process that engages and embraces the ambiguities and complexities of ritual action.

In practice, this means engaging with those who perform ritual action. It is a process that listens carefully to participants' everyday thoughts, experience, and opinions concerning the ritual action itself. It is an immersion and submission into the heart of ritual action. This listening seeks to understand ritual action on its own terms, without forcing it into strong categories such as metaphysics or structuralism. It is listening for the sake of listening. However, listening on its own is not enough. It requires us to go even further. In *différance*, we embrace ambiguity, search for complexity, and play with difference. *Différance* provides us the space for engaging all the various elements of ritual action. It encourages us to play with personal experience and tradition, language and action, and the spiritual and mundane. It pushes us beyond just a description of ritual action. *Différance* is the encouragement to live in it. Living *différance* requires that we face the complexities, strangeness, and mystery of life. Therefore, our goal is not to solve ritual action like a puzzle. Ritual action is not a problem needing our explanation. It is not a machine that we need to disassemble. *Différance* has no interest in such trivialities. It pushes us to seek questions not answers. It asks us to think without the end. *Différance* opens us to the event within ritual action.

EVENT

Différance encourages us to go further into ritual action. It opens us toward the space where we can see not only what is happening, but what is occurring *in the happening itself*. *Différance* points us toward the event.[99] The event is the undefinable, undetermined, and unexpected occurring in ritual action. No one cannot point to it and say, "here it is!" The event is not identifiable in a tangible way. We cannot describe it as a part of a structure or sequence. Like *différance*, events lack a real, defined presence.[100] Having

---

not get off at the first stop." Caputo, *Radical Hermeneutics*, 147.

99. Caputo defines event as "not what happens, which is what the word suggests in English, but something going on *in* what happens, something that is expressed or realized or given shape in what happens." Caputo, "Spectral Hermeneutics," 47.

100. Caputo clarifies that "it is not something present, but something seeking to

no presence, events are not an addition to ritual action. Events do not come from above or outside ritual action. They do not stand apart from ritual action. Like *différance*, event has no home to call its own. Because it is weak, it is stuck between presence and absence. It has no power to announce itself. Where *différance* suggests play, events point to what is happening *within* ritual action.

Name and Event

Events have no realm or place of their own. We cannot find an event apart from the names that contain them. Names and events have a symbiotic relationship. Within names are structured forms. They provide tried and true patterns that we can identify. From actions to texts, names can consist of a variety of different things. Caputo describes names as "historical, contingent, provisional expressions in natural languages."[101] A name is something we use to help identify a person, place, or thing. It gives us a sense of control. Naming a phenomenon is the first step toward understanding it. For example, someone's name is typically the first question we ask when meeting new people. Knowing someone's name helps to stabilize the situation. We may know nothing about the other person, and yet there is a sense of comfort that comes from knowing a name. Without the name, there is a nagging sense of incompleteness. The other needs to be identifiable. You must have a name! This is that same concern Moses had when he encountered God through the burning bush. Moses needed to know God's name for himself and the Hebrews.[102]

Names are strong terms. They represent far more than personal labels. Names point to the known and establish limits of what is known. We cannot name the unknown. Consequently, names consist of the traditions, texts, and actions that comprise the observable and predictable. Names help to mark and organize the past. They are crucial for us to identify the *what* of what has happened. Names can represent the powerful, and thus mark important institutions and occurrences of the past. Names also carry historical baggage. The names of institutions carry a variety of meanings.[103] For

---

make itself felt in what is present." Caputo "Spectral Hermeneutics," 47.

101. Caputo, *Weakness of God*, 48.

102. Ex. 3:13–14 (NRSV).

103. "Names can accumulate historical power and worldly prestige and have very powerful institutions erected in or under their name, getting themselves carved in stone, whereas the voice of events is ever soft and low and is liable to be dismissed, distorted, or ignored." Caputo, *Weakness of God*, 2.

example, the names *White House, Catholic Church,* and *Wall Street* suggest power, honor, and even corruption. However, names are also conditional, working within a defined set of boundaries.[104] A name such as the *White House* represents a stable institution and carries with it an agreed upon definition. Its definition is based on its function.

Though names represent stability, they also contain the unstable event. A name is never just a name. Within it moves something both miraculous and wonderful. The event draws us to the name and provide us with an unquantifiable factor that grasps us in its presence.[105] We already know what to expect with a name. Defined and historical conditioned, a name leaves very little room for the unexpected. Yet events are the moment of surprise within the name. Coming from nowhere, events provide us with the unexpected joy or thrill when encountering mystery within the stable.[106]

Event is the unexplainable grasp, some might say conviction, we feel when observing or participating in a worship service. It has no limits, and it can occur anywhere and at any time. Thus, the most moving experiences do not necessarily occur at a *proper time*. Indeed, it is often not the predetermined *events* that are moving but the unintentional ones. We might encounter the event in a spoken word, an image, a movement, or even the comical. Religious activities, like ritual action, are obvious candidates for events to occur. However, events are not bound to predefined religious activity. The beauty of the event, having no defined presence, is that it has no limits. A simple drive around town, talks with friends, and even walking down the aisle of the local grocery store are all candidates for the unexpected. Events can surprise us in the most unlikely of circumstances.[107] Life itself seems designed around such moments of extreme astonishment.[108]

104. Names "belong to conditioned and coded strings of signifiers." Caputo, *Weakness of God*, 2.

105. We are drawn to the name by the event within it. Caputo describes events as "provocations and promises, and they have the structure of what Derrida calls the unforeseeable 'to come.'" Caputo, "Spectral Hermeneutics," 48.

106. An event "is something we cannot see coming that takes us by surprise, like a letter that arrives unexpectedly in the mail with news that changes your life for ever, for better or for worse." Caputo, *Truth*, 75.

107. "Daily life is full of such unexpected events, sometimes very subtle, like an aside by a teacher that changes the course of a student's life. The teacher does not know this has happened and at the time neither does the student. That is the event." Caputo, *Truth*, 75.

108. For example, Cupitt describes the universe as "just one great Event (or pulse), a vast explosion of energy still slowly scattering and dying. It is not, as they say, 'going anywhere'; it's going everywhere, and its history does not fulfil any purpose." Cupitt, *Fountain*, 24.

Though unexpected, the event leaves us in a state Rudolf Otto describes as the *"mysterium tremendum."*[109] The words *mysterium*[110] and *tremendum*[111] indicate the simultaneous state of enchantment by both mystery and fear. This is a state of overwhelming mystery and awe that comes on suddenly and without warning. And yet, it can be very gentle. Such events can be calming, providing comfort and security. The event is strange, pushing you from the known to the unknown. Otto calls this "creature-feeling,"[112] referring to the sense of awe we have when encountering the event. Tillich calls it the experience of "ultimate concern."[113] Events are moments of feeling grasped by the unknown. It is the experience of being *consumed* by the other.

The event has an element of the unintelligible. It is unlike anything else and is therefore beyond comparison. The event thrives on the edge or reason, continually playing on the mind.[114] At times we may even believe that we can hold and identify it. The event itself provides us hope that it can be grasped in some manner or form.[115] And yet, the event cannot be

109. Rudolf Otto describes the state of *mysterium tremendum* as a feeling that "may at times come sweeping like a gentle tide, pervading the mind with a tranquil mood of deepest worship. It may pass over into a more set and lasting attitude of the soul, continuing, as it were, thrillingly vibrant and resonant until at last it dies away and the soul resumes its 'profane', non-religious mood of everyday experience." Otto, *Idea of the Holy*, 12.

110. According to Otto, "*mysterium* denotes merely that which is hidden and esoteric, that which is beyond conception of understanding, extraordinary and unfamiliar." Otto, *Idea of the Holy*, 13.

111. *Tremendum* is related to *tremor* or fear. This is not fear in the normal sense, but the stirring ofsomething "'uncanny', 'eerie', or 'weird'. It is this feeling which, emerging in the mind of primeval [human], forms the starting-point for the entire religious development in history." Otto, *Idea of the Holy*, 14.

112. Otto describes this creature-feeling as an encounter with divine. There is no need to make that connection yet. Now it is enough to say that an encounter with an event is also an encounter with our finitude. Events can make us acutely aware of our own existence and mortality. Otto writes that creature-feeling "is the emotion of a creature, submerged and overwhelmed by its own nothingness in contrast to that which is supreme above all creatures." Otto, *Idea of the Holy*, 10.

113. Ultimate concern is a total act of the self. It is that which concerns us ultimately. Tillich describes it as that which "is unconditional, independent of any conditions of character, desire, or circumstance. The unconditional concern is total: no part of ourselves or of our world is excluded from it; there is no 'place' to flee from it." Tillich, *Systematic Theology, Volume 1*, 12.

114. Otto uses the phrase "wholly other" to describe an event "which is quite beyond the sphere of the usual, the intelligible, and the familiar, which therefore falls quite outside the limits of the 'canny', and is contrasted with it, filling the mind with blank wonder and astonishment." Otto, *Idea of the Holy*, 26.

115. Otto's own project holds on to this hope that the event does not escape

grasped fully. Names may carry events within them, but these names are not complete translations of events. It is necessary to make a careful distinction between the historical contingency of names and the ahistorical event happening within.

Exceeding the Name

Names are a way to understand the event. It is an attempt to translate the event to understand it. This translation is a never ending historical process of engaging the event. Names are temporary and never meant to be for all time. They change with the times as new generations attempt to understand the event housed within the name.[116] Names are therefore the caretakers of the event. Names have the special task of carrying and evoking the event itself. Moreover, names offer that initial push to get things started.[117] They prepare us for the event, and then slip away into the background.

Names are special because they provide us with a point of engagement with the event. They bring a concrete manifestation to an ever-evolving event. Thus, the name should must not be mistaken for the event itself. We should not create systems out of names, instead events resist systematization. Events seek to escape the limiting boundaries of systematic thinking. Names are and should be deconstructible.[118] Names do not have the final say, for the event is never bound to a name.

Events live in excess.[119] Within the name, the event pushes against the bounds of the name. Though a name may contain the event, it does so temporarily. The event always moves us forward, toward something promised. Uncomfortable with the status quo, the event stirs within the name. This stirring and shaking is not for its own benefit. Events do not deconstruct for the sake of deconstructing. What appears as deconstruction is actually an

---

rationality. He writes that "though it eludes the conceptual way of understanding, it must be in some way or other within our grasp, else absolutely nothing could be asserted of it." Otto, *Idea of the Holy*, 2.

116. Names are translatable according to Caputo. As he puts it, "Names are endlessly translatable, whereas events are what names are trying to translate." Caputo, *Weakness of God*, 3.

117. Caputo states, "Names are asked to carry what they cannot bear toward a destination they do not know. Names are trying to make things happen, while events are what is happening." Caputo, *Weakness of God*, 3.

118. "Words and things are deconstructible, but events . . . are not deconstructible." Caputo, "Spectral Hermeneutics," 48.

119. Events, according to Caputo, "overtake us and outstrip the reach of the subject or the ego. . . . The event arises independently of me and comes over me, so that an event is also an *advent*." Caputo, *Weakness of God*, 4.

invitation.[120] It is our invitation to consider new possibilities resulting from the play of differences. Event is potential. It is not interested in what has been, but what *can be*.

Events are like a seed within the *what is*, which is hidden away, shifting from place to place. It seeks the right soil to grow and to flourish.[121] Therefore, it is not a matter of if it will grow, but *when*. The event must grow, for it carries something of immense importance. For within this seed is something that will forever change the experiences of all who come into its presence. The event only needs room to grow and nutrients to feed it. If conditions are favorable, the event can grow into something truly magnificent and awe inspiring. From a sapling to a mighty oak, the event reaches to the sky using every ounce of its energy to go further and further. Events change the look and shape of the world they inhabit. Like the oak, they draw our gaze. Events create seemingly sacred moments out of mundane ones so that we encounter that sense of transcendence that brings our fullness into being. It is a transcendence that makes the trivial special and the sacred inspiring.[122] This transcendence does not force us to gaze away, as if to ignore the moment at hand. It allows us to look at the beauty or awe within things themselves.[123] The event, Otto describes, puts us into a "*stupor . . .* blank wonder, an astonishment that strikes us dumb, amazement absolute."[124] This can only be described as an encounter with the infinite.[125] The infinite is the draw of the event.

The event's infinite nature, being both uncontainable and unlimited, is precisely its appeal and source of power. The infinite holds the desire of

120. The event is described by Caputo as "something signaling us from afar, something waiting for us to catch up, something inviting, promising, provoking, and let us say, for this is a word that packs a special punch in theology, something *promised.*" Caputo, "Spectral Hermeneutics," 52.

121. Caputo characterizes events as "tender shoots and saplings, the most vulnerable growths, a nascent and incipient stirring, which postmodern thinking must exert every effort to cultivate and keep safe. Postmodernism is the garden of the event, the thinking of the event, offering events shelter and safe harbor." Caputo, "Spectral Hermeneutics," 48.

122. Events modify the world around them. Caputo explains that "events take on the specific look or sound or feel of the sacred, when the sparks we experience in words and things are sacred sparks, divine promptings, or holy intensities, then we have stepped upon the terrain of postmodern theology." Caputo, "Spectral Hermeneutics," 49.

123. To understand the event theology must keep "its ear close to the heart of the pulses or pulsations of the divine in things." Caputo, "Spectral Hermeneutics," 49.

124. Otto, *Idea of the Holy*, 26 (emphasis original).

125. Tillich writes that the "human heart seeks the infinite because that is where the finite wants to rest. In the infinite it sees its own fulfillment." Tillich, *Dynamics of Faith*, 13.

the human heart.[126] This infinite desire is a desire for something we know to be ultimate. This ultimate we can know and recognize, which is why events are so moving. They are not strange for the sake of being strange. An event's strange and awe-inspiring experience comes from its intense familiarity. It calls us toward the promise contained within all things.[127] This is not a promise for a faraway place or distant future. This promise is within the here and now. It stirs within all things and waits to emerge. What waits to emerge is nothing other than the way things *should be*. Thus, we should be prepared to listen to the event. When the event calls, we must be ready to respond with a resounding "yes."[128] Yet listening is easier said than done. We must learn how to listen. It is not a skill reserved only for priests, pastors, or rabbis. In fact, it may be even harder for religious leaders. Entrenchment within an institution makes it much harder to think outside its bounds. The event requires us to *let go*. To listen we ought to let go of the various *names* of systematic, structural, and institutional thought. It means suspending reality, if only for little while, so we can see what is happening *within* the name. We will miss the event if all we can see are institutions. The *noise* of institutions can overpower the still small voice of the event.[129]

Knowledge and Desire

The event draws us to the event. Its movement is an eternal back and forth movement that never ends. The event wants us to hear it. It does not want to

126. As Tillich explains, "[A human] is driven toward faith by his [or her] awareness of the infinite to which he [or she] belongs, but which he [or she] does not own like a possession. This is in abstract terms what concretely appears as the 'restlessness of the heart' within the flux of life." Tillich, *Dynamics of Faith*, 9.

127. For example, Caputo describes the event as "already ahead of us, always provoking and soliciting us, eternally luring us on with its promise. The truth of the event is its promise to come true." Caputo, "Spectral Hermeneutics," 55.

128. Caputo affirms that a "religious faith . . . takes the form of a 'yes, yes' '*oui, oui,*' *within* the general affirmation, the *oui, oui* by which we all respond to the language before language, which must be repeated from moment to moment." Caputo, *Weakness of God*, 59.

129. Names are not about containing the event. Caputo explains, "When something happens that contains an event, it contains precisely what it cannot contain. To exist would mean to exhaust the event, which means the event that is named in or under the name of God can never take final form, can never exist and exhaust itself on the ontical or ontological plane, neither in some highest being up above nor even in Being itself, even as it can never be conceived in some logically adequate expression or concept." Caputo, "Spectral Hermeneutics," 56.

remain a mystery. The event wants us to know it,[130] and we desire it.[131] We can never be sure about the contents of what we desire. We only know that the desire is there. Desire for what we cannot answer, yet the desire *remains* nonetheless.[132] This desire represents our need for connection and experience with something, anything. Thus, desire explains what keeps us coming back to things such as ritual actions. Desire prepares us for the event with ritual action. It makes us available and ready for what can occur.[133] Ritual action, in all its physical, repetitive, and intimate characteristics, carries the event. It carries the heart of our human desire.

To fulfill this desire, the event must be known. The experience of the event and its grasp represent an intimate form of knowing. This knowledge goes beyond trivial knowledge or knowledge of a skill. It is a knowledge based on connection, one that overcomes estrangement. It represents a union between the event and the other, and the precise moment of being grasped by the event.[134] A knowledge that *grasps*[135] is a deeper experience than knowledge that is merely informative or interesting. To be grasped is a deeply personal experience. It brings together the separated. The event reaches out to overcome a bridge or gulf so that we can know it.[136] In this knowledge, the unknown, strange, and even frightening become familiar. The event's goal is not to destroy or change experience. No, the event does

130. The event does not wish to remain hidden. Caputo remarks that the event "solicits and calls to us from within what exists, which is why events are a matter of prayers and tears. . . . Prayer has to do with hearing, heeding, and hearkening to a provocation that draws us out of ourselves." Caputo, "Spectral Hermeneutics," 57.

131. Caputo describes this desire as a lifetime of "hoping, dreaming, sighing for the event, praying and weeping over the event, praying for the coming of the event." Caputo, "Spectral Hermeneutics," 58.

132. "We are all along in the dark about what we desire, about what is desiring us, about what is desiring *in* us." Caputo, "Spectral Hermeneutics," 59 (emphasis original).

133. We need to be prepared for the event. Caputo maintains that one must "make oneself available for the event, to be prepared to be unprepared, to leave oneself unprepared for the unforeseeable." Caputo, *Truth*, 76.

134. Tillich describes knowledge as a union. He writes that in the "act of knowledge the knower and that which is known are united; the gap between subject and object is overcome. The subject 'grasps' the object, adapts it to itself, and, at the same time, adapts itself to the object." Tillich, *Systematic Theology, Volume 1*, 94.

135. To define this grasp, Tillich writes that being grasped "means only that we did not produce it, but found it in ourselves. It may have developed gradually, it may sometimes be the result of a dramatic experience. But it does not really occur . . . through the establishment of a method for achieving it." Tillich, *Ultimate Concern*, 9.

136. Therefore, according to Tillich, "In every act of knowledge want and estrangement are conquered." Tillich, *Systematic Theology, Volume 1*, 95.

something wonderful. It is part of our human experience. We are grasped by what comes from within.[137]

CONTINUING THE CONVERSATION: RITUAL ACTION AND THE NEED FOR WEAKNESS

Deconstruction is not a successor to metaphysics, semiotics, structuralism, or any other method of engaging ritual action. Deconstruction does not follow anything. Instead, it helps us further the conversation begun by hermeneutics. This use of deconstruction echoes Richard Rorty's use of hermeneutics.[138] Much like Rorty's conception of hermeneutics, deconstruction is a manner of entering conversation rather than establishing grounded rules of conversation. As if conversation needed mastering like a science. Deconstruction is not concerned with making conversation fit the mold of normal discourse. Not all conversations are normal. Deconstruction accepts that conversation does not always fit the normal. Deconstruction embraces "abnormal discourse."[139] Hermeneutics may be the study of abnormal discourse, but deconstruction delves further into the abnormal.[140] Unlike hermeneutics, deconstruction does not position itself as normal. Deconstruction is an immersion into the abnormal.

This immersion means resisting the urge to fit the abnormal into the normal. It is instead an honest engagement with the abnormal as abnormal. Deconstruction is a recognition that activities, such as ritual action, resist normal categories. Ritual action, like other abnormal discourse, resists

137. For example, Tillich states, "Something which was strange, but which nevertheless belongs to us, has become familiar, a part of us." Tillich, *Systematic Theology, Volume 1*, 95.

138. See Richard Rorty, "I am not putting hermeneutics forward as a 'successor subject' to epistemology. . . . In the interpretation I shall be offering, 'hermeneutics' is not the name for a discipline, nor for a method of achieving the sort of results which epistemology failed to achieve, nor for a program of research." Rorty, *Philosophy and the Mirror*, 315.

139. Rorty explains that "normal discourse is that which is conducted within an agreed-upon set of conventions about what counts as a relevant contribution, what counts as answering a question, what counts as having a good argument for that answer or a good criticism of it. Abnormal discourse is what happens when someone joins in the discourse who is ignorant of these conventions or who sets them aside." Rorty, *Philosophy and the Mirror*, 320.

140. For example, Rorty writes that "hermeneutics is the study of an abnormal discourse from the point of view of some normal discourse—the attempt to make some sense of what is going on at a stage where we are still too unsure about it to describe it." Rorty, *Philosophy and the Mirror*, 320–21.

categorization into semiotic, structuralist, or metaphysical molds. Listening to abnormal discourses, such as ritual action, requires humility. It requires honesty about what is known, can be known, and cannot be known.[141] Honesty is listening for the sake of listening. It is the ability to listen to abnormal discourse without letting our filters determine the listening itself. This process of de-centering helps us listen to the stories of ritual action.[142] It is the joy of listening for the first time, being genuinely surprised as to what will come next. It is listening in the present moment and allowing ourselves to be grasped. No one enters a conversation with the expectation of how it will go or conclude. The encounter of conversation remains a mystery until the end.

Ritual action is a conversation with mystery. It does not matter if we already know the moves, liturgy, symbols, dress, and so on. Genuine conversation is remaining honest that we have no idea about what will happen in the moment.[143] It relaxes our expectations so that the unexpected can occur. Such relaxation of expectations can only occur in a weak position. A strong position sets out to define and control. A weak position accepts conversation for what it is. Weakness accepts that conversation will not necessarily be clear and precise. Sometimes it will be no more than a whisper.[144] Ritual action will likely be incommensurable, and this is perfectly acceptable.[145] The powerful assumption that the incommensurable ought to conform to something is not only unhelpful, but dangerous.[146] It stifles the event and makes ritual action predictable and boring.

141. "We must be hermeneutical where we do not understand what is happening but are honest enough to admit it, rather than being blatantly 'Whiggish' about it." Rorty, *Philosophy and the Mirror*, 321.

142. Scharen and Vigen clarify that by "de-centering, we mean that while it is impossible (and not desirable) to cast off completely our own views and values as researchers and as people of faith, it is both possible and helpful to put them off to the side in order to focus on the stories, perspectives, and lived realities of others—who may or may not share the lenses we bring." Scharen and Vigen, *Ethnography as Christian Theology*, 16.

143. "Whenever it is suggested that the distinctions between theory and practice, fact and value, method and conversation be relaxed, an attempt to make the world 'malleable to human will' is suspected." Rorty, *Philosophy and the Mirror*, 342.

144. The writer of Ecclesiastes writes, "The quiet words of the wise are more to be heeded than the shouting of a ruler among fools." Eccl. 9:17 (NRSV).

145. Incommensurable discourse should "not cause despair." For example, Rorty states, "There is no metaphysical reason why human beings should be capable of saying incommensurable things, nor any guarantee that they will continue to do so. It is just our good fortune (from a hermeneutical point of view) or bad fortune (from an epistemological point of view) that they have done so in the past." Rorty, *Philosophy and the Mirror*, 347.

146. Writing of a unified language, Rorty remarks that "epistemology—as the

Therefore, deconstruction is important and necessary. It takes knowledge away from experts and returns it to the people. Deconstruction corrects the injustice of others telling practitioners what ritual action means. It challenges our powerful positions, age-old traditions, and unquestioned assumptions as to what ritual action is supposed to mean. Deconstruction is not about knowing.[147] It is about embracing *not-knowing*. It is the joy in the continual conversation of discovery. It is a position of weakness rather than strength. If others banish it to the peripheral, then so be it.[148] Deconstruction is about accepting that position. It is about accepting that risk[149] and burden.[150] Deconstruction is not about winning a popularity contest. As the Teacher puts it, "Vanity of vanities says the Teacher, vanity of vanities! All is vanity."[151]

All this follows from a deconstructionist point of view. It embraces weakness and remains satisfied with being obscure and difficult. Deconstruction is never about building great systems of thought. It is an edifying philosophy.[152] Closely tied to present situations and circumstances. Decon-

---

attempt to render all discourses commensurable by translating them into a preferred set of terms—is unlikely to be a useful strategy. The reason is not that 'unified science' works only for one metaphysical realm and not for another, but that the Whiggish assumption that we have got such a language blacks the road of inquiry." Rorty, *Philosophy and the Mirror*, 349.

147. For example, Rorty makes this same case for hermeneutics. He writes that, "hermeneutics is not 'another way of knowing'—'understanding' as opposed to (predictive) 'explanation.' It is better seen as another way of coping." Rorty, *Philosophy and the Mirror*, 356.

148. Rorty comprises a list of peripheral philosophers. He states, "On the periphery of the history of modern philosophy, one finds figures who, without forming a 'tradition,' resemble each other in their distrust of the notion that [humanity's] essence is to be a knower of essences. Goethe, Kierkegaard, Santayana, William James, Dewey, the later Wittgenstein, the later Heidegger, are figures of this sort." Rorty, *Philosophy and the Mirror*, 367.

149. Tillich knew very well the risk theologians must take. He writes that the theologian "cannot affirm any tradition and any authority except 'through a 'No' and a 'Yes.' And it is always possible that he [or she] may not be able to go all the way from the 'No' to the 'Yes.' He [or she] cannot join the chorus of those who live in unbroken assertions. He [or she] must take the risk of being driven beyond the boundary line of the theological circle. Therefore, the pious and powerful in the church are suspicious of him [or her], although they live in dependence upon the work of the former theologians who were in the same situation." Tillich, *Systematic Theology, Volume 1*, 25–26.

150. The writer of Ecclesiastes writes that "in much wisdom is much vexation, and those who increase knowledge increase sorrow." Eccl. 1:18 (NRSV).

151. Eccl. 1:2 (NRSV).

152. In describing edifying thinkers Rorty declares, "These peripheral, pragmatic philosophers are skeptical primarily *about systematic philosophy*, about the whole project of universal commensuration." Rorty, *Philosophy and the Mirror*, 368 (emphasis

struction is not concerned with setting itself up for eternity. It lets system collapse for the sake of the other. It lets go so the other has an opportunity to speak. Rorty describes the difference between systematic and edifying philosophy as follows:

> Great systematic philosophers are constructive and offer arguments. Great edifying philosophers are reactive and offer satires, parodies, aphorisms. They know their work loses its point when the period they were reacting against is over. They are *intentionally* peripheral. Great systematic philosophers, like great scientists, build for eternity. Great edifying philosophers destroy for the sake of their own generation. Systematic philosophers want to put their subject on the secure path of a science. Edifying philosophers want to keep space open for the sense of wonder which poets can sometimes cause—wonder that there is something new under the sun, something which is *not* an accurate representation of what was already there, something which (at least for the moment) cannot be explained and can barely be described.[153]

Perhaps there is a world outside deconstruction's current focus, but it can never replace what is happening *now*. It will never be as interesting as what deconstruction encounters every day. Listening to people will forever be the task of deconstruction. Thankfully, deconstruction is uniquely qualified for this task. Its emphasis on undecidability gives us a unique perspective on ritual action.[154] Undecidability means that the conversation never ends. There is always more to learn from the other. Ritual action can never be deciphered. It is a mystery that draws us back again and again. Deconstruction is the promise that we will never solve, quantify, systematize, or solidify ritual action (as if we could do that anyway). This is the position of humility. Approaching ritual action from humility will go a long way toward connecting with ritual action. It is time for scholarship to embrace weakness. It is time to stop talking and start listening.

---

original).

153. Rorty, *Philosophy and the Mirror*, 369–70 (emphasis original).

154. Caputo writes, "Deconstruction is a quasi-theory of undecidability, and it works well for everything from architecture to literary criticism, from religion to politics. Deconstruction is an exploration of as many 'instants' of undecidability as it has time (as it is given time) to study." Caputo, *Prayers and Tears*, 225

LISTENING TO THE RHYTHMS: PREPARING FOR THE CONVERSATION

A conversation is a wondrous thing. It represents the joy of connecting with the life of another. Though this simple act, conversation brings together human experience. It represents a unique intimacy in the life of another. This level of intimacy is not something achieved. We cannot make conversation happen. A more helpful analogy is to say that we *fall* into conversation. No one really remembers how a conversation started. We may be able to remember some of the first words or even the first question, but this is not where conversation starts. We cannot pinpoint the moment simple words became connection. The moment is a blur, and only after reflection do we realize what has just occurred. We have crossed some previously unknown border between connection and solitude. And in this crossing, we can almost feel the vibration of the other. We have begun to hear the other. We have just experienced the rhythm of another. Listening has begun.

Once we learn to listen, what we hear might be shocking. Once we let go of the noise, a new world of sound begins to unfold. This sound consists of the rhythms of everyday life and experience. It is pure, unfiltered rhythm. It is what we feel when we let go of the expected. It is not a scholarly, philosophical, or theological rhythm. It is the rhythm of life. This rhythm is what we experience the moment we leave the house, walk through the city, or enter a worship service. Every experience of rhythm holds the potential of conversation.

Here starts our journey toward conversation. This conversation with the unexpected and unknown has no explicit purpose or goal. The only requirement is to give ourselves to the conversation. To give in, we must allow the rhythms of conversation to overtake us.

Rhythms

Rhythms prepare us for conversing with ritual action, though there are no rules for how it should be done. There are no predetermined parameters of where, when, or how a conversation must occur. During genuine conversation, there is no fear of the other suddenly saying, "stop, you are doing it wrong!" There are, however, certain helpful ways of attuning ourselves to listening and conversing. This can be especially useful for listening to ritual action. This preparation does not require us to do anything. We do not need any special training to listen to the movements of everyday life.

Special training in semiotics or metaphysics is neither desired nor required. Listening to ritual action only requires the self.

Henri Lefebvre describes this listening as *rhythmanalysis*. Rhythmanalysis is a non-reductive mode of listening to everyday life and experience, including ritual action. It implies that "everywhere where this is interaction between a place, a time and an expenditure of energy, there is rhythm."[155] Rhythm occurs through both the linear and cyclical, along with difference and repetition. Everyday life consists of both cyclical and linear patterns that continually exert themselves. There is a natural repetitive essence to both nature and human activity. Cyclical cycles consist of cosmic motions such as changing seasons, day and night cycles, ocean and sea tides, and so on.[156] Linear cycles emerge from human action and behavior. The linear is essentially social.[157] These linear cycles have a definite beginning and end while cosmic cycles appear eternal and consistent. Cosmic cycles comprise the background of all human activity and behavior. Because they are cosmic, human behavior cannot escape their impact. Cyclical and linear cycles interact with one another. The cyclical and linear measure against one other. Therefore, Lefebvre states, "everything is cyclical repetition through linear repetitions."[158] Rhythm occurs as these two poles interact with one another.

Rhythm is both measurable and immeasurable. It serves as a bridge between both the quantitative and the qualitative.[159] The natural and the social are irrevocably intertwined with one another. Human beings act within the natural cycles of life. Since the beginning of time, cosmic cycles have regulated how human beings behave and react. Cosmic cycles represent the ordered and rational cycle of movement and time. Yet within this rational and quantifiable universe are irrational and contradictory linear cycles of human action. Cyclical and linear time struggle with each other.[160]

155. Lefebvre, *Rhythmanalysis*, 25.

156. Lefebvre, *Rhythmanalysis*, 18.

157. Lefebvre explains that linear cycles "would come rather from social practice, therefore from human activity: the monotony of actions and of movements, imposed structures," Lefebvre, *Rhythmanalysis*, 18.

158. Lefebvre, *Rhythmanalysis*, 18.

159. "Rhythm reunites quantitative aspects and elements, which mark time and distinguish moments in it—as qualitative aspects and elements. . . . Rhythm appears as regulated time, governed by rational laws, but in contact with what is least rational in human being: the lived, the carnal, the body." Lefebvre, *Rhythmanalysis*, 18.

160. The cyclical and linear, Lefebvre explains, "penetrate one another, but in an interminable struggle: sometimes compromise, sometimes disruption. However, there is between them an indissoluble unity: the repetitive tick-tock of the clock measures the cycle of hours and days, and vice versa. In industrial practice, where the linear repetitive tends to predominate, the struggle is intense." Lefebvre, *Rhythmanalysis*, 85.

Rhythm establishes itself through repetition and difference. Undifferentiated time, such as the mechanical tick-tock of a clock, is not rhythmic.[161] Rhythm is the diversity of actions occurring through cyclical and linear cycles. It is both logical and illogical.[162] Repetition may be orderly, but there is no guarantee that it will remain so. There is always room for variation and change.[163] It has an ebb and flow that is neither mechanical nor predictable. Mechanical repetition erases itself. A machine will perform the same task, the same way, over and over until it breaks down. Any variation is a sign the machine needs repair. Each moment repeats over and over.[164] Nothing is carried over from past experiences. Once a machine performs its task, everything that preceded is erased. Mechanical time has no past and no future. It will never perform its task any differently. The mechanical has repetition but no rhythm. Therefore, rhythm is intimately connected to organic life. Lefebvre writes that, "rhythm enters into the lived."[165] Thus, rhythm is the intersection between place, time, and energy.[166] Rhythm is a process of becoming.[167] No moment or activity is defined or set in stone. The day grows into itself instead of a predetermined mold. There are no guarantees that events always occur the same way. Rhythm suggests that experience implies memory, growth, and difference. Mundane repetitive tasks can fill the everyday experience. However, within the everyday lies the possibility of the unexpected. Each day and every moment bring with it the hope of difference and the not yet. There is an embedded promise in each day that the future is not set. Each day we may walk out the door, toward the same job, follow the same route, and end our day by returning home in much the same way. There are no guarantees that the next day will be like

161. "For there to be rhythm, there must be repetition in a movement, but not just any repetition. The monotonous return of the same, self-identical, noise no more forms a rhythm than does some moving object on its trajectory." Lefebvre, *Rhythmanalysis*, 86.

162. See for example Lefebvre's explanation that "rhythms escape logic, and nevertheless contain a logic, a possible calculus of numbers and numerical relations." Lefebvre, *Rhythmanalysis*, 20.

163. There should be "strong times and weak times, which return in accordance with a rule or law—long and short times, recurring in a recognisable way, stops, silences, blanks, resumptions and intervals in accordance with regularity, must appear in a movement. Rhythm therefore brings with it a differentiated time, a qualified duration." Lefebvre, *Rhythmanalysis*, 86.

164. "Mechanical repetition works by reproducing the instant that precedes it." Lefebvre, *Rhythmanalysis*, 87.

165. Lefebvre, *Rhythmanalysis*, 86.

166. Lefebvre, *Rhythmanalysis*, 25.

167. Lefebvre, *Rhythmanalysis*, 87.

the last. We may walk out that same door only to discover a new route, make a life changing decision, have a profound idea, or even fall in love. Rhythms presuppose variation and difference. Rhythms never remain the same.

Rhythm and the Body

The human body is the starting point for rhythmic listening. The body is not just a subject, it is "the first point of analysis, the tool for subsequent investigations. The body serves us as a metronome."[168] The body is rhythmic consisting of various beats, thumps, and frequencies working together.[169] In combination with its social setting, the body is never silent. The body calls so that someone might listen.[170] In order to listen we cannot ignore the body. We must be in tune with our bodies to connect with the surrounding rhythms. Escape from the body, either into the mind or some metaphysical plane, keeps us from listening. It dulls our senses. Without the body, we cannot hear the rhythms of others.

The body helps us connect with the rhythms of our environment. The rhythms of everyday life are always moving and changing. Rhythms, both natural and social, continually vibrate and interact with one another. The wind and the rain, the gentle rustling of tree leaves, running water, and many others create a symphony of natural rhythms.[171] The earth is continually moving, vibrating, and shifting. The rhythms of nature and society, cyclical and linear, lead us into an immersive experience. We need to be grasped in order to enter this experience, to listen to the rhythms, and join its conversation. Lefebvre explains that "to grasp a rhythm it is necessary to have been grasped by it; one must let oneself go, give oneself over, abandon oneself to its duration."[172] We must immerse our bodies into the heart of the everyday.[173] Immersion into the everyday helps us to approach others

168. Selden, introduction to *Rhythmanalysis*, 6.

169. "The body consists of a bundle of rhythms, different but in tune." Lefebvre, *Rhythmanalysis*, 30.

170. Lefebvre believes that philosophy has ignored the body. He writes, "The body. Our body. So neglected in philosophy that it ends up speaking its mind and kicking up a fuss. Left to physiology and medicine." Lefebvre, *Rhythmanalysis*, 30.

171. According to Lefebvre, for the one that listens "nothing is immobile. He [or she] hears the wind, the rain, storms; but if he [or she] considers a stone, a wall, a trunk, he [or she] understands their slowness, their interminable rhythm. This *object* is not inert; time is not set aside for the subject. It is only slow in relation to our time, to our body, the measure of rhythms." Lefebvre, *Rhythmanalysis*, 30 (emphasis original).

172. Lefebvre, *Rhythmanalysis*, 37.

173. "He garbs himself in this tissue of the lived, of the everyday." Lefebvre,

as a living whole and less like an object to study. Ritual action is a living presence. It lives in the moments of life and is therefore full of meaning. We must listen for its organic rhythm. Ritual action is a living and changing movement comprised of living and changing people. Everything about ritual action is alive. Its rhythm is more akin to a heartbeat rather than a mechanical clock. Understanding that ritual action has a rhythm will enable us to form a relationship with the story of foot washing.[174] It is necessary that we immerse ourselves into the conversation.

CONVERSATION WITH FOOT WASHING

It is time to enter the conversation and listen. Now is the moment of practice. Doing so requires humility to enter a new world of possibility and experience dictated by the other, waiting and wanting to be heard. Finding a conversation partner is not the difficult part. Once we are open to conversation, the world is expanded beyond our imaginations. We only need to listen.

Engaging the ritual action of foot washing in conversation serves as an example of what is possible when we listen to ritual action. In this conversation, foot washing is the voice of weakness. Its voice is not of power or strength. It lacks the glamor of other Christian ritual actions such as communion and baptism. Feet are ordinary. They are associated with smell and kept out of sight.

As a ritual action based on weakness, it is an excellent conversational partner. It shows us what we can learn from ritual action, especially when ritual action is uniquely situated in weakness. Further, this conversation is not generic. This is not just about any group. This is foot washing as practiced by the congregations of the Original Free Will Baptist denomination. Being a small voice, the Original Free Will Baptists provide a small, weak way of entering the conversation. The only goal here is conversation itself. It is now time to step aside and let this ritual action speak for itself. It is time to listen to the Original Free Will Baptist practice of foot washing.

Rhythmanalysis, 31.

174. Lefebvre explains that "rhythmanalysis transforms *everything* into presences, including the present, grapsed and perceived as such. The act does not imprison itself in the ideology of the *thing*. It perceives the *thing* in the proximity of the *present*. . . . The act of rhythmanalysis integrates these things—this wall, this table, these trees—in a dramatic becoming, in an ensemble full of meaning, transforming them no longer into diverse things, but into presences." Lefebvre, *Rhythmanalysis*, 33 (emphasis original).

Chapter Three

A Conversation with the Original Free Will Baptists

INTRODUCING THE CONVERSATION

The Original Free Will Baptists[1] are our guide for encountering ritual action. We will explore ritual action through their experiences and stores. The OFWBs provide an opportunity for us to explore how ritual action shapes its practitioners. Therefore, foot washing[2] is a gateway for interpreting ritual action. Foot washing exposes the fundamental weakness of interpretations that treat action as arbitrary and secondary. Exploring foot washing is an effort at taking ritual seriously. It is an effort toward understanding how action holds meaning and demonstrating how action is critical for theological reflection.

Foot washing comprises simple movements and simple things. At first glance, it appears that there is little to say about it. Foot washing is not glamorous or awe inspiring. It lacks colorful vestments, powerful words, and careful choreography. Yet within these actions and objects lies a beautiful and rich story. This is a story hidden and unknown by many. The foot washing story of the OFWBs is one patiently waiting to be told. It is a story of humbleness, equality, and dignity.

---

1. In what follows, *OFWB* will be used for Original Free Will Baptist.

2. Other names include: "washing feet," "washing of the disciples' feet," and "feet washing." For simplicity, the term "foot washing" will be used whenever possible.

GATHERING THE NARRATIVE

OFWBs have little to no written theology on foot washing, however there is an abundant unwritten tradition and theology. Therefore, I focused on the stories and experience of pastors and laypersons. These experiences ranged from the personal testimonies and history to participant observation. Foot washing is fundamentally a ritual action made possible by its participants. My research focuses on foot washing participants.

I used multiple approaches to listen to the OFWBs. Listening to the their experience of foot washing involved self-administered questionnaires, interviews, focus groups, and participant observation. These approaches compiled a narrative of the OFWB foot washing experience. I employed ethnography as a guide to build the OFWB narrative.[3] Consequently, I did not create this narrative, this is a narrative created by the participants. These approaches brought together both my voice and the voice of the OFWB. Thus, we became co-collaborators and co-authors in the narrative.[4] Ethnographic approaches make it possible to "get a deep reading of what is there—on its own terms."[5]

Questionnaires

Gathering the narrative began with the construction and distribution of a self-administered questionnaire.[6] This self-administered questionnaire consisted of open-ended questions designed to enter the lives and experiences of OFWB participants. These open-ended questions delivered "insights into the minds, beliefs and opinions of individual respondents in a way that closed questions cannot."[7] The self-administered questionnaire consisted of non-random questionnaires based on convenience. The questionnaire invited members and pastors to complete three multiple choice and four open-ended questions. The multiple-choice questions gathered simple information on how and when foot washing was practiced in the respondent's church. The purpose of the multiple-choice questions was to help stimulate

---

3. This use of ethnography shares Scharen and Vigen's conviction that the "aim is to understand what God, human relationships, and the world look like from their perspective—to take them seriously as a source of wisdom." Scharen and Vigen,"What is Ethnography?," 16.

4. Scharen and Vigen,"What is Ethnography?," 19, 22.

5. Scharen and Vigen,"What is Ethnography?," 27.

6. See Navarro-Rivera and Kosmin, "Surveys and Questionnaires," 395.

7. Navarro-Rivera and Kosmin, "Surveys and Questionnaires," 409–10.

the written responses. The following four questions consisted of open-ended reflection questions on the practice of foot washing.

I distributed questionnaires via mail and email across the OFWB denomination. I first mailed these questionnaires to churches. Out of the 240 OFWB churches, I choose fifty to receive questionnaires. The fifty comprised a theoretically representative sample of OFWB congregations. Each church received a packet containing twenty-five questionnaires, a letter of introduction and instructions, a sign-up sheet for interviews/focus groups, and a postage-paid return envelope. I also distributed the questionnaire digitally using an OFWB email mailing list. I invited participants to complete the questionnaire using Google survey. Out of the fifty questionnaires packets mailed, thirteen churches responded totaling 109 returned questionnaires. Thirty-eight responded to the online version of the questionnaire.

Interviews

Telephone interviews followed self-administered questionnaires. Eight laypersons and eleven ministers volunteered for one-on-one telephone interviews. All interviews were audio recorded. Participants indicated their willingness to volunteer on the questionnaire. Due to the small population and regional size of the OFWB denomination, nineteen interviews were determined to be sufficient. Several studies have demonstrated that when studying homogenous groups, theoretical saturation tends to be met after twelve interviews.[8]

Following individual interviews, I conducted two focus group to gain perspectives from individuals in conversation and group exchange.[9] The first focus group consisted of five ministers and the nine laypeople comprised the second. I conducted both focus groups in person and recorded these with an audio and digital video recorder. All interviews followed an in-depth, semi-structured interview protocol. Interviews focused on how participants understood foot washing. I encouraged participants to share their stories and experiences of foot washing. Focus remained on OFWB feelings and attitudes toward foot washing. Interviews included questions on meaning and how foot washing forms identity and community.

---

8. Bremborg lists several studies on theoretical saturation, See Bremborg, "Interviewing," 314.

9. Bremborg, "Interviewing," 313.

Participant Observation

The final stage was participant observation. I both participated in and observed an experience of foot washing. I complied in-depth notes and the recorded the entire experience with a digital video recorder. I choose the observed congregation based on availability and interest. As an OFWB minister and member, this experience added to my own personal experiences of foot washing as a child and adult.

FOOT WASHING THROUGH HISTORY

Foot washing does not belong exclusively to the OFWB. Foot washing appears in some form throughout Christian history. Before its initiation by Christ, foot washing was a practice of hospitality. The earliest biblical examples of foot washing are found in Genesis. For example, Abraham offered water to three visitors for washing their feet.[10] Lot offered the angels of the Lord an opportunity to wash their feet and spend the night.[11] Other mentions include Genesis 43:24, Judges 19:21, and 1 Samuel 25:41. The book of Exodus links it to a religious ceremony in 30:19[12] and 40:30–32.[13]

Foot washing was widely practiced in the Greco-Roman world.[14] It was an act of hospitality and courtesy for guests. Open sandals on dusty and dry roads made this practice a necessity for guests. It was generally expected that a host would make arrangements for guests to have their feet washed.[15] But it was Jesus that gave this act particular significance as found

10. "He said, 'My lord, if I find favor with you, do not pass by your servant. Let a little water be brought, and wash your feet, and rest yourselves under the tree.'" Gen 18:3–4 (NRSV).

11. "He said, 'Please, my lords, turn aside to your servant's house and spend the night, and wash your feet; then you can rise early and go on your way.'" Gen 19:2 (NRSV).

12. "You shall make a bronze basin with a bronze stand for washing. You shall put it between the tent of meeting and the altar and you shall put water in it; with the water Aaron and his sons shall wash their hands and their feet." Ex 30:18–19 (NRSV).

13. "He set the basin between the tent of meeting and the altar, and put water in it for washing, with which Moses and Aaron and his sons washed their hands and their feet. When they went into the tent of meeting, and when they approached the altar, they washed; as the Lord had commanded Moses." Ex 40:30–32 (NRSV).

14. Richard E. Allison writes, "In the Greco-Roman world, foot washing was done for several reasons: (1) as a ritual; (2) domestically, for reasons of personal comfort and hygiene; (3) as an expression of hospitality, a gesture of greeting, or in preparation for a banquet; and (4) as a service by servants or slaves." Allison, "Foot Washing," 322.

15. For example, in Luke the text reads, "Then turning toward the woman, he said to Simon, 'Do you see this woman? I entered your house; you gave me no water for my

in John 13:1–17. In the upper room, Jesus served the disciples by washing their feet, thus reversing the roles of master and servant.[16] Jesus' actions are interpreted by most as an act of humility in contrast to the disciples' hubris.[17] The early church continued this practice of foot washing.[18] There is evidence that church fathers practiced it, including Tertullian, Origen, Chrysostom, and Augustine.[19] In 694 CE, the Catholic Church adopted washing of the feet, or *pedilavium,* as a Holy Thursday liturgical rite at the 17th Synod of Toledo in Spain.[20]

Today, several Christian groups trace their history to the radical reformation practice of foot washing as an ordinance, meaning the practice is understood to be established by Christ. This includes Brethren and Mennonite groups as well as some Baptists.[21] Roman Catholics and Anglicans conduct foot washing as part of the Holy Thursday liturgy.[22] Recently, Pope Francis has brought renewed attention to foot washing.[23]

INTRODUCING THE ORIGINAL FREE WILL BAPTIST COMMUNITY

The OFWBs are small in number, with fewer than 40,000 adherents,[24] but they have a long history. The OFWB community traces its history to the English General Baptists, who as early as 1700 were worshiping in North

---

feet, but she has bathed my feet with her tears and dried them with her hair. You gave me no kiss, but from the time I came in she has not stopped kissing my feet. You did not anoint my head with oil, but she has anointed my feet with ointment."' Luke 7:44–46 (NRSV).

16. Allison, "Foot Washing," 322.

17. "Jesus' washing of feet is usually explained as teaching the need for humility in the light of the disciples' obvious lack of self-abasement in the upper room (Luke 22:24–30)." Kent, "Foot Washing," 419.

18. There is evidence in 1 Timothy that foot washing was a practice of the early church. Describing widows, the text reads, "She must be well attested for her good works, as one who has brought up children, shown hospitality, washed the saints' feet, helped the afflicted, and devoted herself to doing good in every way." 1 Tim 5:10 (NRSV).

19. Allison, "Foot Washing," 322.

20. Fischer, "Washing of Feet," 653.

21. Kent, "Foot Washing," 419.

22. Allison, "Foot Washing," 322.

23. Winfield, "Holy Thursday."

24. Association of the Religion Data Archives, "Convention of Original."

Carolina.[25] The OFWB community is proud of its General Baptist heritage. The denomination's own articles of faith originated from the *1660 English General Baptist Confession of Faith*[26] and the 1812 revision.[27] The community traces its history to Paul Palmer, who established and pastored the first General Baptist church in Chowan County, North Carolina.[28]

Today, North Carolina remains the home of the OFWBs. Two-hundred and forty OFWB churches stretch across Eastern and Central North Carolina, including a small number in South Carolina and Georgia.[29] These churches are organized into eight different geographically based conferences. These conferences coordinate and regulate the work of the denomination, as well as examining and ordaining ministerial candidates.[30] Despite its small size, the OFWB has several ministries. These ministries include foreign missions, a children's home, printing press, and a university.[31]

Throughout its history, the denomination has gone through several cycles of growth and decline.[32] The denomination survived early competition from the Particular Baptists[33], the Campbellite Crisis, and a denominational split with the National Association of Free Will Baptists.[34] Despite difficult circumstances, the denomination sees itself as having remained true to the "spirit and simplicity of the Palmer General Baptist background."[35] This includes the practice of foot washing, more formally called the "washing of the saints' feet."[36]

HISTORY OF FOOT WASHING AMONG ORIGINAL FREE WILL BAPTISTS

The OFWB denomination has consistently practiced foot washing throughout its history. Beginning with its General Baptist heritage, the practice of

25. North Carolina State Convention, *Articles of Faith*, xxvii.

26. Pinson, *A Free Will*, 5.

27. Pelt, *A History*, 104.

28. McBeth, *Four Centuries*, 712.

29 The Convention of Original, "Directories/Resources."

30. North Carolina State Convention, *Articles of Faith*, 103–4.

31. The Convention of Original, "Our Ministries."

32. North Carolina State Convention, *Articles of Faith*, xxix–xxxvii.

33. Particular Baptists referred to General Baptists as "Free-Willers." North Carolina State Convention, *Articles of Faith*, xxxii.

34. Cherry, *An Introduction*, 25–35, 47–51.

35. McBeth, *Four Centuries*, 716.

36. North Carolina State Convention, *Articles of Faith*, 52.

washing feet was conducted almost universally. Although not required for church membership, most considered it an ordinance.[37] Foot washing remained a prominent practice among early Free Will Baptists throughout the 1700s. The adoption of its 1812 confession included a recommendation that foot washing be practiced every quarter.[38] This 1812 confession was the first Arminian Baptist confession to formally describe foot washing as an ordinance.[39]

In the denomination's history, several prominent pastors have reaffirmed the OFWB commitment to foot washing. In 1927, J. C. Griffin argued in his booklet, *The Upper Room Ought*, that it is not enough to know that Christ washed the disciple's feet; rather, Christians ought to do it.[40] Free Will Baptist historian George Stevenson describes foot washing as a way to open us to humility and love, which "serves to strengthen in us a bond of fellowship and brotherhood, to confirm the strength of our faith, and to reveal our weaknesses to us."[41]

Today, OFWBs consider foot washing to have equal standing with baptism and communion. Their *Articles of Faith* states that foot washing "teaches humility, the necessity of the servanthood of every believer, and reminds the believer of the necessity of a daily cleansing from all sin."[42] Foot washing is not unique to the OFWBs, but "it is one of [their] distinctive beliefs and practices, and it makes a very strong theological statement about the stance of the [OFWB] Church and the attitude for ministry (service) among both clergy and laity."[43] Foot washing is also incorporated in the OFWB logo. This logo pictures a basin of water and a towel sitting at the foot of the cross.[44]

Foot washing is traditionally practiced following communion, whereby members wash one another's feet. Typically, men and women are separated.[45] Usually involving only basins of water and girded towels, it is simple in design but powerful in meaning. Thus, significance is not in the things used, but in the actions performed. It is important to note that foot

37. Pelt, *A History*, 18.

38. Stevenson, "A Humbling Act," 5.

39. Pinson, *A Free Will*, 19.

40. Griffin, *Upper Room Ought*, 29.

41. Stevenson, "A Humbling Act" 5.

42. North Carolina State Convention, *Articles of Faith*, 52.

43. Cherry, *Original Free Will*, 120.

44. The logo can be found on http://www.ofwb.org/.

45. This is for modesty purposes. Men and women may go to separate rooms or to private areas in a fellowship hall or a large room.

washing often occurs during Sunday night service, which is also one of the least attended services.[46]

THE NARRATIVE OF FOOT WASHING AMONG ORIGINAL FREE WILL BAPTISTS

Foot washing is a simple practice.[47] Its movements and gestures do not require any special effort to mimic and learn. The movements and items themselves are not far removed from daily life. They carry a certain degree of familiarity.

The items used in foot washing are, for lack of a better word, common. The plain pails of water and towels do not have any special significance. Simple and unadorned, the pails and towels are unattractive and insignificant in themselves. The pails hold just enough water to immerse your foot. Towels are modest, simple, and uninteresting items rarely given a second thought in the process. Thin and frayed from age, you simply pick up one of the towels and gird it around your waist. Neither the pails nor the towels are considered blessed or holy. They hold no divine powers. They are what they are, and nothing more.

After girding yourself, you wait for the other to remove his or her shoes. While waiting, you kneel as the other slowly places his or her foot into the pail of water, one foot at a time. While kneeling, you take the other's foot and lightly sprinkle water over it. Cradling the foot in one hand, you gently run water across the foot. Delicately running your fingers through the water, the water slowly drips onto the foot. The water from the hand passes to the foot, connecting participants with the shared water. After drying the other's foot with the girded towel, the process continues with the other foot. Once completed, participants exchange places. Each person has the opportunity to give and receive. The whole process is quick, lasting only a few minutes.

Once each person has had the opportunity to wash and be washed, the pails and the towels are washed, cleaned, and stored away until needed again. Hugs and words of love are exchanged, prayers given, and the community is brought together. Participants sing hymns and give words of

46. A pastor states, "Sunday nights we have twenty or twenty-five for regular church Sunday night service. Those are usually the twenty to twenty-five there for washing of the saints' feet. So, it's a small crowd, but it's usually the small [crowd] that's there for Sunday night services too." Focus group interview with members and pastors, June 28, 2015.

47. Recorded video of OFWB Church foot washing service, June 28, 2015.

praise. No prescribed words exist, no one follows a written rubric. Instead, the people simply gather together in love and fellowship.

How Do OFWBs Explain Foot Washing to Others?

To explain foot washing, many pastors and members go directly to scripture in John 13. Understanding begins with the story as presented. Without hesitation, a pastor declares, "You've got to go to the text, and in the context of why Jesus did it. My understanding, because you got to go to Luke, disciples were upset about who was going to be the greatest."[48] Many OFWBs point to Jesus' command that the disciples should continue this practice. Since Jesus *ordained* foot washing, all Christians should practice it. One pastors describes Jesus' command as the most important part. He says that "rarely can I say that I'm doing something that the Lord has asked me to do and he has asked me to do this and it's a privilege for me to do. It's something I look forward to when we have it. . . . If I try to describe it to someone who has never done it, I try to tell them I try to be obedient to the scriptures."[49] Other pastors explain it through Jesus' example in scripture. A pastor describes that he introduces it through the scriptures and explains why Jesus did it. He does this to "give people an understanding of why we do [foot washing]. He [Jesus] has given us a mandate. He didn't say you ought to, he just said you need to do these things. If I have done yours, you ought to wash the other. I usually introduce it that way."[50]

Members also refer to the scripture when explaining foot washing to others. One longtime member of the OFWB states, "I personally just take God's word literally. I think that's one of the things he wanted us to do, and when I get down on my knees to wash somebody's feet I really appreciate the opportunity to do that for God."[51] Other members also reinforced this same idea. For example, one member shares that she "would explain that we do this because Jesus at the last supper, when he had the bread and the wine, [Jesus said] 'do this in remembrance of me,' but he also said when we wash feet, 'do this, I wash your feet you should wash one another's feet.' So, we do that and to literally do that is to humble yourself."[52]

Members and pastors have unique ways of explaining and sharing foot washing to those unfamiliar with it. Conversations demonstrate that

48. Focus group (A) interview with OFWB pastor, June 28, 2015.

49. Interview with OFWB pastor (H), February 3, 2015.

50. Interview with OFWB pastor (A), April 7, 2015.

51. Focus group (B) interview with OFWB member, June 28, 2015.

52. Interview with OFWB member (G), January 29, 2015.

OFWBs have rich and insightful theological viewpoints on foot washing. Many already have experience in explaining foot washing to other Christians. OFWBs are prepared to teach, explain, and defend their practice of foot washing.

A former member of the OFWB, now living outside of North Carolina, has had to explain it to Christians unfamiliar with foot washing. He has opportunities to talk about foot washing in his Sunday school class. He emphasizes "the humility of doing it as Jesus Christ washed feet, and his sacrifice. . . . It's personal but it's not. It's like the Lord's Supper, it's personal but it's also public in that you are participating with other believers and you are letting others know that you are among the chosen."[53] Another member makes it clear that "you're not going to get a bar of soap as some people might would think."[54] He declares, "It is a humbling experience that you would wash someone else's feet even though you just place it in the water, and rinse it off and dry it with a towel. Its humility, I guess, in one of its greatest forms to me."[55]

Pastors have developed their own methods for explaining foot washing to new members in their congregations. For example, one pastor describes that he will "explain to [new members] what it is, what it means, what it represents. I first tell them how we do it physically. And then I go into a little more detail in what that represents."[56] Following the basics he goes on to say, "I'm going to tell them that it means, that it represents that we are no better than anyone else, but that we are willing to be considered lower than the other to be able to help someone."[57] Sometimes a pastor may wait to share foot washing with those who want to join the church. A pastor explains, "We don't really advertise it as something to people who are visitors. Usually that's the kind of thing that kind of causes people to not [join the church]."[58] He typically waits until they are serious about joining the church before explaining foot washing and other doctrines of the church. He tells prospective members "what it means to wash the saints' feet. Why we do it, what's the process. I always tell them it's not anything rude. . . . Most people have already washed their feet before they come."[59] OFWB pastors are aware and

---

53. Interview with OFWB member (C), June 30, 2015. It should be noted that this particular individual is now a member of a Calvinist Baptist denomination. As such, his use of the word 'chosen' would not be typical among most OFWBs.

54. Interview with OFWB member (H), January 26, 2015.

55. Interview with OFWB member (H), January 26, 2015.

56. Interview with OFWB pastor (E), March 27, 2015.

57. Interview with OFWB pastor (E), March 27, 2015.

58. Interview with OFWB pastor (G), February 6, 2015.

59. He goes on to say, "I tell them about the incarnational nature of it. What it

sensitive to the fact that foot washing can make some people uncomfortable. It is something that may take time to get used to. Foot washing must be "voluntary, you know if you choose to do it. Which is really the only way that you can do it. You can't force anyone to do it by any means. Things of that nature would remove the emphasis off of what it's supposed to be doing to demand that you got to do it."[60]

Other pastors make sure newcomers have the opportunity to watch and participate. In foot washing, pastors sometimes pair newcomers with a church leader, usually the pastor or a deacon. This helps to reduce some of the unfamiliarity and uncomfortableness. No one is ever forced to participate. It is okay to just sit and observe before making the decision to participate or not. Typically, one pastor explains, "If you don't want to participate, just observe. See what takes place you know. Then I kind of pair them up. If I have new members that have never practiced that, I try to make sure that when they do wash feet that they're paired with someone who really understands what it's all about. I think that's a part of discipleship. With someone that really understands the meaning of washing feet."[61] Observation is important for those who have no prior experience with foot washing. It takes patience and careful explanation to make newcomers comfortable. One pastor discovered that "if you would talk to them and tell them exactly what happens [and what] they'll experience one time, and I encourage them just to go back and observe. I find that when you do that, and encourage and love them along, that they really want to participate."[62] This same pastor describes how after observing foot washing, a new member told him, "I was very uncomfortable leaving the sanctuary, going to another room to be with other ladies knowing that I was going to have my feet washed and wash someone else's feet. I was real uncomfortable but then when we got in there it was really more like a worship service."[63] Even for pastors from other denominations, observation is necessary to understand foot washing. OFWB pastors sometimes describe playful joking from other pastors, outside the tradition, about foot washing.[64]

---

means the fact that we're embodied. . . . We really do believe that Christ cares about the human person as a whole." Interview with OFWB pastor (G), February 6, 2015.

60. Interview with OFWB pastor (D), March 30, 2015.

61. Interview with OFWB pastor (I), February 2, 2015.

62. Interview with OFWB pastor (E), March 27, 2015.

63. Interview with OFWB pastor (E), March 27, 2015.

64. A pastor shares, "In one of our pastoral ministry classes at [seminary], we were supposed to perform something [from a] pastoral point of view and I did feet washing in one of my seminary classes and they were in shock. They were all Southern Baptist except for me. It was a small group, about seven of us I think, and I did the feet washing

When teaching foot washing, pastors try to teach and model the aspects of servanthood and servant leadership to their congregations. Toward newcomers, pastors use foot washing to demonstrate that they are not above the church or an authoritarian figure. When teaching a class of new members, a pastor states, "I feel like I have an advantage. I get to talk to some of the people I teach in the intro class. We can sit there and tell the stories of the beatitudes and how Jesus is switching everything around we always thought to be normal. . . . At the end of the day all of the talking meant nothing until he got down on knees, girded himself with a towel and started [washing the feet] of his disciples, of his disciples. His disciples! That's what I look at."[65] Speaking of foot washing, he continues, "To me that's very important and [I] think that's what Christ shows, because it easy for us to have all of the sudden an authoritative figure on [the] pulpit."[66] This is why it is not unusual to see an OFWB "pastor washing possibly one of the least fortunate financially members of the church."[67]

First and Memorable Experiences of Foot Washing

Foot washing is a vitally important aspect of participants' memories and experiences. Many of these experiences began in childhood (twelve and younger). First experiences for children typically invoke feelings of strangeness, even reluctance or uncomfortable feelings.[68] Much of this has to do with the general stigma involving feet.[69]

OFWB childhood experiences are both strange and fascinating. A first experience of foot washing can cause feelings of nervousness and anxiety. A member recalls being nervous the first time "because I didn't know what to do. So, I looked and observed. One of the deacons kind of took me under his wing, showed me what [foot washing] was, he washed my feet first. I remember that."[70] As a nine-year-old, one pastor remembers how captivat-

---

service and their jaws were just dropping and it really surprised them. Because they had kind of joked about it, talked about it, and everything else to me so when they really saw it done the way the scriptures have it clearly spelled out in John, it suddenly changed their understanding of it. It really did. When they saw it acted out instead of just joking about it, it changed their attitude. It really did." Interview with OFWB pastor (H), February 3, 2015.

65. Focus group (A) interview with OFWB pastor, June 28, 2015.

66. Focus group (A) interview with OFWB pastor, June 28, 2015.

67. Interview with OFWB member (H), January 26, 2015.

68. Focus group (A) interview with OFWB pastor, June 28, 2015.

69. Focus group (A) interview with OFWB pastor, June 28, 2015.

70. Focus group (A) interview with OFWB pastor, June 28, 2015.

ing it was for him to do it for the first time. He said that is "because to a child when you experience that for the first time it's an eye-opening experience because it's something you've never pictured yourself doing."[71]

Sometimes children can observe what is happening before participating.[72] Most childhood experiences occur sometime after baptism. For children it is a hard action to understand, but they quickly get over those feelings.[73] It becomes second nature even though they may not understand it. As a child, one pastor recalls not understanding foot washing: "It was just that's what you did so you did it. As you grow, become more familiar with the teaching and understand what it is, then it becomes much [clearer.]"[74] This same pastor continues, "That the folks then, if I remember correctly, they didn't take much time to explain it either. That's what we did as OF-WBs. That's what you did."[75] Another pastor echoed this same sentiment explaining, "I didn't understand it. It was just something that I went over there and did. . . . I didn't really absorb it until probably until I was married. In my mid-twenties before it started to mean more to me."[76]

OFWB pastors and members describe being in awe during foot washing.[77] Part of it is the feeling of inclusion, especially when most of those doing it are older. A pastor recalls, "One thing that always struck me was that it was all different generations doing it together. That was a time when we could interact with people who weren't necessarily our own age and so a lot of the older women would wash the female children's feet and vice versa.[78] There are feelings of acceptance and inclusion when OFWBs experience foot washing for the first time. It is an opportunity to learn from the older members of the congregation.[79]

71. Interview with OFWB pastor (K), February 12, 2015.

72. One pastor recalls, "It would not be unusual for me, after communion, to go back there with the men and to observe what was going on. So, I've really grown up with it all of my life." Interview with OFWB pastor (E), March 27, 2015.

73. Foot washing can become a natural action. A questionnaire respondent reports that she has "been doing this [foot washing] my whole life, [it] was strange to learn other churches didn't do it." Questionnaire response from OFWB, Church (H), April 2014.

74. Interview with OFWB pastor (D), March 30, 2015.

75. Interview with OFWB pastor (D), March 30, 2015.

76. Interview with OFWB member (H), January 26, 2015.

77. One pastor remembers that "my first reaction would be like in awe, of grown men washing each other's feet. And of course, not understanding what all that mean and what all it represented." Interview with OFWB pastor (E), March 27, 2015.

78. Interview with OFWB pastor (F), March 5, 2015.

79. A questionnaire respondent writes that the most important aspect of foot washing was "being with the elderly people when I was young and learning from them."

Participating in foot washing often brings you into contact with the older more prominent members of the congregation. It places you on equal footing with the deacons, Sunday school teachers, and other spiritual leaders in the church. For example, a pastor remembers at "eight or nine years old, I thought I had arrived. This was fantastic, this was something that I've not done. And to hear them singing while they were washing feet, the men in the room, it didn't matter if I was a young boy, I was included with what was going on."[80] It is especially meaningful when a family member washes your feet.[81] Washing the feet of your mother or father can create a moving experience.[82] Experiences with family members are often remembered later in life.[83] Even indirect experience involving family members can create powerful memories. As a boy, a pastor remembers his grandfather washing the feet of a mentally handicapped man. This man frequently walked to church. He remembers "his feet looked terrible. His toenails hadn't been cut, and I remember my granddaddy dropping right down on his knees and washing those feet. I was thinking how could you do that? I could never do that. As I have looked back over the years it really made me realize that if you can't wash feet like that, then you can't wash feet. You're missing the whole point."[84]

Remembering her first experiences more than sixty-five years ago, a member shares how she felt excluded as a child. Because she had not accepted Christ and been baptized, she was not allowed to attend.[85] She

---

Questionnaire response from OFWB, Church (A), May 2014.

80. Interview with OFWB pastor (B), March 26, 2015.

81. One pastor remembers his grandfather washing his feet for the very first time. He remembers "growing up in the church after I was saved and baptized going through the ritual of feet washing, even having my grandfather to wash my feet. I can remember that as well. I was twelve or thirteen-year-old boy. That mean a lot to me that my grandfather would do that." Interview with OFWB pastor (H), February 3, 2015.

82. Describing her first experience of foot washing, a questionnaire respondent writes, "I remember washing my mother's feet, and she washed mine. To be able to do that for my mother was very touching." Questionnaire response from OFWB, Church (F), September 2014.

83. One pastor recalls an experience with his uncle. He remembers being in a Sunday school classroom at his church when he was ten years old. He shares, "One of my uncles took the lead and would lead the singing when men would go back there for washing of feet and we had several persons at that who were new members. . . . One of the respected leaders of the church took on the new candidates and washed their feet and showed them how we practiced that at the [church name] church. Then my uncle would lead the singing. I was ten years old, but I still remember being in that classroom." Interview with OFWB pastor (C), February 4, 2015.

84. Interview with OFWB pastor (A), April 7, 2015.

85. Practices can also have a shadow side. Here exclusion marks this member's

remembers "watching the men go to one side and the women the other and not understanding."[86] When she finally was allowed to participate, she recalls how much of an honor it was to participate with the ladies in her church. These were the women that taught her in Sunday school. They were the ones "who always made the biggest cakes at homecoming. They were the most special people, I guess if there was anyone next to God I thought those ladies were."[87] Sixty-five years later, she describes those moments with those ladies with a degree of reverence and awe. Sitting in simple wooden chairs, they girded themselves with old torn towels that looked more like sheets. In front of each chair was a plain white pail filled with water. These ladies would then kneel to wash the other's feet. She recalls how they "wore hose on each leg, not the pantyhose, and they would take them off so that their feet could be washed. . . . I remember in later years when they would just sprinkle the foot with the hose on."[88] For her it was an amazing experience.

Sometimes first memories are humorous. It is not unusual for participants to see the lighter side of the practice.[89] Remembering his own experiences as a child over sixty years ago, he remarks about a time his father asked him to get water for foot washing (the building lacked running water). Not knowing any different, he returned with ice water instead. Afterwards he and his father had a "conversation" about foot washing.[90]

Children sometimes find the experience more meaningful than adults. One member recalls how impressed she was by a child's first experience of foot washing. Speaking of this child, she remembers, "I got to see it through her eyes, and [it was a cold day] she said, 'Wow that makes you warm inside

---

perception of foot washing as a child.

86. Interview with OFWB member (B), March 31, 2015.

87. Interview with OFWB member (B), March 31, 2015.

88. Interview with OFWB member (B), March 31, 2015.

89. For example, this pastor describes how one night a "lady said she really was happy that we were doing communion that night because that meant she got her pantyhose washed." Interview with OFWB pastor (D), March 30, 2015.

90. His father and several other men of the church were constructing the church at the time. Following work, the men were going to have communion and foot washing. He explains, "They were out there working, and daddy sent me, his sister lived just a short distance from the church, daddy sent me up to her house to get a pail of water. . . . Well I didn't know any different, so I went up to get the pail of water. His sister's name was [name], and Aunt [name] wanted to know what they wanted it for. I said, 'I guess they're working. I guess they're wanting to drink it.' So, she fills it full of ice. When I get back, that's when daddy took me aside and he said 'we need to talk about feet washing' [he begins laughing]." Interview with OFWB pastor (D), March 30, 2015.

and out when you do that!' It was so sweet and to see her from a child's viewpoint, and I thought that was great."[91]

A children's pastor includes foot washing as a part of the church educational program. As expected, children are initially reluctant to do foot washing for the first time. She explains, "My first group of kids were very reluctant. Some of them were very grossed out by the thought of touching someone else's feet. Some of them were almost embarrassed of taking their own shoes and socks off in front of someone else."[92] Slowly through a process of education, children in her church have become more familiar with it. She makes sure to have lessons throughout the year, including a Lenten lesson.[93] She also teaches foot washing on Sundays when a new member is baptized. In her church, deacons wash a new converts' feet before baptism. She has the older children help her demonstrate washing their feet. Now her children, she explains, "have become more familiar with it . . . they don't typically have that reaction that they used to because they have at least seen it, even if they haven't experienced it. They usually . . . if they are a new kid and they haven't seen it before then they might be a little bit reluctant, but once they see the other kids doing it then they realize that this isn't so bad, I can do this."[94] Another pastor describes how, "A couple of years ago in our Bible school, our director washed all the children's feet, and talked about why we were doing that. And the little children would run up and sit there. I was amazed, I sat and watched, and they sat there so quietly. It was like they were in awe, I can't believe you're doing this."[95] Foot washing can be an amazing experience for children in OFWB churches.[96]

First experiences for adults often bring the same feelings of reluctance, embarrassment, and hesitation. It can be especially difficult for those with no prior experience with it. First time participants are unsure because it is so different from everything else they do in church.[97] After returning to

91. Interview with OFWB member (G), January 29, 2015.

92. Interview with OFWB pastor (F), March 5, 2015.

93. About Lent she says, "Yes we include it in the lessons. I cover Jesus' last week of his life. During the lent season in junior church. So that's one of the lessons." Interview with OFWB pastor (F), March 5, 2015.

94. Interview with OFWB pastor (F), March 5, 2015.

95. Interview with OFWB pastor (A), April 7, 2015.

96. An eleven-year old questionnaire respondent writes that foot washing is "like I'm literally walking in His [Jesus'] footsteps." Questionnaire response from OFWB, Church (J), July 2014.

97. For example, a pastor describes foot washing as "probably unusual, weird, strange I guess. Being such a different event from anything else that takes place in the church, certainly the community at large, and I think that most of the individuals that participated in it, kind of felt that they too felt a level of 'un-sureity.'" Interview with

church in his early twenties, a pastor recalls, "I'll never forget just the weird-ness of taking your shoes off and somebody washing your feet and doing the same."[98] Despite the *weirdness* of it, or maybe because of it, this pastor observes, "it made me see the elderly gentlemen in our church in a way I'd never seen them before, very vulnerable."[99] Foot washing is a practice you need to grow into. The first experience of it can be off putting and unusual. A member states, "I was a little embarrassed by it . . . but then as I have grown over the past four years spiritually I see it as a very humbling experience."[100]

The first experience of foot washing is a kind of boundary crossing. This is not an imposed barrier, but a self-imposed one. It is, as a member says, a "barrier you have to cross in letting down your guard to participate in that."[101] You must deal with your own issues regarding feet, the body, and intimacy. You must let go of preconceived ideas and notions regarding touching feet. Foot washing can be very easily misunderstood and feared. This same member explains, "It's not foot washing like you think of washing something. It is, don't worry, you don't have to touch my foot if you don't want too. You can hold the back of the leg, splash a little bit of water and you're done."[102] There are also misconceptions involving women's clothing and what one ought to wear to participate.[103]

Once you overcome these physical and mental barriers, important experiences can take place.[104] Participants are often surprised by their emotions afterwards.[105] The first time, in particular, can be powerful and over-

---

OFWB pastor (J), February 26, 2015.

98. Interview with OFWB pastor (G), February 6, 2015.

99. Interview with OFWB pastor (G), February 6, 2015

100. Interview with OFWB member (A), March 3, 2015.

101. Interview with OFWB member (D), February 5, 2015.

102. Interview with OFWB member (D), February 5, 2015.

103. A pastor describes her frustration in trying to organize foot washing in a non-OFWB setting. She was attempting to organize foot washing as part of a divinity school chapel service with other members of a worship teams. She says, "I remember someone said, 'well a lot of our women wear pantyhose and so they couldn't take off their panty-hose and participate.' And I looked at them and said, 'What? You don't have to take off your pantyhose to participate. You're just sprinkling water on the foot. It's pretty much just absorbed. It dries very quickly.' That was something that I would never even thought of as being a hindrance to washing feet. I guess for someone who had never participated in a foot washing service those were the kind of things that came to their mind." Interview with OFWB pastor (F), March 5, 2015.

104. A questionnaire respondent describes how she now has "feelings of joy!" Questionnaire response from OFWB, Church (H), April 2015.

105. A questionnaire respondent writes, "My first time, I was twenty-five years old and it brought the most spiritual feeling over me! I felt nothing but peace." Questionnaire response from OFWB, Church (A), May 2014.

whelming.[106] Recalling a Holy Thursday service, a pastor remembers how "we washed feet and at least three or four men were there who had never washed feet before. They participated, and I heard them talking. They said, 'I've never done this before, but this is awesome, it's an awesome feeling.'"[107] This same pastor continued, "I think that for people that do it for the first time, it's an overwhelming experience."[108]

Speaking of a friend who grew up as a Southern Baptist, a pastor recalls the hesitation this friend had the first time he participated. Realizing that his friend was uncomfortable he told him, "'Come on, let's do this together.'"[109] Years later he shares how this person still tells "me how he will never forget that first night we washed feet together. Now he's a deacon in our church, so that means a lot [to me]."[110] An OFWB member shares how much it meant to him when the pastor washed his feet as a new member. The pastor "washed my feet and to me that meant something to me because here I am a new member of the church and the pastor's washing my feet. . . . I felt it through the Holy Spirit and what he was doing, but it meant a lot more that the, you know, he's the pastor of the church."[111] The newness of it, combined with intimacy and physicality of foot washing, help first experiences as adults to be particularly meaningful and inspiring. Once you cross the self-imposed barrier of discomfort, the first experience can help put "things in a whole new light."[112] Some never forget the person who first washed his or her feet. For one respondent, it was a bonding experience that forever changed his relationship with another member. He explains that he "wouldn't necessarily say we're friends, he was always cordial. But when he washed my feet that first time and he looked at me and told me said, 'Look, I'm glad you're back in church and I love you and I'm glad you're here,' and he gave me a hug. There was no more authentic experience in this church."[113]

---

106. A questionnaire respondent writes that the first time, "There was a whole new way of looking at my faith." Questionnaire response from OFWB, Church (D), May 2014.

107. Interview with OFWB pastor (A), April 7, 2015.

108. Interview with OFWB pastor (A), April 7, 2015.

109. Interview with OFWB pastor (H), February 3, 2015.

110. Interview with OFWB pastor (H), February 3, 2015.

111. Focus group (B) interview with OFWB member, June 28, 2015.

112. This member stated that, "I knew what washing feet was about. I understood and had read the passage. Until I experienced it. Yes, it puts things in a whole new light. After I understood it in its fullest I wondered why more churches weren't doing it." Focus group (B) interview with OFWB member, June 28, 2015.

113. Focus group (B) interview with OFWB member, June 28, 2015.

The Pastor's Role in Foot Washing

Explaining how foot washing teaches service and servanthood is shown rather than said. Pastors recognize they have an uphill battle. Some newcomers are cautious of anything that appears ritualistic. One pastor describes how "we [OFWBs] have an inherent bias and/or fear of anything that almost seems or thinks or smells of sacramentalism that . . . magically something is going to happen."[114] Overcoming this fear means a concerted effort to reach out and form relationships with those hesitant. A pastor follows up explaining that, "The only way we can get this in the people's thoughts is through relationship. If we don't have intimate relationships with people, if we don't engage people, if we don't disciple people, in these things we can say this is required, [but] it's useless. People are doing because they feel like they got to. We have to build relationships with people to be able to explain it to them."[115]

Some pastors and members describe frustration and disappointment when foot washing it is not taken seriously. One member remembers how much of an impact her experiences as a young married woman had on her. She recalls how one group of women made foot washing a spiritual occasion. She describes how she can still remember "those ladies . . . when they went back, when they went to the room, there was no talking. It was quiet, and they sung the old hymns. They sung *Amazing Grace*. I still get chill bumps. I remember just what I was feeling of how special that was. It was a different sound then singing at the church. It was just really different, and those ladies were serious about it."[116] She compares this to OFWB churches that do not take foot washing seriously. She remembers, "I have been in some places, it was not taken to me, seemingly very seriously. Talking and laughter and that's probably fine, but that wasn't the way that to me it seemed it should be because it was a very serious time."[117] She goes on to state how after visiting one particular church, she "came away very upset because they had [washed feet] and it didn't seem anybody took it seriously. I had no idea churches could do it that way. Because what I had experienced, even through my earlier years, it was very quiet . . . it was spiritual. It was a spirit filled time. If I ever felt that I could feel the Holy Spirit almost touching, that was a time

114. Focus group (A) interview with OFWB pastor, June 28, 2015.
115. Focus group (A) interview with OFWB pastor, June 28, 2015.
116. Interview with OFWB member (B), March 31, 2015.
117. Interview with OFWB member (B), March 31, 2015.

that I could do it."[118] In her experience it was "just a very reverent time. . . . When those older ladies were so reverent, it was just special."[119]

This feeling of reverence can come in a variety of ways. Since OFWBs do not have a rubric for foot washing (other than John 13), congregations are free to follow their own customs. Each congregation has its own way to make foot washing special, meaningful, and reverent. Pastors may experience several variations of foot washing during their ministerial careers. This pastor explains that,

> There [are] some settings it's very quiet. And that's not something that's limited to just one area of the OFWB. I think it depends on the setting going on in the congregation at that time. [If] there's been a tragedy or something then it affects what's taking place as you do feet washing. [At] other times, you would have a conversation which is usually leading toward biblical conversation. . . . And then at other times you will have somebody that will break out singing *Amazing Grace* or *Old Rugged Cross* or some of those older hymns that they can sing without having to have a book in their hand. So, it's not, it's kind of split across all three in a sense. It just depends on the atmosphere at the time.[120]

Pastors express frustration when other OFWB pastors do not conduct foot washing in a way that is meaningful and reverent. One pastor explains that, "it's the kind of service you really put forth your very best and do the very best you can do in a service. For people to have that opportunity to understand what's happening to us . . . in the whole process as we experience that renewal, from the example that we have set, that he [Jesus] set, that we are now doing ourselves and renewing ourselves in him . . . but I don't think today that our ministers are emphasizing it enough."[121] A pastor puts it this way, "It can be completely not [spiritual] if I'm being honest with you. I've been in feet washing services where everyone is talking about the ball games, the weather, and not even thinking about what we're doing and it [does] not mean that much to them."[122] This level of conversation can lead some to believe that foot washing is losing its meaning.[123] It can be, as a

118. Interview with OFWB member (B), March 31, 2015.

119. Interview with OFWB member (B), March 31, 2015.

120. Interview with OFWB pastor (D), March 30, 2015.

121. Interview with OFWB pastor (B), March 26, 2015.

122. Interview with OFWB pastor (H), February 3, 2015.

123. Describing this lost meaning, a questionnaire respondent writes that "everyone is talking about different things like the weather, or their backache rather than concentrating on Jesus during this act of humility. It almost seems to have lost its meaning and purpose when the discussion is on anything and everything but Jesus." Questionnaire

pastor stated, "as unholy an experience as you can imagine. I think it should be celebrated, this is a celebration. It should be uplifted."[124] Another pastor affirms the same point: "We must keep [foot washing] as holy as we possibly can. . . . It's time for me to be still and know and be in a very worshipful atmosphere if I'm expecting to experience his divine love in my life at that moment. I guess the word would be high reverence."[125] If that level of reverence can be achieved, foot washing becomes more about the worship and less ritualistic.[126]

To emphasize the reverence of foot washing, some OFWB pastors try to explain the importance of foot washing to their congregations. In an effort to instill this practice early, one church makes it a tradition to wash the feet of new converts before they are baptized.[127] Others pastors suggest that participants should sing hymns while washing feet.[128] Pastors may even devote an entire service in preparation for foot washing.[129] Some pastors suggest that it must be conducted in complete silence so that the only sounds are those of the water and pots.[130] Some will have married couples

---

response from OFWB, Church (I), June 2014.

124. Interview with OFWB pastor (C), February 4, 2015.

125. Interview with OFWB pastor (B), March 26, 2015.

126. Explaining her most memorable experience of foot washing, a questionnaire respondent writes, "We actually had warm water and soap. It was at night. The lights were not bright. It was the most reverent, humbling feet washing service I have ever been in. It was more than just a ritual. It was truly a worship service." Questionnaire response from OFWB, Church (G), May 2014.

127. One pastor describes the custom, "the deacons come wash the new convert's feet before they're baptized, and then they go to the baptism. . . . If there are ladies or girls involved they have their wives do the young girls. The deacons don't do the young girls. That's paired off the same way. That takes place prior to a baptism service. You see it done in different ways in different settings." Interview with OFWB pastor (D), March 30, 2015.

128. "I've actually made our men, this past time and the time before, to try to sing acapella *Amazing Grace* while they're involved in it. And that really slows them down. That brings in the Holy Spirit. Not concentrating on the ball game or the weather but concentrating on what they're doing." Interview with OFWB pastor (H), February 3, 2015.

129. "It's really the preaching about it, about the significance of it more than the act itself. The service prepares us for it before we actually do the act." Interview with OFWB member (F), March 17, 2015.

130. She describes that "in more recent days, our pastor suggested that during the time of Jesus all you could hear was the sound of water and the sounds of the pots and the water and things, and so we've been told to be silent during this and see how this affects you. So that more recently that's what we've done. It's kind of a solemn occasion trying to remember what it was like for Jesus and the disciples." Interview with OFWB member (G), January 29, 2015.

wash each other's feet. A pastor shares, "I've heard of a minister that had his married couples pair up and wash one another's feet. When he did that, he said, 'Those couples had said they never washed the feet of their spouse in the church.' That was one of the most memorable times that they have ever experienced that ordinance when they did that."[131]

Despite these efforts, because foot washing involves moving around, some OFWBs see foot washing as less serious than other worship practices. A pastor who regularly deals with this issue explains,

> I . . . explain to them that this is a reverent part of the service. Just because we're moving around and washing each other feet, doesn't mean that it's a time that you can be irreverent. I encourage them to be quiet and holy. To be prayerful. If someone breaks out in singing, join along and sing. But just think about what you're doing and what it represents. I found out that if you'll talk to them ahead of time; if you'll prepare them for what's about to happen. When you're washing each other's feet, it's not a time to talk about the weather or how the crops are doing or if you been fishing lately, something like that. It's actually a part of the service.[132]

Other pastors attempt to modify how and where foot washing is done to keep it reverent. The simplest method is to conduct it in the sanctuary rather than dividing men and women into separate parts of church. This pastor explains his procedure,

> I had space, like at the front of my church in [city], and I would have the ladies together on the front pews. Then I had the men set up at the back of the church, so we were all in the same room and this created a more reverent time. Sometimes when you leave the sanctuary and congregated yourself to rooms to wash feet, other people would get off track of [why] we were there. . . . I stay at the center and remind them that this is not the time that we do that. This is a time we need to be reflecting on what this ordinance means and just spiritually reviving us to really be the servants that God has called us to be.[133]

OFWB pastors increasing like to have their congregation do foot washing in the same location, together, not separated by gender. As a young man, one pastor did not like the idea of separating men and women before

---

131. Interview with OFWB pastor (I), February 2, 2015.
132. Interview with OFWB pastor (E), March 27, 2015.
133. Interview with OFWB pastor (I), February 2, 2015.

foot washing. He decided to put a table in the fellowship hall between the men and the women. He says, "Women on one side, men on the other. But we're in the same room. We still gather, basically holding hands and sharing testimony, but we do it with the women. So that we're all together."[134]

Education about foot washing is not just for the congregation alone. Sometimes even deacons and other leaders of the church need a reminder about how foot washing should be practiced. One pastor explains that before practicing foot washing, or any ordinance, he will "talk about the meaning of the practices. I will take the time to talk about what we're doing and why we're doing that. I'll talk with deacons in the churches about how we actually practice it."[135] This same pastor also serves as a professor at a university, where he made foot washing especially meaningful for a group of students. Student fellowship invited him to lead a Holy Thursday service in the campus chapel. He decided to make foot washing the focus of the evening. He describes the scene:

> I had the basins and the towel. We had the students and I talked to them about it and I explained what we were doing and why I felt that it was important. I think that there were about twelve students that were there, so very informal, and I invited the students to participate if they wanted to. I had one of the students that I'd already spoken to who was willing for me to wash his feet so that the others could see actually how it could be done. Right on down to me girding myself with the towel and rolling up my shirt sleeves. All twelve of the students participated and most, including me, with tears in their eyes. It was a very meaningful experience.[136]

The People's Role in Foot Washing

Often it is the people, not the pastor, who make foot washing meaningful. Pastors may set the scene, but the people bring foot washing to life. The relationships formed during foot washing bring long time practitioners back to the practice. OFWBs look forward to it.

Foot washing brings the congregation together. A member explains that foot washing creates a much tighter bond among those who participate. She does not have that same feeling of closeness to other members

---

134. Interview with OFWB pastor (G), February 6, 2015.

135. Interview with OFWB pastor (C), February 4, 2015.

136. Interview with OFWB pastor (C), February 4, 2015.

of her church. She explains, "It definitely draws you closer . . . there is a different type of closeness there. It's on another level. They are even more family. I guess it would be more akin to it being your immediate family versus your extended second [or] third cousin, great great aunt kind of. It's a much, much tighter bond."[137] For her, it creates a safe space where she has "a chance to put down that barrier that we put up and see that people really aren't going to make fun of us there, not going to talk about us you know. These people really are my family. And they really do have my back."[138] She continues explaining that younger members are awed when they wash the feet of older members.

> My favorite part is, there's this one lady in our church. She's almost 92. A faithful, faithful woman. It is such an honor when I get the chance to wash Miss Helen's feet. She's going to make sure she's there. Her health is not great, but she is going to be there no matter what. Just the example she has set, and I've known her all my life, and so I've known the struggles that she's been through in her life. Seeing how poised she has always been and how Godly she has lived her life despite all the hardships she's been through, to get the opportunity to serve her is just wonderful.[139]

Foot washing can also bring about the unexpected. There are occasions where people act uncharacteristically emotional following foot washing. For example, there was an older man in a pastor's congregation who was known to be very quiet and reserved. He hardly ever spoke a word. However, following foot washing, this man would break his silence in a very emotional and powerful way. It was the custom of this church to hold hands together in a circle, giving time so that each individual could share or give a prayer request. It just so happens, "every time it came to him, he gets tears in his eyes and he just kind of squeezed the guy's hands to the right and to the left so that guy could say his [prayer request] or whatever. This one guy, he never said anything out in public. In that room, with tears in his eyes . . . what he was saying was, 'You know I love you guys, I love all of you guys.' Something like that every time. That's all he would say."[140] He goes on to say that in that circle, it was not unusual to see "grown men you've looked up to all your life . . . big guys don't cry, weeping you know it really does change

---

137. Interview with OFWB member (D), February 5, 2015.
138. Interview with OFWB member (D), February 5, 2015.
139. Interview with OFWB member (D), February 5, 2015.
140. Interview with OFWB pastor (G), February 6, 2015.

the way you see people."[141] The love OFWB people experience during foot washing creates opportunities for emotional participation. It may help motivate individuals to share, especially those who might otherwise stay silent. As OFWBs practice foot washing, "It's kind of like saying I love you, and most of the time when I wash, I try to make sure I do a different [person] every time. I try to respond with a different person every time, and usually when I complete that task one of the things I do before I stand up is to look up at them and say, 'I love in Christ.' That's what I think it says."[142] Everyone is expressing that same love, and "everybody is on the same level doing the same thing and very seldom do you ever hear any argument or any discord or anything in that direction."[143] Because you have already opened yourself up to another person, there is an incentive to open yourself up to the larger group.[144]

Foot washing is also a chance to bring in people on the outside. Pastors and members describe it as an inclusive experience that helps to break down feelings of animosity that can develop between individuals. For people on the outside, it gives them a chance to become a part of the church family.[145] It helps to develop a "sense of familiarity and the sense of family, belonging, when you do something like that. The people who have been on the fringe, might would feel it [foot washing] brings them into the group."[146]

141. Interview with OFWB pastor (G), February 6, 2015.

142. Interview with OFWB pastor (D), March 30, 2015.

143. Interview with OFWB pastor (D), March 30, 2015.

144. A member explains that "there are people who open up with a prayer request or a praise report who otherwise wouldn't have done it in a larger setting. But with [the] smaller setting, I think it is, it comes after you've opened yourself up as to 'hey I've already opened to doing foot washing. I'm just going to jump right on in and ask for this prayer for this problem that I'm having." Interview with OFWB member (D), February 5, 2015.

145. For example, a pastor reached out to a troubled member of the community to teach how foot washing demonstrates humility, love, and service for all. Remembering, a pastor says, "We just happened to have a visitor that Sunday. I'll be frank with you, he wasn't just a visitor. He had a little bit of a reputation because he had experienced some trouble with the law. I'll just go that far. He was the guest of one of my lay people, so I approached him before the worship service and I was very frank with him [and I said to him], 'Would you be offended if I washed your feet during this service?' He was very gracious, and he agreed. I got one my teenage boys and I said, 'Look I want you to get a pitcher of warm water, have it ready to go, and at the appropriate time I will nod and that will be the signal for you to go get it because I'm going to demonstrate feet washing.' I came to that part of the service and that's exactly what I did." Focus group interview (A) with OFWB pastor, June 28, 2015.

146. Interview with OFWB pastor (A), April 7, 2015.

Foot washing is a way for OFWBs to demonstrate the value and importance of each person, especial those who feel like they do not deserve it.[147]

For OFWBs, foot washing is an opportunity to bring together people as equals.[148] In foot washing, it is not unusual for the old and the young, rich and poor, the powerful and weak, and so on to wash each other's feet.[149] It is a moment where status no longer matters. What is important "is the drawing of you and I as brothers to the point that we can hug one another in Christian atmosphere and say, 'I love you brother.' I think it's that . . . that humbles you, both of you, to the point where you recognize you're now equal regardless of your station in life. I think that's important, that we meet one another as equals at the foot of the cross."[150] Foot washing is a way of telling people, "Nobody's too great to wash feet. Nobody is not worthy of having their feet washed. They're all valued but we're all equally valued. I think it's kind of an equalizer."[151] All people deserve to be treated with dignity and respect.[152]

It is this sense of love and equality that helps to strengthen, deepen, and repair relationships among OFWBs. Foot washing is a continually reminder of the desire for love and compassion between one another.[153] Each time it is practiced, it creates opportunities that allow members to become better connected to one another. It reinforces the need to serve one another, especially towards those who are in conflict or disagreement.

147. A member shares how "it was almost like being exalted when somebody kneeled down and washed my feet. I thought to myself, 'I'm the last person that needs their feet washed. I need to wash everybody's feet in this church. Set it up on a regular basis.' That's how ashamed I was of my actions before I turned to Christ. That guy still told me he loved me." Focus group (B) interview with OFWB member, June 28, 2015.

148. Explaining this equality, a questionnaire respondent writes, "When I get down on my knees and wash my sister's feet and they in turn do the same, for me no sister is greater than the other." Questionnaire response from OFWB member, Church (C), June 2014.

149. At that moment, position and status no longer matter. A member shares in a focus group that, "The washing of the feet kind of brings you closer to your fellow Christians because . . . it takes away your earthly positions. Everybody's equal, they're all the same." Focus group (B) interview with OFWB member, June 28, 2015.

150. Focus group (B) interview with OFWB member, June 28, 2015.

151. Interview with OFWB member (G), January 29, 2015.

152. A questionnaire respondent echoes this sentiment writing that foot washing is an "opportunity to bow before the Saints of our church and wash their feet to let them know that we love and respect them." Questionnaire response from OFWB, Church (C), June 2014.

153. A questionnaire respondent believes that foot washing, "creates a desire for love and compassion for others." Questionnaire response from OFWB, Church (F), September 2014.

I think [foot washing] builds connections amongst the membership of the church. [It] does deepen the intimacy that is called
to be held within the church, so it strengthens our commitment
to serve to those who sit next to us in the pews. I think that it is
also a way of healing and repairing broken relationships. . . . I
think the practice of foot washing can be and in many instances
is a way for people who have had differences or disagreements
to meet in a sacred space, and to share in a moment of repair, if
you will, to a broken relationship.[154]

Forgiveness

Foot washing can be a way to heal broken relationships. It is a moving experience for both the washer and the one being washed. It brings individuals
together into a shared path of love and forgiveness. Foot washing offers an
alternative when words do not work. Not all people can say, "I am sorry,"
and for some, foot washing can begin a healing process. A pastor described
two ladies who verbally attacked one another for years. The relationship
had completely deteriorated. Yet, one night, the "Holy Spirit convicted this
other lady of her things and she turned around and they switched places
[during foot washing] and before they left that night their difference had
been healed through the fact that they were washing each other's feet. It only
happened because one of them was willing to empty themselves and say,
'look whatever I've done let me wash your feet.'"[155] Experiencing this first
hand, one member describes how foot washing helps her repair relationships with others. She describes moments when "I've been a little irritated
with somebody and I've had to wash their feet, and that sort of gives you a
perspective. That's happened to me twice. You realize that this person is very
precious, and I think it's a real humbling thing, especially if you're irritated
with someone. You've got to have the right attitude."[156]

OFWB pastors help to make space for moments like this, but they cannot force these moments. OFWBs make these moments happen. It is not
about the status and importance of the pastor. Foot washing involves everyday people undergoing real issues, disagreements, and complex situations.
In the OFWB, foot washing is a way to live in community. Foot washing

154. Interview with OFWB pastor (J), February 26, 2015.
155. Focus group (A) interview with OFWB pastor, June 28, 2015.
156. Interview with OFWB member (G), January 29, 2015.

can be a first step toward reconciliation and renewing the bonds within the community.[157]

For example, two deacons were feuding over the placement of a landfill within their community. Being on opposing sides of the issues, there was a deep seeded animosity between them. According to their pastor, "This thing went around and around and one of the men, the one who was opposed to it, had some documents put in his mailbox, basically not too nice and polite about his opposition. He thought that other guy in the church did it and he blamed him for it publicly. Well, he found out that those documents came from someone else."[158] After falsely accusing his fellow deacon, this man scheduled an emergency meeting of the deacon board and "he went before the other deacons and publicly acknowledged 'I have sinned against my brother, and I'm profoundly sorry, and I don't believe that I can officiate at the table tonight until I've made peace with my brother.' We prayed together, he served at the table, and then he washed his feet."[159] For OFWBs, foot washing is "fleshing out what it means to be a person that would call himself out to the name of Jesus. As a servant people we have to learn to forgive, there can be no genuine community apart from forgiveness. I think that washing of feet fleshes out that community."[160] You can be led into the experience of love and forgiveness without needing words.[161]

Relationship

OFWBs are not surprised that foot washing can lead to these experiences. It is not a mystery for OFWBs. Because foot washing forms intimate and familial bonds, members who practice are naturally closer to one another. OFWBs themselves make the experience of foot washing special. As a pastor puts it, "I think for me, the individuals, [in the past] I've had the opportunity to share in that practice, it does deepen one's relationship. As a pastor I think it would be safe to say that for me, overall, I was closer to the men with whom I participated in foot washing as opposed to those who didn't

157. Foot washing is a reminder, according to a questionnaire respondent, "to always treat others as Jesus would. No matter what comes our way." Questionnaire response from OFWB, Church (H), April 2014.

158. Interview with OFWB pastor (C), February 4, 2015.

159. Interview with OFWB pastor (C), February 4, 2015.

160. Interview with OFWB pastor (C), February 4, 2015.

161. Foot washing reminds OFWBs of the need to serve and be forgiven. A questionnaire respondent writes that foot washing "reminds me to have a servant's heart and that we have to allow Jesus to cleanse us of sin." Questionnaire response from OFWB, Church (D), May 2014.

practice it or didn't attend those services. Not that there weren't friendships there, I think it made a difference in the connections that I had with members of the congregation."[162] Another pastor believes that foot washing is, "a shared experience. . . . It's a unifying thing once you let it."[163] Foot washing is a way to build communal relationship among OFWB congregations. Drawing individuals closer together, foot washing promotes community rather than individualism.[164] Foot washing, according to an interviewed pastor, "is a tool to develop relationship and develop that community, and that is an avenue and model that is in John 13 for us to emulate. Not the individualist idea that we have. A community of fellowship and intimacy."[165]

These experiences inspire OFWBs to continue foot washing. As a multigenerational practice, it enables them to reflect on the history of the practice and those deceased members of the community.[166] For many, they are doing the same thing their parents and grandparents did. These experiences last a lifetime for OFWBs. At each instance of foot washing, they re-connect with the past and the present. It is an experience that OFWBs want to pass on to their children and grandchildren.[167] Even the pails and the towels carry the history of those who came before. As you prepare for foot washing, a deacon shares:

> You're getting those pails out, these are the same pails that were potentially used forty or fifty years ago. It's just a feeling of history and a feeling of foundation in the church when you're getting those [pails] out. And those long towels that you try to wrap around your waist, and they seem to get shorter as time goes on. You're using the same towels, potentially, that we used twenty years ago. Only used four times a year so they'll last a long, long time. It's not only a spiritual thing, but it puts you up with the history of the church and the history of the denomination. That you're still doing it the old way. There's not any modern way of washing feet itself. Taking the pail and getting down on your

162. Interview with OFWB pastor (J), February 26, 2015.

163. Interview with OFWB pastor (H), February 3, 2015.

164. A questionnaire respondent writes, "I feel it draws me closer to my church family." Questionnaire response from OFWB, Church (A), May 2014.

165. Focus group (A) interview with OFWB pastor, June 28, 2015.

166. A questionnaire respondent writes that she is "grateful to have shared this experience with family and elder church members that are no longer with us." Questionnaire response from OFWB, Church (H), April 2014.

167. A member shares that "it was an honor to be able to wash my son's feet. I hope it would carry on to him. We have a grandchild now, he's two and a half. I hope it will carry on with him. For my grandson to pass on that feeling, and I think it will. I really do." Interview with OFWB member (H), January 26, 2015.

knees putting their feet in the pail, in little pans. And using these old chipped pans and these old towels like that, it sort of adds an importance and a solemnity to it. I don't know what the right word is, but it enriches it so much more and this is nothing that the world can really change or modernize. It makes it maybe a little bit sweeter and a little bit more important doing it that way.[168]

THE EFFECTS OF FOOT WASHING ON ORIGINAL FREE WILL BAPTISTS

Foot Washing and Humility

OFWB pastors and members have a lot to say regarding foot washing and humility. OFWB participants consider this a rich practice. Three words define foot washing: "humility, service, servant."[169] I asked interviewees to describe what words came to mind when they thought of foot washing. Almost every interviewee named one of these words or a common synonymn. For example, fifteen out of nineteen interviewees named humility as a word that they associated with foot washing. Repeatedly, interviewees and questionnaire respondents named humility as the defining quality of foot washing.[170] Foot washing is "an expression of humility, humbleness, being willing to become that low with your brothers and sisters in Christ."[171] One former member, when remembering his experiences as a boy, responded by saying, "The beauty, the solemnity, the humility that washing of the saints' feet demonstrated to believers is, I don't know how to say, it's very humbling to do that."[172] For others, there is a direct correlation between the humility of Jesus and the humility of foot washing. When asked what first came to mind about foot washing, a pastor proudly proclaimed, "First is humility, seeing the example of Christ and [he] bowing and kneeling before his disciples and washing their feet knowing what he was about to go through very soon, and

168. Interview with OFWB member (H), January 26, 2015.

169. Interview with OFWB member (F), March 17, 2015.

170. One questionnaire respondent writes that every time foot washing is practiced "I experience a feeling of humbleness and a little anxiety." Questionnaire response from OFWB, Church (B), June 2014.

171. Interview with OFWB pastor (D), March 30, 2015.

172. Interview with OFWB member (C), June 30, 2015.

knowing the reality that he had to wash Judas' feet. That's a very humbling thing in my heart. It really is."[173] This idea of humility goes beyond a mere knowledge of the act. The connection between foot washing and humility is more than association. It is connecting with a feeling that goes beyond explanation. One interviewee described her first reaction to foot washing as follows, "The very first word I think, I know the feeling, if I could just get the word. . . . Humility, I guess that's probably the very first. It's a very humbling experience."[174]

Naturally and without hesitation, foot washing provokes rich and profound feelings of humility for interviewees. The mention of foot washing brings them to a special state or place connected to their own knowledge and experience of humility. This connection between foot washing and humility flows from the OFWB heritage regarding foot washing. The OFWB *Articles of Faith* describes foot washing as way to teach humility.[175] OFWB pastors and members have developed their own ideas and definitions on humility, its connection with foot washing, and the example of Jesus Christ. The life, teachings, and examples that Jesus set are never far from the minds of the OFWB. When asked to describe humility, a pastor describes it as "being able to realize that . . . it's an honor to reach out and help someone else or to serve someone else."[176] Humility connects to the way you think about yourself. To be humble is to place yourself before God and recognize that you are no greater than any other person. Humility, a pastor explains, "means humbling myself before God and other people, to do the things that would serve them."[177] According to a member, humility begins with God, so much so that it is "giving God all the credit and glory for the things that he's done, who we are and the blessings we've received."[178] Humility is for some a spiritual feeling. It is opening yourself to the invitation of the Holy Spirit.[179] The presence of God creates that space where you can learn, experience, and live humbly. It is not just an individual experience according to OFWBs. Humility directly translates into your life and ministry. It is "being able to

173. Interview with OFWB pastor (H), February 3, 2015.

174. Interview with OFWB member (B), March 31, 2015.

175. North Carolina State Convention, *Articles of Faith*, 52.

176. Interview with OFWB pastor (E), March 27, 2015.

177. Interview with OFWB pastor (A), April 7, 2015.

178. She continues saying, "It's not looking for recognition or credit for anything we do personally but knowing that all that we do is through God." Interview with OFWB member (A), March 3, 2015.

179. "[Footwashing] causes me to humble myself to be the follower that [God] has asked me to be and to do [foot washing] with my brother, and at that point I am recommitting myself to my own call. Interview with OFWB pastor (B), March 26, 2015.

understand that others are just as important as you. Knowing that their lives are things that matter and [are] important. That you're willing to humble or lower yourself to the point where you'd be a servant."[180]

Foot Washing, Service, and Servant Leadership

First thoughts of foot washing inevitably come to service and servanthood for OFWBs.[181] Foot washing plants the seed for service.[182] It is, as one pastor describes, "Absolutely the first thing that comes to my mind."[183] Like humility, OFWB interviewees have strong thoughts and feelings regarding service. A pastor stated that she defines it as, "Anything that we do for someone else. Especially something that we would be doing for someone that we wouldn't normally do . . . or normally come in contact with or lowering of ourselves in order to help someone else in need."[184] OFWB interviewees express service as putting other people first. Pastors and members argue that service is a necessary part of the Christian experience. First and foremost, service is the ability "to do something for the good of someone else. To help someone else."[185]

Foot washing and service have a direct connection and relationship according to interviewees. Foot washing is a practical practice that "if you understand it correctly . . . teaches us about our role as servants of the kingdom."[186] Foot washing helps to impart the servant leadership for pastors both in and outside the church walls.[187] Members echo this same sentiment when asked what service and servanthood means to them. An interviewee says that to her, servanthood means, "We are to serve each other, and I think

---

180. Interview with OFWB pastor (H), February 3, 2015.

181. "[Foot washing] reminds me to be a servant to all people, rich and poor, saint and sinner." Questionnaire response from OFWB, Church (A), May 2014.

182. A deacon claims, "I'm not saying that's [foot washing] the only way, but it can plant a seed to make you more community minded in giving and service." Interview with OFWB member (H), January 26, 2015.

183. Interview with OFWB pastor (C), February 4, 2015.

184. Interview with OFWB pastor (F), March 5, 2015.

185. Interview with OFWB pastor (E), March 27, 2015.

186. Interview with OFWB pastor (I), February 2, 2015.

187. "I have tried to emphasize in my churches for the people that don't know it, it's really not necessarily washing the feet for cleansing. That's what we practice now in person, but I think we practice it for the purpose of teaching us what it means [to be a] fellow Christian. You're their servant, you are to serve with them." Interview with OFWB pastor (I), February 2, 2015.

foot washing is a way to show that and to experience that and the experience of closeness it brings as part of fellowship."[188]

For OFWBs, service ties you directly to the example set by Jesus Christ.[189] Jesus, as stated by a member, "though he was Lord, he presented himself as a servant in the sense that he was going the servant's path by washing the disciples' feet. Even though he was their Lord."[190] Jesus Christ is the standard bearer of what it means to be a servant.[191] OFWBs see foot washing as a visible reminder of the standard of humility and service set by Jesus, which all people are called to emulate.[192] This same member says, "Feet washing in itself is not an end, it's just a beginning of a service that we should look to, to continue this humility and servanthood that Jesus set the example for."[193]

The service component of foot washing carries with it a tangible connection to the physical world.[194] It is a reminder that Christ calls Christians to serve the physical world.[195] A pastor suggests that foot washing is an incarnational act. It reminds believes that Jesus was incarnate in the flesh. Foot washing is a deeply physical and "fleshy"[196] act that reminds you that service is physical. Foot washing shows OFWBs that they should be doing things for others.[197] Serving, a member explains, "is serving people as chil-

188. Interview with OFWB member (G), January 29, 2015.

189. A questionnaire respondent shares that foot washing is a reminder "that we are to be servants to others just as Jesus was a servant to the disciples. Jesus is much more important that I am. If he humbled himself in this way, how much more so should I." Questionnaire response from OFWB, Church (E), September 2014.

190. Interview with OFWB member (F), March 17, 2015.

191. A questionnaire respondent shares, "I feels so close to those whom I am participating and with Him. He is a part of [foot washing]. I want to be like Him." Questionnaire response from OFWB, Church (B), June 2014.

192. A pastor believes that "if it was good enough for our Lord to do and he saw the necessity of us doing it, it's something that we should likewise do as well." Interview with OFWB pastor (K), February 12, 2015.

193. Interview with OFWB member (F), March 17, 2015.

194. Writing about this connection with daily life, a questionnaire respondent explains that foot washing "is a reminder to be humble in all that you do. Also, to always put others before yourself." Questionnaire response from OFWB, Church (E), September 2014.

195. For example, a questionnaire respondent writes, "Kneeling and splashing water on a fellow Christian's feet reminds me of the importance of humility, servant-hood, and the need for daily cleansing of my sins." Questionnaire response from OFWB, Church (B), June 2014.

196. One pastor repeatedly used this term to describe foot washing's physicality. Interview with OFWB pastor (G), February 6, 2015.

197. This pastor makes the theological argument that "[Jesus] came in the flesh to

dren, serving the world by showing his love and his mercy and his kindness and forgiveness."[198] Foot washing suggests that it is better to serve than to be served.[199] Service requires humility. Foot washing is a reminder of those two concepts so that you are equipped to help "another person be a better person and lower yourself to not feel greater or bigger or wiser or smarter or anything than anyone else."[200]

OFWB interviewees and questionnaire respondents agree that, to some degree, foot washing demonstrates or represents the concepts of humility and service. It is the living expression of these themes, more importantly; it connects to the person and ministry of Jesus Christ who embodies these themes. These are "virtues that have been embodied by Christ throughout his life and ministry and it's that sort of virtuous living that Christians are expected to embody in their own life. And I think the practice of foot washing is a . . . tangible way that believers are able to show what that is supposed to look like in the world."[201] Foot washing demonstrates the OFWB character. Through humility, service, and servanthood, foot washing "fundamentally portrays how we're called to live as a redeemed people."[202] According to one pastor, the thought and experience of foot washing inspires the feeling that "this is what Christianity is really all about. It's about getting on your knees and serving."[203]

Pastors and members both share ways that foot washing has helped to shape their views on service and servant leadership.[204] The actions teach and remind practicing OFWBs of the roles they serve both in their churches and outside into the larger community. Every time OFWBs practice foot

---

minister to people who are in the flesh. . .it reminds [Christians] that we are obligated to serve our brothers and sisters in Christ, in the flesh, in the body." Interview with OFWB pastor (G), February 6, 2015.

198. Interview with OFWB member (A), March 3, 2015.

199. This same member goes on to say, "I see people that take things for granted and expect to be served instead of serving in the Christian community and that bothers me. There are not enough people willing to take on a servant's role. They expect the church to serve them." Interview with OFWB member (A), March 3, 2015.

200. Interview with OFWB member (B), March 31, 2015

201. Interview with OFWB pastor (J), February 26, 2015.

202. Interview with OFWB pastor (C), February 4, 2015.

203. Interview with OFWB pastor (A), April 7, 2015.

204. For example, a questionnaire respondent writes, "[Foot washing] helps me understand and appreciate the humble attitude we must assume to do as [Jesus] would have us do. A person cannot lead until he knows how to follow." Questionnaire response from OFWB, Church (F), September 2014.

washing, there is an intent that participants should gain a desire to serve others.[205]

Many OFWBs see service as the explicit goal of foot washing. Take for example this pastor who states, "I think that it is a formative practice. Much like someone getting on a treadmill every day to lose weight or better their level of fitness. I think the practice forms us and shapes us to more rightly reflect the image of Christ. In that act of kneeling and washing another person's feet, I think it demonstrates the level of service, commitment, or devotion that we are called to have not only [to] people in the church, but more importantly the people out in the community.[206]

At each performance, members and pastors are reminded of the need to serve one another. Because each person has the opportunity to serve and be served, members learn the importance of equality.[207] This moment is not only for the pastors and deacons, it is for all who are willing to get on their knees and serve. Foot washing can be a powerful motivator, especially when you realize that it is something you receive and give. A member explains her feelings when she realizes "that we all are serving and yet we serve one another. So, you're not just a servant, you're being served as well. And that's an amazing thing about the church, if the church in general realized that we are here to serve each other. So, we're all being served, but we are all serving. Nobody is just a servant, and nobody is a master. We're all the same."[208]

Pastors take this equality seriously. For pastors, foot washing is an opportunity to demonstrate servant leadership. It reminds the congregation that the pastor is a servant.[209] Perhaps more than other denominations, the role of an OFWB pastor is to serve the congregation as an equal. Pastors are not immune to the temptation of power and influence. Foot washing is a physical and visible embodiment of the dangers of power. Working in a higher education setting, this pastor describes how "washing of the saints' feet reinforces my need to fear power. Particularly my own . . . I have

205. Foot washing gives participants a first taste of service. A questionnaire respondent explains that foot washing is important for "experiencing the opportunity to have the servant heart and attitude." Questionnaire response from OFWB, Church (H), April 2015.

206. Interview with OFWB pastor (J), February 26, 2015.

207. Foot washing helps one questionnaire respondent to "remember that everyone is important, no matter what/who they are or their circumstances." Questionnaire response from OFWB, Church (H), April 2015.

208. Interview with OFWB member (G), January 29, 2015.

209. "I think it's something that brings me back down to earth. Sometimes you get so caught up in the day to day work, and it's easy to get bigger than ourselves. When we wash feet, I am reminded as I get down that this is where the Lord was, this is where he expects me to be." Interview with OFWB pastor (A), April 7, 2015.

basically been trained to be fearful of power."[210] Foot washing teaches him that "in the exercise of power I must first and foremost be a servant of Christ and his church. The people I seek to lead, I have to first and foremost be their servant. I have to be reminded of that because left to my own devices I don't think I would like me very much. . . . I need those tangible reminders."[211]

Foot washing reminders pastors that everyone is equal. Pastors are not more important than anyone else.[212] A pastor explains that in "the church as well as anywhere, there's always someone who thinks I've gotten a little bit higher office or I've got a little bit more important role to play in the church. They get a basin of water and put a towel around their waist, there's no greater or higher levels of anybody. We're all on equal ground."[213] He continues, "You wash feet to bring you to that point where everybody is on the same playing field. Servant hood is not that difficult of a thing. It's more of a joy then it is a duty. . . . It becomes more of a servant attitude that's coming from my heart instead of a ritual or from duty."[214] In this way, OFWB leaders see foot washing as setting the leadership standard. Foot washing "shows servant leadership and the need for leaders within our church, within any of our organizations to serve instead of necessarily taking all of the glory that the position can hold."[215]

Foot washing is a way to remind OFWB pastors of their duty to serve the congregation and community. It is their moment of self-reflection. It is an opportunity to look back and see if you have truly been a servant leader. Foot washing is a necessity for pastors, for if "I'm not willing to wash someone else's feet, I can't expect anyone else to. It's just one of those things. Not only is it a humbling experience for me, it's an opportunity for me to lead the people. That's why we do that publicly when we are ordaining deacons and other things because I want them to see that."[216] In OFWB churches, foot washing is the public acknowledgement that pastors are equal to everyone else. One pastor insists that foot washing teaches him that "I'm on the same level as my members, as far as spirituality goes. I might have been called to be a pastor, but that doesn't mean I'm above them. We are

210. Interview with OFWB pastor (C), February 4, 2015.

211. Interview with OFWB pastor (C), February 4, 2015.

212. For example, this pastor claims that foot washing "reminds me that just because I'm in a leadership position within a congregation, that doesn't mean that I'm any better than anyone else and that we're all on an equal playing field in God's eyes." Interview with OFWB pastor (F), March 5, 2015.

213. Interview with OFWB pastor (H), February 3, 2015.

214. Interview with OFWB pastor (H), February 3, 2015.

215. Interview with OFWB member (D), February 5, 2015.

216. Interview with OFWB pastor (A), April 7, 2015.

workers together. . . . So, I think it reminds us that we're all the same level; when you kneel down to wash someone's feet."[217] Foot washing is an identity many OFWB pastors take without hesitation.[218] Without this identity, a pastor wonders if "I would actually be as communally minded, and service minded, and socially minded as I am."[219] He goes on to explain that, "Our symbols for our denomination actually has the basin and the towel on it. . . . For me that speaks volumes of what the Christian experience is supposed to be. We take up our cross like we're supposed to and go into the world to service."[220] As an OFWB, foot washing has completely shaped and formed his personal theology.[221]

Foot washing encourages OFWBs to become more socially and community minded. Service is part of the intent and meaning of foot washing. Of course, much of this depends on the pastor's involvement. Foot washing can teach service, but it "depends on the leadership of that church along with the minister and how he does it."[222]

Pastors hope that foot washing triggers the response to serve, at least for those receptive to it. Those who have never served may be inspired to serve. Foot washing can be that experience that "triggers something within them as they are out in the community . . . to respond in different ways to the needs of the community. Because I have now become a servant and that's really what we're supposed to do."[223] It helps "you see the importance of what you do outside of church."[224] While there is some uncertainty as to whether it inspires service, there is an intention and hope that it will.[225]

Ultimately, OFWB foot washing initiates you into a different level of service. It initiates you into an intimate, personal, and hands on service. Among OFWBs there is the hope that foot washing will set you on the path

217. Interview with OFWB pastor (I), February 2, 2015.

218. This pastor shares that "I wear a little lapel pin that has a basin and a towel. That speaks of a servant. That's what Jesus intended it to be, serving each other." Interview with OFWB pastor (D), March 30, 2015.

219. Interview with OFWB pastor (G), February 6, 2015.

220. Interview with OFWB pastor (G), February 6, 2015.

221. He explains, "To me my whole theology is shaped by OFWB doctrine [of] washing of the saints' feet." Interview with OFWB pastor (G), February 6, 2015.

222. Interview with OFWB pastor (B), March 26, 2015.

223. Interview with OFWB pastor (D), March 30, 2015.

224. Interview with OFWB pastor (K), February 12, 2015.

225. A member claims, "I think it probably [inspires service] does within our church. The wider community, I'm not sure it inspires service, but it may inspire service for those within our church to serve the wider community; to go out, to witness, to share the blessing that we received." Interview with OFWB member (A), March 3, 2015.

toward a deeper level of service. It is a service based on relationship and connection. It is not enough that you serve others, rather there should be a spiritual and familial bond to that service. It is, as one young minister describes, "a different type of servitude. It's not going out and washing [someone's] clothes or washing [their] car. This is touching another man's [or woman's] foot or feet. I think this is just one of those barriers that, I think, if not broken down, [is] maybe the reason why Christianity is not doing as well in society today. Because you've got worthy people doing services all day. You got big companies out there doing it all the time. This is [what] differentiates us from the world."[226] It differentiates OFWBs through their embrace and encouragement of relationship, which takes them beyond the abstract. It is an incarnational act.[227]

OFWBs believe foot washing is an act that should continue outside the church. It suggests a better way to live and act in the world.[228] Thus, OFWBs argue that foot washing is not just a ritual. Rather the goal is "letting the imagery of washing the saints' feet play out in everyday life. As you love and respect your fellow man [or woman]."[229] OFWBs see foot washing as something that carries over into everything you do. Foot washing is not an end, rather, "Let that be the beginning. . . . We're supposed to carry that attitude of feet washing into our daily walk in serving the Lord by serving others."[230] Foot washing reminds you that "we're to serve, not wait for somebody to pat us on the back and say what a good singer you are or good preacher you are or good deacon you are. That's not what our job is. Our job is to set an example of humbleness and servitude."[231]

Foot Washing and Transformation

Most experiences of foot washing are not instantly transformative. It is a gradual change that adds to your Christian experience. OFWB pastors and members describe foot washing's effect as gradual and subtle. For many, it is hard to describe how foot washing has changed their Christian experience.

226. Focus group (A) interview with OFWB pastor, June 28, 2015.

227. A pastor explains that foot washing "is one of the most incarnational things that we do. There is nothing more incarnational than the washing of the feet." Interview with OFWB pastor (G), February 6, 2015.

228. According to a questionnaire respondent, foot washing "helps me to remember that we should always remember to be humble in our daily lives as commanded by our Lord." Questionnaire response from OFWB, Church (G), May 2014.

229. Interview with OFWB pastor (E), March 27, 2015.

230. Interview with OFWB member (F), March 17, 2015.

231. Interview with OFWB member (F), March 17, 2015.

This pastor says, "I don't know because it's always been a part of my life. So it's not like I've ever known the Christian walk without foot washing."[232] Another pastor explains, "In terms of something I would compare to a Damascus road type or Philippian jailer, I've not seen anything like this, but I've seen more in the term of persons recognizing a more noble calling of what the Christian life is supposed to look like."[233] Therefore, pastors will typically use words like "enriched"[234] and "enhanced"[235] rather than transform. Foot washing works in the background, carefully shaping the Christian character of OFWB participants. Its enhancing effects, a pastor explains, "Makes me a better pastor, a better believer, a better servant. . . . Laity they think the pastor is a little bit more theologically advanced and more in touch with God or little more holier than thou, but once you get that basin and towel together you're all on the same plane. Everybody is equal in the Lord's sight there."[236] Foot washing effects are not immediate, instead it adds to what is already present. Therefore, foot washing does not change the Christian experience, instead "it adds a sweetness to it. . . . It helps make it sweeter because you're following the commandments of Christ, and I think any time you follow the instructions of Christ, it sweetens your faith and your Christianity."[237]

OFWBs experience foot washing's effects corporately as a community more so than individually. Foot washings effects are only noticeable in community. A member believes that she does not "think the act of foot washing has really transformed anyone that I know personally in a significantly different way other than to make them more humble and to make all of us feel like a Christian community, that Christian bond. I think collectively it's transforming."[238] It is this collective experience that bonds the participants together. It is not the experience of foot washing alone that makes it meaningful. Having your feet washed in isolation would not have the same effect it does within a wider community. Without foot washing, a long-serving pastor noted, "I don't believe you would have the bond of fellowship that you have with other believers in the same faith. I don't think it would be there. That is something that kind of bonds you together. Because to me it makes you realize that what we do is broader than I am and there's more

232. Interview with OFWB pastor (F), March 5, 2015.

233. Interview with OFWB pastor (C), February 4, 2015.

234. Interview with OFWB pastor (C), February 4, 2015

235. Interview with OFWB pastor (H), February 3, 2015.

236. Interview with OFWB pastor (H), February 3, 2015.

237. Interview with OFWB member (H), January 26, 2015.

238. Interview with OFWB member (A), March 3, 2015.

people that really believe just like I do."[239] Without it, he believes, you would miss that connection. For OFWBs, foot washing creates a bond that goes beyond believing and doing the same thing. Foot washing brings OFWBs together in a way that other practices cannot. Without foot washing, "I don't think it would be that way because what do you have that would really tie you together like that does? I mean you may believe the same things, you may do different things within that belief, but . . . I think there's a bond there that [foot washing] creates that wouldn't be any other way."[240]

The communal aspect for OFWBs helps both members and pastors shift their perspective. It moves you from an inward perspective to an outward one.[241] For many, foot washing means "I'm not better than anyone than anyone else or I'm not as good as I think I might be. It keeps me in perspective, looking at myself in perspective."[242] For OFWBs, foot washing is a continual check against pride, selfishness, and individualism. OFWBs need foot washing to maintain a healthy Christian spirit of humility. Pastors repeatedly explain that foot washing is necessary to understand humility. If OFWBs did not have foot washing, a pastor explains, "I think that what would be missing without it is to bring me to that point of understanding humility. That it causes me to remember that every time I do it. If I fought with my brother and have not [repaired that relationship], it will remind me that I need to get that done."[243] Foot washing's transforming effects are found in the ways it continues to draw participants back again and again. It can create a longing and desire for the type of community that it presents. A member describes times that she has missed foot washing. She states how, "There's been times where the kids had school the next day, and service was running late, and so we skipped foot washing that night [the evening service]. I know that I missed something. A part of me still wanted to be there even though for whatever reason I couldn't that time. I really did, I craved, wanted to be back there."[244]

Foot washing's transforming effects can help prepare you for serving the outside world. It is a gradual process of molding you to engage the outer community and world. A member explains, "I think it's all made me who I am today. I do . . . I go back to those stories, to those experiences. It's

239. Interview with OFWB pastor (D), March 30, 2015.

240. Interview with OFWB pastor (D), March 30, 2015.

241. A questionnaire respondent shares that foot washing, "keeps me closer to his example of serving and not thinking too much of myself." Questionnaire response from OFWB, Church (H), April 2014.

242. Interview with OFWB pastor (E), March 27, 2015.

243. Interview with OFWB pastor (B), March 26, 2015.

244. Interview with OFWB member (D), February 5, 2015.

definitely a part of my life. I do know, and maybe the reverence side of it has made me appreciate, the part of serving more. I think that is one of my gifts maybe because I love doing things for other people. I love that."[245] Another interviewee agrees with this sentiment stating, "I think that [foot washing] has changed my outlook on what I think our Free Will Baptist denomination can be in its local [setting] and in its community, wherever it can thrive."[246] Foot washing creates a thankful and appreciative attitude among OFWB participants.[247] Thus, it prepares you for future service and action. Looking back at his life, an interviewee believes that foot washing has "driven me to my knees more. It makes me appreciate more what Christ did for us. It also makes me thankful. It's not something that I'm proud of. I'm just thankful and I think there's a difference. . . . It took me awhile to learn that."[248] It is a process of learning, learning from foot washing and from others. You cannot expect foot washing to immediately change you. Foot washing is "a process of getting me to where I am today. It's taken all those people, it's taken all of that learning of service. It's taken learning more about who Jesus is and what he did and how he taught the disciples. There are so many things that I look at differently, so much differently. . . . I'm not the same person I was then."[249]

FOOT WASHING AND THE SPIRITUAL

Connection to Jesus

Participants take foot washing seriously because of its connection to Jesus. OFWBs see great value in reenacting something done and commanded by Jesus.[250] Practicing foot washing means that you are being obedient to Jesus's call. Jesus tells us to wash feet, and therefore it must be done. When washing feet, OFWBs are trying to be faithful to scripture. Being very candid,

245. Interview with OFWB member (B), March 31, 2015.

246. Interview with OFWB pastor (J), February 26, 2015.

247. A questionnaire respondent shares that foot washing "makes me consider how willing I am (or not) to accept help, encouragement from others." Questionnaire response from OFWB, Church (B), June 2014.

248. Interview with OFWB member (C), June 30, 2015.

249. Interview with OFWB member (B), March 31, 2015.

250. A questionnaire respondent explains this connection stating, "Knowing my Lord was humble enough to wash the Disciples feet and we should be humble in our daily life." Questionnaire response from OFWB, Church (C), May 2014.

one pastor declares, "It's certainly a direct initiative from the Lord himself. I think it connects us because he has asked us to do it. I'm being obedient to his call."[251]

OFWBs have a strong desire to obey Jesus and follow his example. Foot washing provides a physical tool for learning about Jesus and his message. More importantly, for OFWBs, foot washing is "an effort to be more like [Jesus]. Trying to be more like him in our daily walk and activities and the things that we do, keeping us cognizant of what he did for us and our salvation."[252] Jesus sets the example.[253] Therefore for OFWBs, foot washing is "following the example of Christ. And by following the example we are to do likewise."[254]

Besides being an example, foot washing can be a commandment for some. Pastors and members point to the passage on foot washing as being a direct commandment from Jesus. For example, a pastor argues, "One of the direct commandments from the New Testament, in my opinion, is to go out and do [foot washing]. He didn't say let's just do it tonight. The way I read it, it was do it now."[255] This pastor clarifies that this command is for a purpose. Jesus commands foot washing with the hope that "it would help carry over more and to you helping [your] fellow man [or woman] outside the walls. To helping the poor and the sick and things like that because it puts you in that frame of mind."[256]

OFWBs see foot washing as a way to learn about Jesus. You must experience foot washing to understand what Christ's ministry was all about. Foot washing should never be done just for sake of doing it. OFWBs practice foot washing "so people can understand why you're doing this and what the love of Christ [does]. . . . He set that example for us to do."[257] The experience "connects you to him in that this is what he did, and you know it's not simple and easy. . . . It can be humbling for us and we can relate to him in that way and what it means to be a servant."[258]

---

251. Interview with OFWB pastor (H), February 3, 2015

252. Interview with OFWB member (A), March 3, 2015.

253. Foot washing is a reminder of the personal and universal implications of Christ's life, death, and resurrection. A respondent writes that foot washing "brings remembrance of what Jesus did for mankind, for me personally. It gives me a closer feeling of Jesus' brotherhood." Questionnaire response from OFWB, Church (E), September 2014.

254. Interview with OFWB pastor (K), February 12, 2015.

255. Interview with OFWB pastor (H), January 26, 2015.

256. Interview with OFWB pastor (H), January 26, 2015.

257. Interview with OFWB pastor (B), March 26, 2015.

258. Interview with OFWB member (G), January 29, 2015.

Foot washing draws OFWB participants closer to Jesus. OFWBs are connecting to Jesus on historical, emotional, and spiritual levels. It draws them closer to their savior and helps them feel that they have done something important. An OFWB member shares, "I think that it makes you feel closer because you're doing something you know he did. It just makes you feel closer to him. I think it also makes you feel that he's pleased with what you're doing. I think that would be a lot of it, the closeness. You're pleasing because it goes back to the teaching part of what he was trying to teach his disciples. I think that maybe you feel like sometimes, maybe I got it."[259]

Foot washing is therefore a way to enter the life and experience of Jesus.[260] For OFWBs, it makes Jesus feel real and tangible.[261] Jesus and his ministry becomes accessible to everyone. Foot washing establishes a connection between Christ and everyday life for OFWBs.[262] When you are drawn closer to Christ it inevitably draws you to others. OFWBs do foot washing because "it's a reminder to them that Jesus was one of us, and that he cared enough for his disciples, and we are his modern-day disciples that he would have stooped down to wash their feet. So, I think it's a way of us connecting with that New Testament story. Remembering that Jesus wasn't just some superhero type person. He was truly human."[263] Following this realization, foot washing puts Jesus in a different light. OFWBs are able to see "what Christ really did, how he served not just ones he loved and that loved him, but how he served those that hated him anyway, but he still did it and he did it lovingly. When I think about that, and I try to make myself . . . remind myself of that intentionally every time when I'm doing foot washing."[264]

Foot washing's connection to Jesus reinforces the idea among OFWBs that they are to be a servant. A pastor suggests, "If our Lord came to be a servant, who do we think we are if we're not following that example? There again the practice itself reinforces the behavior of what it means to be a part

259. Interview with OFWB member (B), March 31, 2015.

260. When practicing foot washing, a questionnaire respondent writes, "I feel like it is a wonderful way to express love for Jesus and of Jesus to try to walk in his ways." Questionnaire response from OFWB, Church (G), May 2014.

261. Expressing this tangible connection, a questionnaire respondent writes that when washing feet, "I feel like I am following one of His examples and that makes me feel closer to Him." Questionnaire response from OFWB, Church (E), September 2014.

262. Foot washing "reminds me of Christ's true nature, which is that of a servant, which is what I should be." Questionnaire response from OFWB, Church (E), September 2014.

263. Interview with OFWB pastor (F), March 5, 2015.

264. Interview with OFWB member (D), February 5, 2015.

of the Christian community."[265] As a Christian community, OFWBs seek to establish their communities in the image of Jesus. Individuals bring Jesus to each other every time foot washing takes place. It is a way to reminding one another that Jesus lives in each person. When you kneel and wash another person's feet, it is as if you are washing the feet of Jesus. Therefore, "Christ says I was hungry and you feed me, I was naked, and you clothed me, I was homeless, jobless, I think what we do for others and do unto others [is] what Christ Himself ultimately [does] to that person. . . . In fact, I think it connects the person to Christ because it is Christ that is doing the kneeling and the washing."[266]

Connection to the Holy Spirit

Foot washing can also be a spiritual experience for OFWBs. While OFWBs typically think of Jesus in connection with foot washing, many acknowledge that the Holy Spirit has an important role to play. The intimate setting, fellowship, and prayer work together to create an experience that invites the Holy Spirit. On one level, the Holy Spirit connects participants with Jesus.[267] During foot washing, it is the Holy Spirit that "teaches us how to grow in Christ, and I think the experience of washing feet too is an experience of growing in Christ and growing in love for your fellow believers. It teaches us how we love unconditionally."[268]

While the Holy Spirit can help OFWBs grow in Christ, they also believe that the Holy Spirit adds a unique feeling to the experience. Some see the Holy Spirit has having a major role in foot washing. One member believes that the Holy Spirit is "very involved. That's part of the beauty of it. Those that do participate . . . do it through the Holy Spirit. And the Holy Spirit humbles us and it's certainly a big component of foot washing."[269] She goes on to describe foot washing as a "spiritual cleansing." This cleansing, she describes, is the work of the Holy Spirit "cleansing our hearts and minds

265. Interview with OFWB pastor (C), February 4, 2015.

266. Interview with OFWB pastor (G), February 6, 2015.

267. A questionnaire respondent describes the presence of Jesus during foot washing. She believes that when "girding myself with the towel and getting down to humble myself to wash my sister's feet. There is a closeness among us, we can all feel Jesus near. I feel His Spirit near." Questionnaire response from OFWB, Church (G), May 2014.

268. Interview with OFWB pastor (I), February 2, 2015.

269. Interview with OFWB member (A), March 3, 2015.

and consciences. Which is liberating knowing that through Christ's example we can [be cleansed], it makes it more real, makes it more tangible for us."[270]

The close intimate gathering of foot washing provides a spiritual opportunity for OFWBs. It is an opportunity to do something you do not normally do. In that small room, OFWBs enter an experience not found in any of their other services. A pastor explains, "We are doing something that we do not normally do, that it's somewhat of an anomaly to anything we might do in life."[271] He continues stating, "Of the three ordinances that we have, it's the only one that to me brings us together in a room quietly doing things that we do not normally do because the Lord said do it. To me, it's probably the most Spirit-filled thing we do."[272]

Through the Holy Spirit, participants come closer to each other and to God. The Holy Spirit becomes a part of foot washing. However, the Holy Spirit is not in the things used. The Holy Spirit, for OFWBs, is not bound to the pails or the towels. The space used is neither holy nor unique. OFWBs experience the Holy Spirit through one another. The atmosphere of foot washing heightens a presence already there but not normally felt. A member explains, "I think it's just a time of feeling closer than during ordinary time, which it shouldn't be probably. I think it's the atmosphere, I think it's something that permeates everything at that particular time that just makes it, makes you feel closer."[273] The Holy Spirit, a pastor claims, is "totally involved. It's hard for me to sit here and say that anybody partaking of the washing of the saints' feet cannot be wrapped in the Holy Spirit. Because that's too close to you, that's too close to each other."[274]

Foot washing invokes a spiritual sense of closeness to one's fellow believers. OFWBs see this as evidence of the presence of the Holy Spirit. OFWBs also find evidence of the Holy Spirit's presence in prayer and singing. A member explains that since it is a "smaller more intimated group of very like-minded believers, you really do feel [the Holy Spirit's] presence there. . . . I have just felt his presence there so heavy [during the] times when you heard those speak you really didn't know they could speak. They've never spoken in church before. When he's involved those have been the very best times."[275] At the movement of the Holy Spirit, "that's when the singing breaks out or that's when a person is prompted to tell about something

270. Interview with OFWB member (A), March 3, 2015.

271. Interview with OFWB pastor (A), April 7, 2015.

272. Interview with OFWB pastor (A), April 7, 2015.

273. Interview with OFWB member (B), March 31, 2015.

274. Focus group (A) interview with OFWB pastor, June 28, 2015.

275. Interview with OFWB member (D), February 5, 2015.

going on in their life."[276] Another OFWB pastor describes this as a "stirring" experience. He describes how the Holy Spirit motivates you to change your behavior. The Holy Spirit is moving you to take action, both during that moment and afterwards. He claims, "When you think of the Holy Spirit being there and being involved, that comes from . . . thinking about the atmosphere, the silence. Sometimes just biblical conversation and sometimes the singing. I think the Holy Spirit is stirring hearts to move in that direction instead of us just saying 'okay this is what we want to do.'"[277] Through foot washing, the Holy Spirit shows how you are to live. The Holy Spirit "speaks to you, that this is what you're expected to do in your Christian life, not to just wash feet but to go out and help other people. It's a teaching experience."[278] It is an experience that "is incredibly real and present and here. Your feet are dirty and I'm bowing down in front you to wash your feet . . . washing the saints' feet cannot get any more real, cannot be anymore present and here and now."[279]

DISCORDANT VOICES OF FOOT WASHING

Not all OFWBs practice foot washing. Many OFWBs do not participate in foot washing regularly. There are some OFWBs who have never experienced foot washing. Despite its importance within the denomination's history, foot washing can be a fringe practice. Both pastors and members are concerned by its poor attendance and a lack of younger participants. Even within the OFWB, foot washing's participants are desperately trying to keep the practice alive. Foot washing has a dedicated core group of participants. They believe in the practice of foot washing, but this conviction has not translated into large groups of participants. The OFWB story of this practice is also one of frustration and disappointment. The future of foot washing within the denomination has yet to be determined.

Pastors and members both acknowledge that participation is a problem. A member shares, "It's one of our most poorly attended services. We try to get attendance, but it is, every time, one of our most poorly attended services."[280] A member estimates, "I don't have a percentage, but in our church, I would say 10 percent of the population wash feet, 10–15 percent. That's the lowest attended service that we have. And from what I understand,

276. Interview with OFWB pastor (E), March 27, 2015.

277. Interview with OFWB pastor (D), March 30, 2015.

278. Interview with OFWB member (H), January 26, 2015.

279. Focus group (B) interview with OFWB member, June 28, 2015.

280. Focus group (B) interview with OFWB member, June 28, 2015.

it's low in a lot of other churches too, but I can't measure other churches. I know in ours it is."[281] Another pastor also shares that participants of foot washing are low. He estimates that "about 25 percent participate and 75 percent don't."[282] A children's minister also describes low numbers of participations. She says, "We run like 150 on Sunday morning and we might have thirty-five at a business meeting. Of those thirty-five, we typically have anywhere from three to five women who participate in the foot washing. We may have ten men that participate."[283]

Foot washing can carry a stigma for some. It is something to avoid.[284] It is not unusual to see people "shy away from it. Especially people who did not grow up Free Will Baptist. . . . When you say you're going to have a feet washing service, your numbers are not going to be as large as you would on a normal Sunday night."[285] Those who are available to wash feet do not always participate. Because communion and foot washing can occur during the same service, many "come and stay in the sanctuary and just don't go to the rooms to wash feet. . . . It just sounds strange to them so they don't participate."[286] Even those who do participate in foot washing acknowledge that it does not always hold the same importance that baptism and communion have.[287]

Participants are usually older adults or elderly. Foot washing does not usually attract youth. Despite education, "the younger folks are chickened out by [foot washing],"[288] therefore, the "older people [wash] more than other people these days."[289] In many OFWB churches, foot washing has acquired an identity as a practice or event for the old and elderly. Pastors have difficult time getting younger people involved in the practice. For older adults, a pastor explains, it is "something that we've done all of our life. It's part of who we are."[290] Unfortunately, younger members may not share this

281. Interview with OFWB member (H), January 26, 2015.

282. Interview with OFWB pastor (A), April 7, 2015.

283. Interview with OFWB pastor (F), March 5, 2015.

284. "At our church, some people avoid it on purpose. Some people just don't see the importance in it." Interview with OFWB member (F), March 17, 2015.

285. Interview with OFWB pastor (H), February 3, 2015.

286. Interview with OFWB member (G), January 29, 2015.

287. A member explains how "When we go over to the fellowship hall, a lot of times that's what we feel like, it's just to go ahead and get it over. . . . In our church it lacks the gravitas that you have here while we do communion." Focus group (B) interview with OFWB member, June 28, 2015.

288. Interview with OFWB pastor (G), February 6, 2015.

289. Interview with OFWB member (G), January 29, 2015.

290. Interview with OFWB pastor (D), March 30, 2015.

identity, "Some of the younger folks of today just don't see any need of it so therefore there's not very much participation."[291]

OFWB pastors and members cite several reasons for foot washing's decline. Some believe that new members, who did not grow up as OFWB, do not carry on the practice.[292] Others argue that touching another person's feet is a barrier many will not cross.[293] Some see it as a practice that ministers force upon the laity, thus causing foot washing to lose its meaning.[294] For these reasons, it is not unusual for there to be OFWBs "that have never washed anyone's feet that have been a Free Will Baptist for many, many years. Some people just won't do it."[295]

Members give several reasons for not doing it. Talking about his reasons for never doing foot washing, a member describes how his experiences of the practice have always been negative. He is not against foot washing, but he does have a problem with the participant's behavior, "I didn't see a reverence to it. I didn't see a seriousness to it. It was just like this is something we do. I'm not keen on 'this is just something we do.' There has to be a purpose. . . . I didn't see what I thought was anything that really I thought was extremely meaningful."[296] He still refuses to do foot washing, citing that "I've had no burning desire to go back. I guess that makes me not a real good Free Will Baptist but, I'm not too concerned about it really."[297] He does acknowledge that his primary problem was with the people rather than the practice itself. He admits that things might be different if he tried it again.[298]

291. Interview with OFWB pastor (D), March 30, 2015.

292. A member describes how "we knew everybody at church and all their family and family history, and they had always grown up in that church. And now as going to college is more prevalent, people move away, and others move in, we've had more people come into the church with no experience of being OFWB before. A lot of times they are more reluctant." Interview with OFWB member (D), February 5, 2015.

293. A pastor says, "I think it's just the opposition of touching somebody else's feet. You know most people have a little issue with that." Interview with OFWB pastor (A), April 7, 2015.

294. He explains that "years and years ago it was one of those things that you had to do. I think that took some of the emphasis, the meaning away from it." Interview with OFWB pastor (D), March 30, 2015.

295. Interview with OFWB member (H), January 26, 2015.

296. Interview with OFWB member (E), January 27, 2015.

297. Interview with OFWB member (E), January 27, 2015.

298. Speaking of his first experiences of foot washing, he shares that there "was a group of people who were all friends. They knew each other well. . . . There may have been a little more comfortable familiarity that existed that may not exist now if I went to another service because of the demographic of the church. I don't have problems with the concept." Interview with OFWB member (E), January 27, 2015.

Though he may try it again in the future,[299] he has a problem with foot washing being part of the OFWB identity. He is not sure what foot washing says about the denomination.[300]

Others object to the practice itself. A deacon describes how foot washing is now outdated. He explains that it no longer has any relevance because it lacks any connection with contemporary life. For him it has nothing to do with the aspect of touching feet, instead foot washing is "a practice that is so unnatural to our society. I guess that's just where I lose it."[301] Foot washing is "busywork"[302] that distracts from actual service projects.[303] It reflects the time of Christ when everyone "would've been familiar with what [Jesus] was doing and why. Today nobody does [foot washing]. It's no longer the lowest position. We do it because we read about it in his word and Christ did it. Some people take that as a command and I understand that. But I think that, I just don't think that it still applies today."[304] Members acknowledge that foot washing can become "very ritualistic . . . it's programmed in a way. A lot of times we don't consciously think about why you're doing it."[305] A final objection is from those who work in healthcare and regularly wash bodies. For them, foot washing feels like what they do during the work week.[306]

299. He shares, "I think we're doing a good job of having a reverent communion in our church and most churches I've been in. We're successful in making that a reverent service. If we could upgrade foot washing to that level, maybe I'd be okay with it." Interview with OFWB member (E), January 27, 2015.

300. Foot washing, according to this member, "almost seems to be a trademark for us. I'm not sure that the people outside the denomination see that. . . . I'm not sure what perception that gives of us in this day and age." Interview with OFWB member (E), January 27, 2015.

301. Focus group (B) interview with OFWB member, June 28, 2015.

302. Focus group (B) interview with OFWB member, June 28, 2015.

303. This member explains, "We do a ton of projects here over the years that are hands on, everybody working together doing something for somebody, serving in any way we can. [We] have food drives, we do all kinds of stuff all year long. I love that stuff. I always want to be a part of everything like that. To me all of that has a tangible point. Maybe that's where I miss it in foot washing. I'm not saying I'm right and everybody stop doing foot washing. To me that's where I lose foot washing. To me it's just, there's no tangible end to it. I haven't helped anybody when I do that." Focus group (B) interview with OFWB member, June 28, 2015.

304. Focus group (B) interview with OFWB member, June 28, 2015.

305. Focus group (B) interview with OFWB member, June 28, 2015.

306. A member says, "I worked in a nursing home most of my life. To me it was like . . . you were a person who worked on a computer day in and day out, the last thing you want to do is go home and get on a computer. In the same sense for almost fifteen years of my life, I worked a nursing home and I bathe people, washed their feet, washed their back, washed their hair, I mean I covered it all. To me I just can't get the true meaning out of it." Focus group (B) interview with OFWB member, June 28, 2015.

WE ARE A PEOPLE OF THE BASIN AND THE TOWEL: OFWB IDENTITY

Despite non-universal participation, foot washing is essential to the OFWB identity.[307] It is a reminder of who they are. It reminds OFWBs of their call to service, servant leadership, and love for all people. Foot washing "identifies who we are. We are servants of the Lord, that's what that towel and basin mean. It's servant-hood, serving others and that we ought to be more like Jesus in doing that. It's a vibrant part of us as a denomination. To me it is a major part of who I am as an OFWB."[308] OFWBs who practice foot washing want to see it remain that way. They want to be known as people who wash feet, not for the sake of foot washing itself, but what it says about who they are "as a church, as a believer, and as a people."[309]

Foot washing is a continuation of the OFWB story. It is "one of the things that designates all people who are part of the Free Will Baptist church, from other Christian faith traditions."[310] OFWBs have a unique story, experience, and tradition worth sharing with others. Their practice of foot washing "makes us unique. I don't think it's something to hide from or think we're wrong or think that we should change because everybody else isn't doing it."[311] It is part of the OFWB history and heritage, and for that reason alone it should not be abandoned. Foot washing is, they argue, "something that we should share and not try to go away from. I think we're trying to go away from it just to try to go along with everyone else, to fit in better. We would rather [sometimes] do away with some of our real heritage. It really makes us unique and I hope that doesn't happen."[312] Foot washing defines their OFWB experience. Without it, their heritage would be in question.[313]

---

307. A prominent pastor says, "A common phrase that I will use is we should never forget that 'we are a people of the basin and the towel.' I haven't listened to enough preaching over the past twenty years to know if that is a refrain of my brother and sister ministers. I sure hope that it would be because I think it's vitally important." Interview with OFWB pastor (C), February 4, 2015.

308. Interview with OFWB pastor (D), March 30, 2015.

309. The full quote from the pastor reads, "I think that we need to bring [foot washing] back to where it belongs . . . even though that's not always done in our church, we should be trying to bring that to our people. Why do I say that? It's because that's who we are, that's what makes us who we are as a church, as a believer, and as a people." Interview with OFWB pastor (B), March 26, 2015.

310. Interview with OFWB pastor (J), February 26, 2015.

311. Interview with OFWB pastor (H), February 3, 2015.

312. Interview with OFWB pastor (H), February 3, 2015.

313. Speaking of the OFWB logo, a concerned pastor shares, "I think if we're not [doing foot washing] we might as well just go ahead and redo our emblem, the whole

Foot washing is bigger than the OFWB heritage. It is part of the larger Christian story of redemption, hope, and love. OFWBs are but one small part of this universal story. Their practice of foot washing is a reminder of that story, and therefore part of the renewal of the world. This renewal begins in Jesus Christ and continues through the Christian story today. As a pastor describes it, "I think he's going to renew [the world]. I think Christ started the process of renewing it and he wants us to join him in it. . . . What more beautiful metaphor of that is there than the servitude of bowing at a brother or sister's feet and saying 'I love you in Christ and it's my privilege to serve you by washing feet.'"[314] OFWBs are continuing that story of renewal. Foot washing is a call to live as a servant. OFWB theologian and educator David Hines writes,

> Christians are a community of the forgiven, of persons who have had their personal stories rewritten according to the story of Jesus. Christians make this story tangible through their symbols: the cross and the sacraments. This collective memory and re-presentation has the power to produce a distinctive way of living. In Baptism we have a new start. In Eucharist we remember how we came to be. Then in the Washing of the Saints' Feet we learn how we are called to live.[315]

---

nine. If we're not going to practice what Jesus said to do, might as well get rid of the whole emblem. The towel and the basin, get rid of it all. And then what leg do we have to stand on? That [foot washing] is what defines us as OFWBs." Focus group (A) interview with OFWB pastor, June 28, 2015.

314. Interview with OFWB pastor (G), February 6, 2015.

315. Hines, "Tell Me the Story."

CHAPTER FOUR

Relation, Space, Story, and Action

THE STORY CARRIES ON

THE EVENT SPEAKS, AND the story is heard. Moving forward, we will not leave the story behind. Although the OFWBs are small, their story is a living one. They renew their story at every practice of foot washing. They speak their message generation after generation. Their ending remains a mystery, but this story of foot washing will surely not end with the OFWBs. Their story is much bigger than that. The OFWB experience connects with the wider human experience. Their story speaks to what it means to be human. Through experience and action, OFWBs share their story for the world. This story connects to the life and experience of Jesus Christ. Conversing with this story only requires us to have an attentive ear and open heart.

Going deeper into a world of ritual action requires time to engage this story. As we enter this world, the goal is not to possess or change it. It is not an object of academic curiosity. Shifting from analysis to understanding allows us to understand how this story speaks today. We read the story to amplify its voice, not to change or misrepresent the story. It is a process of expanding the story's reach and putting it into contact with other modes of expression. Building from the OFWB narrative, we can see how foot washing speaks to relationship, the social, and the everyday. The OFWB voice goes beyond the religious and theological, not to leave them behind, but to expand them.

RELATIONSHIP: BEING-WITH

The OFWB experience of foot washing points to a shared meaning. Meaning is rooted in the experiences shared among individuals. During foot washing, OFWBs live and enact what Jean-Luc Nancy describes as *being-with*. This is the idea that meaning does not begin at that individual level, instead individuals and groups share in this meaning.[1] Being, in the singular, points only to the self, thus meaning has no reach beyond the individual. Being-singular lacks the ability to connect with others. Consquently, it ends at the level of the individual.

Meaning is a dynamic process circulating between persons.[2] It opens in the space between people.[3] It is a matter of contact and reaching out within the space. This space is neither a bridge nor a vacuum. It is a place of action and connection. It is a state of encountering the thoughts, feelings, and experiences of others. It is not an empty space, it is as Nancy suggests, "The heart of a connection, the interlacing of whose extremities remain separate even at the very center of the knot."[4] At the heart of this connection are individuals reaching out to one another. It is a crossing of separate but connected individuals. As individuals reach out, a *between* stretches toward the two.[5] Here being-singular becomes being-with. Being realizes its true existence in the space, and existence lives in "an affirmation of the world."[6] It is taking refuge in being and entering a state of contact between one another.[7]

Existence is contact between people, therefore meaning occurs in the giving and receiving between individuals. It circulates back and forth through a mutual sharing.[8] We cannot control this circulation of meaning.

---

1. Meaning is not tied to an ultimate signifier, instead meaning is generated through shared experience. Nancy writes, "There is no meaning if meaning is not shared, and not because there would be an ultimate or first signification that all beings have in common, but because meaning is itself the sharing of Being." Nancy, *Being Singular Plural*, 2.

2. "Being itself, the phenomenon of Being, is meaning that is, in turn, its own circulation—and we are this circulation." Nancy, *Being Singular Plural*, 2.

3. That is everything, as Nancy puts it, "passes *between us*." Nancy, *Being Singular Plural*, 3 (emphasis original).

4. Nancy, *Being Singular Plural*, 5.

5. "The 'between' is the stretching out and distance opened by the singular as such, as its spacing of meaning." Nancy, *Being Singular Plural*, 5.

6. Nancy, *Being Singular Plural*, 9.

7. Nancy writes that meaning, "is a matter of one or the other, one and the other, one with the other." Nancy, *Being Singular Plural*, 5–6.

8. Circulation is the origin of meaning. Nancy explains that "there is no other

It happens between all things and moves in all directions.[9] Circulation is a process of contact. It reflects that existence is a matter of being-with instead of being-singular.[10] Being must be being-with.[11] Thus, meaning circulates in being-with, and there is no control of meaning from the perspective of an *I*. Existence lives in the circulation between the *I* and the other. Consequently, breaking that connection is tantamount to breaking life itself.

Being depends on being for existence. Being-singular represents a rejection of the other. Being-singular points to the self as its own origin. Accordingly, what occurs outside the self becomes secondary or accidental. Being suffers under the illusion as its own creator.[12] As Nancy describes, the "plurality of beings is at the foundation of Being."[13] Plurality points to a fundamental shift in how we view the self in relation to others. A single self, being, does not represent being to its fullest extent. Being is a static concept alone. Being is not a state or a quality, but an action[14] or a becoming. Being is unfinished within itself. Being must relate with being in order to change and grow. Relationship is at the heart of what it means to be human. Being is existence, yes, but existence for and with others.[15]

Being connects-to-being and being lives in connection with being. The static gives way to the dynamic. To understand our own being or existence, we must reach out to being. We embrace the plurality of being. The origin of our existence does not being with the I, but with the other.[16] At every moment, existence lives in connection. To have being, is to be in the

---

meaning than the meaning of circulation." Nancy, *Being Singular Plural*, 3.

9. Circulation, Nancy describes, "Goes in all directions at once, in all directions of all the space-times opened by presence to presence." Nancy, *Being Singular Plural*, 3.

10. According to Nancy, "Existence is *with*: otherwise nothing exists." Nancy, *Being Singular Plural*, 4.

11. "Being cannot be anything but being-with-one-another, circulating in the *with* and as the *with* of this singularly plural coexistence." Nancy, *Being Singular Plural*, 3 (emphasis original).

12. Nancy suggests that a "single being is a contradiction in terms. Such a being, which would be its own foundation, origin, and intimacy, would be incapable of Being." Nancy, *Being Singular Plural*, 12.

13. Nancy, *Being Singular Plural*, 12.

14. Nancy explains that being "is neither a state nor a quality, but rather the action according to which what Kant calls 'the [mere] positing of a thing' takes place ('is')." Nancy, *Being Singular Plural*, 12.

15. Or as Nancy puts it, "Being is given as existence, being-in-oneself-outside-oneself, which we make explicit, we 'humans,' but which we make explicit, as I have said, *for* the totality of beings." Nancy, *Being Singular Plural*, 12 (emphasis original).

16. For example, Nancy writes, "It is the plural singularity of the Being of being. We reach it to the extent that we are in touch with *ourselves* and in touch with the rest of beings." Nancy, *Being Singular Plural*, 13 (emphasis original).

world.[17] As such, our life in this world is to live for others. Being never lives for the self.[18] Being is shared, and it plays between one and the other. In the in-between, being plays.[19] It plays in this space so it might understand one another. Without this play, this interaction, being has no understanding. It only sees the reflection of the self.[20] We cannot understand being until we understand that "Being is communication."[21]

We Are What We Do

When OFWBs practice foot washing, there is no mention of being, circulation, or plurality. No one provides reasons as to the necessity of being-with. There are no reflections of any kind on how their actions create meaning. Something more important is happening when they practice this ritual action. OFWBs live the idea before its formulation.[22] Action comes before the knowing.[23] OFWBs do not need to be told about being-with. They know it

---

17. To be human is to be "*in* the world insofar as the world is its own exteriority, the proper state of its being-out-in-the-world." Nancy, *Being Singular Plural*, 18 (emphasis original).

18. Being is always for the other. It is not "for just one, but always for one another, always between one another . . . 'one' or 'it' is never other than *we*." Nancy, *Being Singular Plural*, 27 (emphasis original).

19. "Being is put into play among us; it does not have any other meaning except the dis-position of this 'between.'" Nancy, *Being Singular Plural*, 27

20. "The understanding of Being is nothing other than an understanding of others, which means, in every sense, understanding others through 'me' and understanding 'me' through others, the understanding of one another." Nancy, *Being Singular Plural*, 27–29.

21. Nancy, *Being Singular Plural*, 28.

22. In what follows, in this and subsequent chapters, general, all-encompassing language will be used to describe OFWBs and their perspectives on foot washing. Of course, the OFWB perspective is more nuanced and diverse. Not all OFWBs value foot washing. There are a variety of views regarding the necessity, meaning, and importance of foot washing even among the OFWB. Yet for the clarity of argument, and to avoid complicated linguistic gymnastics, a more unified and direct approach is employed. This direct approach reflects the data gained (see chapter 3) from questionnaires, interviews, and participant observation. Thus, this portrayal represents a snapshot of the OFWB experience. However, this snapshot attempts as faithful representation of the OFWB experience as is possible.

23. Sue Patterson describes how Wittgenstein "maintains that acting accordance with a rule is prior to the explicit articulation of or comprehension of the rule. We can play the game in accordance with the rules without ever knowing that it has particular rules. The game is its rules; the rules are enacted, lived." Patterson, *Word, Words and World*, 37.

and live it through foot washing.[24]Every time they practice foot washing, these concepts are physically enacted. Words are not necessary for doing or even understanding the experience.

The experience speaks for itself. Foot washing drives OFWB tradition and behavior. It is a habitual action, which serves as a basis for Christian formation. Consequently, foot washing shapes behavior because it is done rather than taught.[25] It privileges action over doctrine, standing in contrast to a Christianity that privileges thought over action.[26] As OFWBs practice foot washing, they privilege action over thought. The action teaches and shows them how to live. It helps to shift the focus of OFWBs toward others, and helps them to show intimacy, forgiveness, and acceptance for one another. This ritual action teaches through the heart rather than the head.

Foot washing shapes OFWB's being-in-the-world. OFWBs are actors who teach and learn through ritual action.[27] As actors, they allow this action to influence the way they live and view the world. For OFWBs, action comes before reflection. Therefore, foot washing represents how they are to live. Their response is to do first and reflect later. It is not that the intellectual is unimportant, but they express the intellect through what they do. Foot washing is who they are.[28] Foot washing represents how love drives the actions of OFWBs.[29]

24. "Conceptual knowledge ('knowing-that') takes the form of new propositions, concepts or categories whereas a gain to tacit or pre-conceptual knowledge ('knowing how') occurs through activities or practices." Patterson, *Word, Words and World*, 51. OFWBs fall into the latter category. They just know how. It requires no explanation.

25. According to Smith, "The driving center of human action and behavior is a nexus of loves, longings, and habits that hums along under the hood, so to speak, without needing to be thought about. These loves, longings, and habits orient and propel our being-in-the-world. The focus on formation is holistic because its end is Christian *action*." Smith, *Imagining the Kingdom*, 12.

26. Because of modernity, Smith thinks "many models of Christian higher education (and many accounts of discipleship) are fixated on epistemic matters. Seeing Christianity as primarily a set of doctrines, beliefs, and ideas, they implicitly and functionally reduce Christian education to the acquisition of knowledge." Smith, *Imagining the Kingdom*, 12.

27. "I think it's incumbent upon me as a pastor and a teacher to use [foot washing], this is a teachable moment. I'm utterly convinced that the only thing that brings us joy this side of heaven is that which we do to enrich the lives of others. This gives me a very concrete way of illustrating that, what it means, what it looks like." Interview with OFWB pastor (C), February 4, 2015.

28. Smith explains that "those Christian communities we usually criticize for their anti-intellectualism are, in fact, intellectualist in their implicit philosophies of action insofar as they believe that changing what we think will change what we do." Smith, *Imagining the Kingdom*, 32.

29. Action as a way of Christian knowledge is Smith's argument. As he puts it, "But

OFWBs demonstrate that action can come before thought. Pastors educate their congregations on the practice, but education is by no means uniform. Some education can come from sermons; however the primary way of learning is through observing and participating. To learn foot washing, OFWBs must do it. The action determines the rule.[30] What they *do* is an outcome of what they *do*.[31] Thus, OFWBs educate for action through action. They see that the best way to learn about Jesus is to do what he did. By reenacting his actions, OFWBs expect to learn how to follow the example of Jesus.[32]

Foot washing teaches OFWBs to see, act, and live in the world. Seeing the world comes from acting in the world. Their actions determine the proper way to interpret it. Action guides encounter.[33] It trains them on how to respond and behave toward others. For OFWBs, foot washing educates them for encountering the other. Foot washing's concepts, such as humility, service, and forgiveness, guides their interaction with others.[34] In using pairs, foot washing reminds OFWBs that their actions affect others. Their actions teach them that being is being-with. What they *do* is who they *are*.

---

what if we are actors before we are thinkers? What if action is driven and generated less by what we think and more by what we love?" Smith, *Imagining the Kingdom*, 33.

30. Wittgenstein considers this in the case of a road sign. He writes, "I have been trained to react to this sign in a particular way, and now I do so react to it. But that is only to give a causal connexion; to tell how it has come about that we now go by the sign-post; not what this going-by-the sign really consists in. On the contrary; I have further indicated that a person goes by a sign-post only in so far as there exists a regular use of sign-posts, a custom." Wittgenstein, *Philosophical Investigations*, 80.

31. Smith is "pushing back against an 'intellectualist' account of action that assumes that what I *do* is the outcome of what I *think*." Smith, *Imagining the Kingdom*, 33 (emphasis original).

32. Smith believes that intellectualism can "lead us to misunderstand the nature of action, including ethical action. We tend to assume that 'education for action' requires first uploading the relevant rules and axioms into our minds, then equipping agents with the critical thinking skills that will allow them to amass the relevant facts of a situation then make the right decision." Smith, *Imagining the Kingdom*, 34.

33. Seeing the world is dependent on how one acts in the world. Smith writes, "I'm not only primed to see the situation in a certain way. . . . I'm also already inclined or disposed to act in a certain way—not as the result of a decision, but as a sort of 'natural' tendency given the inclinations that I've acquired, the habits that already prime me to 'lean' in certain directions." Smith, *Imagining the Kingdom*, 36.

34. OFWBs use foot washing to teach service. A pastor explains how he does this by stating, "I think it sets a great example of what the Lord has asked us to be as servants. We talk about that a lot. We practice this at different things, the ordination of deacons and that sort of thing. I wash the deacon's feet and his wife's feet. And we talk about why we do that. We are taught to serve, as Christians we are called to service." Interview with OFWB pastor (A), April 7, 2015.

OFWBs and Being-With

OFWB foot washing is a living philosophy of being-with. This living philosophy is taught and applied through action. Thus, OFWBs understand the world through action involving being-with others through humility, love, and forgiveness. Foot washing is this visible action of being-with.[35] It acts out the idea that existence means contact. Christian action becomes bodily action. Bodily action is a physical reaching out within space. This action is a reminder that the body is inescapable. There is no place outside the body. More importantly, there is no place outside bodies.[36]

Any meaning circulates through the body, with the body, and toward other bodies. When OFWBs practice foot washing, the body is inescapable. This action is impossible with one body alone. To do it, a body must touch another body. At its core, foot washing is a being-with instead of being-singular. Its existence, as an action, is dependent on a plurality of being. Its meaning comes from relationship. No one can claim sole ownership of this meaning. Foot washing is a mutual sharing of meaning circulating between the giver and receiver, the *I* and the other. Neither the giver nor receiver control the action. It is a mutual giving and sharing. Both parties remain open to one other. This openness allows the experience of shared existence and meaning.[37]

In foot washing, the water is, literally and figuratively, this space of connection. Everything that occurs passes through this space. In this water are two bodies coming together and sharing an experience.[38] The water is

---

35. Foot washing brings OFWBs closer together. It is their way of expressing being-with. A layperson reflects, "[Foot washing] definitely draws you closer. We have members who are, of course like ever church, you only see them on Sunday mornings. We have those that are there for every service but may not participate in foot washing. But those that do participate there is a different type of closeness there. It's on another level. They are even more family. I guess it would be more akin to it being your immediate family versus your extended second third cousin, great aunt kind of. It's a much, much tighter bond." Interview with OFWB member (D), February 5, 2015.

36. Speaking of the body, Athena Athanasiou makes the case that "the human has no 'proper' place to take outside social situatedness and allocation, including the exposure to the possibility of being undone. The human is always the event of multiple exposures." Butler and Athanasiou, *Disposession*, 32.

37. Judith Butler writes, "If the body opens him toward a 'you,' it opens him in such a way that the other, through bodily means, becomes capable of addressing a 'you' as well. Implicit in both modes of address is the understanding of the body, through its touch, securing the open address not just of this other whom I touch, but of every other body." Butler and Athanasiou, *Disposession*, 81.

38. "I think it brings us all together in a real sense of unity." Interview with OFWB pastor (H), February 3, 2015.

a joined space of creation, and such creation occurs because "existence is creation."[39] If being is being-with, then existence is shared. The water is the origin of a new creation, existence, between the giver and receiver.[40] In that water, the other matters. Each existence matters to the other, because each existence connects to the other. When OFWBs say that foot washing is an opportunity to show humility, love, service, and forgiveness, they are staying that the other matters. Their existence ties to the other's existence. Foot washing is an opportunity to create something new. It is a chance to create a new relationships and experiences.[41] Foot washing demonstrates that OFWB existence is a being-with. Each person lives in relationship with Jesus and one other. Their existence immerses in the existence of others.[42]

BEING SINGULAR PLURAL: THE WITH OF BEING

Foot washing, for OFWBs, suggests a shared existence. Being, individual existence, is not on its own. Being-singular is not an absolute existence, nor is being total and complete. The world has an influence on who or what we are. Being-singular is existence for the self.

The OFWB practice of foot washing suggests a different view of the self. Foot washing opens us toward others, instead of viewing ourselves as enclosed. Likewise, it suggests that the other is not external, but that all existence is co-existence.[43] Co-existence is being-singular-plural. This means

39. The full quote reads, "Existence is creation, *our* creation; it is the beginning and end that *we* are. This is the thought that is the most necessary for us to think. If we do not succeed in thinking it, then we will never gain access to who we are, we who are no more than us in a world, which is itself no more than the world." Nancy, *Being Singular Plural*, 17 (emphasis original).

40. Nancy writes that creation "signifies precisely that there is no Other and that the 'there is' is not an Other. Being is not the Other and that the 'there is' is not an Other. Being is not the Other, but the origin is the punctual and discrete spacing between us, as between us and the rest of the world, as between all beings." Nancy, *Being Singular Plural*, 19.

41. Speaking of foot washing's effects, a pastor recalls, "[After foot washing,] there's an embrace that brings [us] together and there's a literally conversation of 'Thank you brother I appreciate all you do. You meant this much to me.' It's a unifying thing once you let it. It really, really will. We don't practice it enough, we don't get serious enough with it many times. But when really get an understanding and get serious it is a unifying thing in my heart." Interview with OFWB pastor (H), February 3, 2015.

42. "Through our bodies we are implicated in thick and intense social processes of relatedness and interdependence." Butler and Athanasiou, *Disposession*, 55.

43. "That which exists, whatever this might be, coexists because it exists. . . . A world is not something external to existence; it is not an extrinsic addition to other existences; the world is the coexistence that puts these existences together." Nancy, *Being Singular

that all being is both singular and plural.[44] Being is never for itself, the singular does not rule over being. Accordingly, the singular and plural both constitute existence.[45] All that exists, exists in relation. The singular needs to refer to something outside the self. We need a relation, a reference point, to relate to.[46] We come to understand ourselves through others. Consequently, being-singular is a mystery to itself without the plural of discovery. It is not that all beings are the same. For we are all different, and these differences make each of us unique. Yet difference is necessary for being to exist.[47] We knows ourselves through our relationships with others.

Being is relationship. Being-singular-plural reveals that the core of being is not the isolated self. Being-singular is being-plural. Being is being-*with*, and this *with* is the essence of existence.[48] The mind is not the foundation of our existence. We cannot begin with the self to establish the self. For what do we have to gain from living within our mind? Only that which we already know. Therefore, Descartes' well-known maxim, "I think therefore I am" establishes nothing. More fitting would be *I relate therefore I am*. Relation is not an addition to being. The mind does not exist alone. The *with* of being, relationality, is being's true nature. Its form comes from function. Being is not first *is* before it is *with*.[49] Being begins *with* before it does anything.

Plural, 29.

44. "Being is singularly plural and plurally singular." Nancy, *Being Singular Plural*, 28.

45. Or as Nancy describes it, "The singular plural constitutes the essence of Being, a constitution that undoes or dislocates every single, substantial essence of Being itself." Nancy, *Being Singular Plural*, 29.

46. Existence requires relation. Nancy explains "there exists something ('me') and another thing (this other 'me' that represents the possible) to which I relate myself in order for me to ask myself if there exists something of the sort that I think of as possible." Nancy, *Being Singular Plural*, 29.

47. Nancy writes that "there does not exist just these 'me's,' as subjects-of-representation, because along with the real difference between two 'me's' is given the difference between things in general, the difference between my body and many bodies. . . . In a certain way, there never has been, and never will be, a philosophy 'of the subject' in the sense of the final [*infinite*] closure in itself of a for-itself." *Being Singular Plural*, 29 (emphasis and brackets original).

48. Being-singular-plural or being-with lies at the core of Nancy's philosophy. Being-singular-plural "means the essence of Being is only as coessence. In turn, coessence, or *being-with* (being-with-many), designates the essence of the *co-*, or even more so, the *co-* (the *cum*) itself in the position or guise of an essence." Nancy, *Being Singular Plural*, 30 (emphasis original).

49. Nancy emphasizes this point by writing "it is not the case that the 'with' is an addition to some prior Being; instead, the 'with' is at the heart of Being." Nancy, *Being Singular Plural*, 30.

Being-with is being-singular-plural. It brings the self and the world into balance. The self needs the world and the world needs individuality. The goal is not to eliminate one or the other. Tillich declares, "The self without a world is empty; the world without a self is dead."[50] As a result, all beings participate in the world. The world is a place of action. Though the self acts in the world, the self is not one with it. Being-singular signifies estrangement between one another. The self is not fully connected with other selves.[51] Being-singular-plural points to the barrier we must overcome to be *with*.[52] Being-with is our destiny. It is a reaching out across the space between existences. This reaching out completes us. Being-singular, without plural, is hollow.[53] Existence ought to be lived in the *with*.

Living *with* lives in participation with the other. No one, Tillich writes, "exists without participation, and no personal being exists without communal being."[54] Being requires the resistance of other beings. Existence is encounter with existence. For we do not truly know ourselves until we enter the space of the other. Being-singular discovers existence through being-with. Being-singular-plural is representative of the personal encounter needed for us to live and grow. Our individuality remains a mystery until we encounter the individuality of the other.[55] Existence comes through a personal encounter.[56]

Nowhere is this more evident than in the Christian life. Karl Barth states, as "children of God as a creation of the Holy Spirit we have to do with

50. Tillich, *Systematic Theology, Volume 1*, 171.

51. "We can approach other beings only in terms of analogy and, therefore, only indirectly and uncertainly." Tillich, *Systematic Theology, Volume 1*, 168.

52. Tillich describes this separation stating, "Being a self means being separated in some way from everything else, having everything else opposite one's self, being able to look at it and to act upon it. At the same time, however, this self is aware that it belongs to that at which it looks. The self is 'in' it." Tillich, *Systematic Theology, Volume 1*, 170.

53. The self needs the world. "Without its world the self would be an empty form. Self-consciousness would have no content, for every content, psychic as well as bodily, lies within the universe." Tillich, *Systematic Theology, Volume 1*, 171.

54. Tillich continues, "The person as the fully developed individual self is impossible without other fully developed selves." Tillich, *Systematic Theology, Volume 1*, 176.

55. This correlates with Nancy's arguments of existence being an origin and creation. Existence is born out of encounter. It is the creation of a world. Understanding ourselves comes from understanding others. How do we understand individuals unless we push against the barrier of other individuals? Precisely because the "individual discovers himself through this resistance. . . . In the resistance of the other person the person is born." Tillich, *Systematic Theology, Volume 1*, 177.

56. Tillich puts it in the following way, "Persons can grow only in communion of personal encounter. Individualization and participation are interdependent on all levels of being." Tillich, *Systematic Theology, Volume 1*, 177.

a determinateness of human life understood as *being* and *doing*."[57] The call of God is a call to action.[58] Outward action, being-plural, defines a Christian. This outward action, Barth writes, "Means that he cannot cease to testify that God in Christ has found him. Therefore his being makes necessary a very definite doing. He simply cannot suppress or conceal or keep to himself what he is."[59] The call of God is the call to being-with, and being-with is the intended state of all persons. The Christian life does not privilege an inward state over the outward. Our inward nature is pulled toward the outside. The life of Christ does not close us toward others. It opens being-singular to being-singular-plural. The life of Christ is a life lived *with* others.[60]

Being-with whom? Being-with all. Being-with is first and foremost co-existence. It is existence with others and for others. The *with* signifies the *all* of existence. Being is being-with all persons, no matter the other's race, gender, status, or so on. The *with* is sharing. Being-with signifies that existence is a shared existence. It is the recognition that beings are not all the same. Being-with does not erase the differences between beings.[61] Each person is unique, and this individuality is not absorbed by the *with*. The *with* brings individuals together with-one-another. Consequently, being-with reveals each individual's otherness. Every individual is also an *other*.[62] None of us can escape our otherness. Being is being-strange, but it is

---

57. Barth, *Doctrine of Word*, 369.

58. Thus one "confronted only by God, and no one can represent him in the confrontation. But if we look at the doing or outward aspect of this same man [or woman], we find that in spite of his isolation this same man [or woman] is united in society as an individual with the whole Church, related, of course, to God, but in God to others. The impossibility of regarding him [or her] strictly from the one standpoint or the other means that we cannot treat either of these insight as exclusive. The fact is that they belong together." Barth, *Doctrine of Word*, 369–70.

59. Barth, *Doctrine of Word,* 370.

60. "In the freedom of God he [or she] himself [or herself] became free and the child of God. This is the irresistible summons to action. This is what he [or she] has to reveal and declare. This is what his [or her] whole existence has now to proclaim and attest and affirm. It is in this decision that he [or she] now lives." Barth, *Doctrine of Word,* 370.

61. Nancy makes it clear that *with* "does not indicate the sharing of a common situation any more than the juxtaposition of a pure exteriorities does (for example, a bench with a tree with a dog with a passer-by)." Nancy, *Being Singular Plural*, 35.

62. "Being is with Being; it does not ever recover itself, but it is near to itself, beside itself, in touch with itself, its very self, in the paradox of that proximity where distancing and strangeness are revealed. We are each time an other, each time with others." Nancy, *Being Singular Plural*, 35.

being-strange-with-one-another. Being-singular-plural is both sharing and division. It is unity and separation. It is isolation and community.[63]

Being-singular-plural represents what is difficult about relationship. Relationship and sharing are hard. Individuals struggle to move toward each other. Being-singular is difficult to overcome. Therefore, we are tempted to stop at the level of being-singular. It is difficult to look past the self. Existence mistakenly begins with the *I* before the *we*. The *I* cannot fulfill itself without the *we*. Being-with, "Is existence reclaiming its due or its condition: coexistence."[64] It is being for everyone. Being-with is also being-for-all.[65]

The *with* of being does not exist in abstract. Describing *with* is describing something actual. It does not describe a presence outside experience. The *with* of being-with is actual, present, and presentable.[66] The *with* exists between each person through meaningful action and presence. Though difficulty, the *with* represents an actual coming together.[67]

OFWBs present the *with* through foot washing. What occurs during foot washing is actual. The water becomes a place of contact. It is the physical and visible *with* representing the emotional *with* between beings. What Nancy writes abstractly and philosophically is real and concrete between OFWB participants. OFWBs repeatedly stress that foot washing is a coming together of individuals. Individuals that are acting, caring, and loving together. These OFWBs do not need to be reminded about the *with*. They live, act, and embody the *with*.

63. Being-singular-plural, As Nancy puts it, "Is a mark of union and also a mark of division, a mark of sharing that effaces itself, leaving each term to its isolation and its being-with-the-others." Nancy, *Being Singular Plural*, 37.

64. Nancy, *Being Singular Plural*, 42.

65. Or as Nancy puts it, being "must be an ontology for the world, for everyone—and if I can be so bold, it has to be an ontology for each and every one and for the world 'as a totality,' and nothing short of the world, since this is all there is (but, in this way, there is *all*)." Nancy, *Being Singular Plural*, 53–54.

66. "The *with* is not 'unpresentable' like some remote or withdrawn presence, or like an Other." Nancy, *Being Singular Plural*, 62 (emphasis original).

67. Or coming apart. *With* can also be a point of tension. Relationships are never easy and what draws two together can also repel. *With* requires work. Being-with, co-existence, maybe the natural state of existence. This does not mean that existence is free from conflict. Nancy writes, "The 'with' is or constitutes the mark of unity/disunity, which in itself does not designate unity or disunity as that fixed substance which would undergird it; the 'with' is not the sign of a reality, or even of an 'intersubjective dimension.' It really is, 'in truth,' a mark drawn out over the void, which crosses over it and underlines it at the same time. . . . As such, it also constitutes the traction and tension, repulsion/attraction, of the 'between'-us. The 'with' stays between us, and we stay between us." Nancy, *Being Singular Plural*, 62 (emphasis original).

Foot washing is relationship. It is being-singular-plural. When OFWBs come together, they enter as individuals. They enter as individuals from different backgrounds and experiences. They enter as pastors and laypeople, young and old, and rich and poor. OFWBs carry their lives into foot washing. Foot washing begins at an individual level. Therefore, the point is not to eliminate the individual. Foot washing does not erase identity and individuality. It does not erase the being-singular. OFWBs are not saying that identity does not matter. Instead, an individual matters *because* of who he or she is. False plurality erases identity, but true plurality, that is community, is the embrace of being-singular with being-plural. It embraces individual and communal identity. Foot washing is being-singular-plural.

When OFWBs come together, they come together as individuals in community. Modeling Jesus, they accept each other for who and what they are.[68] Without any philosophical argument, they know Jesus to be the embodiment of being-singular-plural.[69] When washing the disciples' feet, Jesus accepts the disciples as sinners, betrayers, and deserters. Despite knowing who they are and what they will do, Jesus embraces them as whole persons. Jesus acts as being-with. He initiates the *with*. Community, the plural, is affirmed through the *with*. And as they kneel and wash, OFWBs connect to Jesus. Moreover, OFWBs are continuing Christ's *with* whenever and wherever they wash feet. Foot washing is the ability to accept and connect with each as person both individually and communally. Foot washing, therefore, is a commitment to being-singular-plural.[70]

The OFWB perspective on humility forms through being-with. Being-with is not important because it is postmodern or philosophical. Being-with, from an OFWB point of view, is humility in action. OFWBs continually stress the importance of humility in foot washing. Humility is a *with*. For OFWBs, foot washing is reaching across the space between persons. Humility overcomes that space to build connections. Being-singular surrenders itself for the sake of washing the other's feet. Thus, foot washing is an act of

68. "[Foot washing] certainly has enhanced my experience as a Christian. It puts me more in touch with feelings of servitude and I can relate more to Jesus." Interview with OFWB member (A), March 3, 2015.

69. Explaining Jesus' example, a pastor says, "The host then becomes the servant, and that's just unheard of. If our Lord came to be a servant, who do we think we are if were not following that example. There again the practice itself reinforces the behavior of what it means to be a part of the Christian community." Interview with OFWB pastor (C), February 4, 2015.

70. This layperson discussed how foot washing draws people together. "I think [foot washing has] drawn us closer together. We are more united in belief in recognizing the significance of what Christ did for us and for his apostles. We have that common bond of belief and unity." Interview with OFWB member (A), March 3, 2015.

recognition, not of the self, but of the plurality of being. As OFWBs wash feet, they connect through humility. Humility physically connects individuals in bonds of relationship, friendship, and love. Foot washing breaks down the barrier of being-singular to *become* being-singular-plural. OFWBs find each other through the *with*.

OFWBS, HABITUS, AND ACTION

OFWBs live as being-with. Foot washing demonstrates their calling toward all people. This calling originates in the life and ministry of Jesus Christ. Additionally, OFWBs are generators of meaning. They actively create new and unique meanings between one another. Foot washing is an ongoing and dynamic process, and its meaning varies from group to group. The way it is practiced, when it is practiced, and the people who practice it affect foot washing's meanings. Its meanings originate in the moment. Personal stories, surprise encounters, good friends, and emotional responses point to the dynamism of ritual action. Foot washing is unique because OFWBs are unique. They play an important role in conveying the meanings of foot washing.

Pierre Bourdieu describes this process as *habitus*. Habitus is a structured behavior that does not necessarily correlate to any established rule or guide. Habitus flows from "systems of durable, transposable *dispositions*, structured structures predisposed to function as structuring structures . . . which can be objectively 'regulated' and 'regular' without in any way being the product of obedience to rules."[71] All action involves a regulated series of moves and behaviors. When groups perform actions, like ritual, these actions appear to be second nature. Participants just know what to do. Habitus is the source and organizer of these series of moves and behaviors.[72] Habitus is not an outside source that controls or programs action. Habitus rejects any mechanized theories of actions.[73] It rejects deterministic action that disregards the experiences and uniqueness of its participants. Habitus organizes group behavior and leads the community toward a likely, but not controlled, action.

71. Bourdieu, *Outline of a Theory*, 72.

72. Bourdieu explains, "The *habitus* is the source of these series of moves which are objectively organized as strategies without being the product of a genuine strategic intention." Bourdieu, *Outline of a Theory*, 73.

73. Bourdieu maintains that it is "necessary to abandon all theories which explicitly or implicitly treat practice as a mechanical reaction, directly determined by the antecedent conditions and entirely reducible to the mechanical functioning of pre-established assemblies." Bourdieu, *Outline of a Theory*, 73.

Habitus suggests that action is strategic. Action builds on action, and participants use past experiences to inform and modify behavior. Foot washing, being a ritual action, incorporates both collective and individual history. Habitus is simultaneously a collector, product, and producer of this history, pointing to action as a collective practice.[74] History matters to the practice of action. Consequently, habitus creates a filter through which participants act. This history suggests the action's performance and the meanings it has acquired. Thus, history is a "matrix of perception."[75]

History and Action

History matters more than the rule of action. As OFWBs practice foot washing, they share a history of the *now*. On one level, OFWBs are connecting with the living history of Jesus. More immediately, OFWBs are connecting with the history of their parents and grandparents. Therefore, the history of fifty to sixty years ago is particularly meaningful to OFWBs. They are connecting and re-presenting that history into the present. This is often an unconscious act. OFWBs do what they have always done. OFWBs, especially those raised in the denomination, just know how to do foot washing. Consequently, it is difficult for them to explain how they know the action. Their history lives within them. Through foot washing, history is re-presented and passed on. Foot washing becomes who they are. The history of their parents and grandparents becomes their history, and history accumulates to produce more history. It is both preserver and creator.[76] History becomes second nature.[77] And history becomes nature.[78]

74. Bourdieu explains that the "*habitus*, the product of history, produces individual and collective practices, and hence history, in accordance with the schemes engendered by history." Bourdieu, *Outline of a Theory*, 82.

75. This habitus is "a system of lasting, transposable dispositions which, integrating past experiences, functions at every moment as a matrix of perceptions, appreciations, and actions." Bourdieu, *Outline of a Theory*, 82–83.

76. For example, Bourdieu suggests that this "accumulated capital, produces history on the basis of history and so ensures the permanence in change that makes the individual agent a world within a world." Bourdieu, *Logic of Practice*, 56.

77. "The 'unconscious' is never anything than the forgetting of history which history itself produces by incorporating the objective structures it produces in the second nature of *habitus*." Bourdieu, *Outline of a Theory*, 79.

78. E. Durkheim writes that "in each of us, in varying proportions, there is part of yesterday's man [or woman]; it is yesterday's man [or woman] who inevitably predominates in us, since the present amounts to little compared with the long past in the course of which we were formed and from which we result. Yet we do not sense this man [or woman] of the past, because he [or she] is inveterate in us; he [or she] makes up the

Everyone becomes an agent of that history. OFWBs produce and reproduce the history, experiences, and meanings of foot washing.[79] Individual participants are not bystanders. They are not doomed to reproduce a meaning of which they have no part. These meanings belong to the OFWB. Their history contributes to the history of their parents and grandparents, creating a new lived present. As they learn and pass on these actions through repeated action, the *habitus* both collects this history and is produced by it.[80] Such practices transmit identity, and foot washing carries what it means to be Christian and OFWB. It is a visible history enacted in the *now*. Collective history is alive through collective practice. These actions pass on a specific way and being-in-the-world.[81] OFWBs pass on their ideas of humility, service, equality, and love through the collective action of washing feet. Therefore, OFWBs know that no one can explain foot washing. Understanding comes from doing it.

This understanding goes beyond the physical mechanics of the action.[82] Understanding incorporates one into a habitus. It is a way of seeing one another and the world. Learning foot washing means an incorporation into a way of behavior. The habitus is sharing a world-view and way of acting in the world, which creates a commonality and being within a group.[83] Action carries more than physical movements. Action carries history and

---

unconscious part of ourselves." Quoted in Bourdieu, *Outline of a Theory*, 79.

79. "Each agent, wittingly or unwittingly, willy nilly, is a producer and reproducer of objective meaning. Because his action and works are the product of a *modus operandi* of which he is not the producer and has no conscious mastery . . . which always outruns his conscious intentions." Bourdieu, *Outline of a Theory*, 78.

80. Bourdieu further understands the habitus "is the product of the work of inculcation and appropriation necessary in order for those products of collective history, the objective structures (e.g. of language, economy, etc.) to succeed in reproducing themselves more or less completely, in the form of durable dispositions." Bourdieu, *Outline of a Theory*, 85.

81. Therefore, for example, Bourdieu notes that groups pass on information collectively. He writes that "the essential part of the *modus operandi* which defines practical mastery is transmitted in practice, in its practical state, without attaining the level of discourse. The child imitates not 'models' but other people's actions." Bourdieu, *Outline of a Theory*, 87.

82. "The fact that schemas are able to pass from practice to practice without going through discourse or consciousness does not mean that acquisition of the *habitus* comes down to a question of mechanical learning by trial and error." Bourdieu, *Outline of a Theory*, 88.

83. The habitus, "could be considered as a subjective but not individual system of internalized structures, schemes of perception, conception, and action common to all members of the same group or class and constituting the precondition for all objectification and apperception." Bourdieu, *Outline of a Theory*, 86.

meaning.[84] Accordingly, doing the action also means *living* the history it contains, which carries history into the present. Doing foot washing also means living in OFWB history. It is living in a history of humility, service, and love. It represents a communal identity of how things can be and should be. These actions demonstrate a specific type of being-in-world shared in community.

Habitus and Community

Habitus highlights the important role that communities play in forming identity through ritual action. Habitus is not programming. Its goal is not to suppress individual thought or deviation from behavior. The habitus is both personal and communal. It works with the individual, being-singular, to create a perception between the self and the world. It teaches us how to be being-singular-plural. Habitus is comprised of both individual and collective experience.[85] As such, it is a collection of individual experience and history. It shows that individual experience does not point to individualism but communalism. Individual experience is experience best shared.

Habitus points us toward possibility. It is an expectation of the world. Nevertheless, this possibility does not originate from the self. It originates in community. Habitus points to what we can expect when sharing existence.[86] It is not telling us what to think, but how we should think together. More importantly, the habitus shows us how to live together. It is learning how to be being-with. It is learning how to be community.

The possibility of the habitus is the possibility of vision. It does not determine the future; rather it is the vision for future behavior. It continually shows us the *what if* of communal action. That is, it orients us toward *possibility*. The habitus is not deterministic, but hopeful.[87] It sets the conditions

84. The habitus is a "system of dispositions—a past which survives in the present and tend to perpetuate itself into the future by making itself present in the practices structured according to its principles." Bourdieu, *Outline of a Theory*, 82.

85. The habitus "has a history that is both collective and individual." Smith, *Imagining the Kingdom*, 83.

86. Smith suggests that "*habitus* is a *condition* of possibility: like horizons of expectation, a *habitus* circumscribes just how we'll be inclined to constitute the world. However, a *habitus* is also a condition of possibility: rather than being some limit on my range of possible experiences, it's what makes any experience possible. The *habitus* both governs and enables perception." Smith, *Imagining the Kingdom*, 84 (emphasis original).

87. "Through the *habitus*, the structure which has produced it governs practice, not by the processes of a mechanical determinism, but through the mediation of the orientations and limits it assigns to the *habitus*' operations of invention." Bourdieu,

for communal life. Through action and perception, it sets the tone of a community.[88] It demonstrates what being-with looks like. More importantly, it shows us how to live as being-with. For OFWBs, habitus shows them what it means to live as an OFWB.

The habitus does not live in the past. This is not the past dominating the future. Instead, the habitus uses the past as a guide for living in the present. It creates a dialectic between the past and present in order to determine how the past can live in the present.[89] The habitus determines a course of action based on what is expected and not on what will occur. Looking to the past, we can expect actions to generate certain outcomes. The past matters, and experiences are not discarded. Therefore, the past provides a starting point for communities.[90] That means action has an origin within the community. The habitus formulates what we can reasonably expect from a given course of action. OFWB's have a perspective of both the past and the present, and foot washing carriers the actions of those who came before. Therefore, OFWBs have a reasonable expectation of what this action means for them in present. Foot washing carries the past within itself. It carries, or represents, concepts such as humility, forgiveness, and service. Each generation encounters and comes to expect these concepts. More importantly, they physically enact them as conditioned by the habitus.[91]

A habitus of foot washing sets up some generally expected behaviors and attitudes. OFWBs know how and when to act when doing foot washing. Through the habitus, OFWBs have a good idea what to expect from one another. OFWBs know that their feet will be washed, hearts will be humbled, and love will be shared. This may include singing hymns, acting in silence, or general conversation. These movements may be performed a hundred times without variation, yet the working of the habitus does not

---

Outline of a Theory, 95.

88. The habitus "engenders all the thoughts, all the perceptions, and all the actions consistent with those conditions, and no others." Bourdieu, *Outline of a Theory*, 95.

89. Bourdieu describes this dialectic by stating that the "*habitus* may be accompanied by a strategic calculation tending to perform in a conscious mode the operation that the *habitus* performs quite differently, namely an estimation of chances presupposing transformation of the past effect into an expected objective." Bourdieu, *Logic of Practice*, 53.

90. Bourdieu writes, "Unlike scientific estimations, which are corrected after each experiment according to rigorous rules of calculation, the anticipations of the *habitus*, practical hypotheses based on past experience, give disproportionate weight to early experiences." Bourdieu, *Logic of Practice*, 54.

91. "Through the *habitus*, the structure of which it is the product governs practice, not along the paths of a mechanical determinism, but within the constraints and limits initially set on its inventions." Bourdieu, *Logic of Practice*, 55.

imply a lack of change. There is change, subtle change, but change nonetheless. The habitus is both static and dynamic. It generates as well as stabilizes. Its framework is a fertile ground for adaptation and unpredictability.[92]

Both predictability and unpredictability bring OFWBs back to foot washing. It is doing the same actions Jesus performed, thus it suggests how OFWBs are to treat other people. Foot washing also points to the creativity of the habitus. There are elements that they can never predict. These include the unexpected feelings of joy, gratitude, and apperception that can suddenly overtake them. They never know when a new friendship might occur, nor can guess how their hearts and minds are being transformed. These experiences are neither mechanical nor forced. When washing feet, OFWBs know to expect the unexpected within the *expected* action.[93]

The habitus brings individual and communal history together. Working through institutions, the habitus brings individual history and experience into a communal framework. On its own, individual experience does not survive past the individual. Being-singular ends as being-singular. The habitus saves those experiences from being lost forever. A community preserves these experiences through the accumulated history of the habitus, and this process makes these communities possible. The OFWB as a community is not possible without the individual stories, emotions, and experiences that comprise it. Foot washing provides the framework for the OFWB being-in-the-world, but individual history makes this worldview possible. The habitus is both singular and plural. It is being-singular-plural.

Action and Counter Action

The being-singular-plural nature enables the functioning of the habitus. The habitus of foot washing works because it is "understood as a system of dispositions common to all products of the same conditionings."[94] Within the institution, there is a mutual understanding between individuals. This mutual understanding creates an environment of sharing and anticipation.

92. *Habitus* works as a balancing force. "Because the *habitus* is an infinite capacity for generating products—thoughts, perceptions, expressions and actions—whose limits are set by historically and socially situated conditions of its production, the conditioned and conditional freedom it provides is as remote from creation of unpredictable novelty as it is from simple mechanical reproduction of the original conditioning." Bourdieu, *Logic of Practice*, 55.

93. The habitus provides the conditions for invention and variation. For Bourdieu, the "*habitus*, like every 'art of inventing', is what makes it possible to produce an infinite number of practices that are relatively unpredictable." Bourdieu, *Logic of Practice*, 55.

94. Bourdieu, *Logic of Practice*, 59.

Individuals know what they can reasonably expect from one another. Each action has an expected action, and action makes possible further action.[95] The physical action and counter actions are obvious in foot washing. Actions such as removing shoes, kneeling, and touching feet provoke further actions. Underneath the surface, a whole series of emotional moves are also taking place. For example, OFWBs learn humility, servant-hood, and forgiveness as a series of actions set within a larger action. Humility becomes a visible action as well as emotional feeling. Humility responds to humility as OFWBs wash each other's feet. Through washing and being washed, humility reacts to humility and love replies to love.

Living the Habitus

The source of these moves is the habitus. They are strategic moves without a governing strategy.[96] As a source, the habitus is not separate from action itself. The source arises within the action itself. The habitus lives within action, in both its past practice and present condition. The practices generated by the habitus continually adapt to the present. Through the habitus, humility becomes the expected reaction. In addition, participants expect other reactions such as love and equality. For OFWBs, emotions such as humility become the communal norm and their being-in-the-world. The habitus of foot washing carriers over into daily life. Foot washing teaches OFWBs how to live as a Christian community.

The foot washing habitus is a continual reminder of how OFWBs are called to live.[97] Foot washing's transformative effects are not immediately obvious. The first experience of foot washing may not provoke drastic change. Instead, as habitus, the effects are long term. Habitus is a slow process that works on individuals gradually. It is a gentle reminder of how to act and be in the world. We do not choose a habitus. We are molded into it.[98]

95. Habitus makes possible this movement of action and counter action. Bourdieu writes, "Each action has the purpose of making possible the reaction to the reaction it induces." Bourdieu, *Logic of Practice*, 61.

96. "The *habitus* contains the solution to the paradoxes of objective meaning without subjective intention. It is the source of these strings of 'moves' which are objectively organized as strategies without being the product of a genuine strategic intention." Bourdieu, *Logic of Practice*, 62.

97. "Through washing of feet we demonstrate how we're called to live as a redeemed people." Interview with OFWB pastor (C), February 4, 2015.

98. "It is the cumulative effect of habituation that shapes you as a native. While you can be born into a community, no one is born a 'native' in Bourdieu's sense because 'nativity' is not genetic—it's not just a matter of blood or location. You are formed into a native. And even if you *want* to join, you cannot simply *choose* to do so." Smith,

Therefore, the habitus is continually adjusting, carrying over into life. We learn how to live the habitus in our own time and circumstances.[99]

For OFWBs, foot washing does not end at the completion of the physical act. Habitus reminds them how to live, and the body enacts the habitus.[100] These reminders, such as servant-hood and equality, are molded onto the physical body.[101] Consequently, the habitus establishes a practical sense. Bourdieu describes practical sense as a "social necessity turned into nature, converted into motor schemes and body automatisms, [practical sense] is what causes practices, in and through what makes them obscure to the eyes of their producers, to be sensible, that is, informed by a common sense."[102] Practical sense goes far beyond seeing the world a certain way. Practical sense, being a communal viewpoint, calls us to act in the world.[103] As Smith describes it, "It's not just knowledge *so that* I can act; it is to know *by* acting."[104] It is knowing how to act without knowing. It is action without concepts.[105] Smith suggests that it is "not just being-in-the-world but *doing-in-the-world*."[106] This action does not follow an internal logic that we can analyze or measure. Instead, both understanding and doing comes from

---

Imagining the Kingdom, 93 (emphasis original).

99. The habitus, as Bourdieu describes it, reminds instead of immediately transforming. The habitus looks at the long term implications of action. He states, "The *habitus* is the principle of a selective perception of the indices tending to confirm and reinforce it rather than transform it, a matrix generating responses adapted in advance to all objective conditions identical to or homologous with the (past) conditions of its production; it adjusts itself to a probable future which it anticipates and helps to bring about because it reads it directly in the present of the presumed world, the only one it can ever know." Bourdieu, *Logic of Practice*, 64.

100. Bourdieu describes this relationship between knowledge and the body. He explains, "The body believes in what it plays at: it weeps if it mimes grief. It does not represent what it performs, it does not memorize the past, it enacts the past, bringing it back to life." Bourdieu, *Logic of Practice*, 73.

101. "Our bodies are students even when we don't realize it, and because we are so fundamentally oriented by this *habitus*, this incarnate education ends up being the more powerful." Smith, *Imagining the Kingdom*, 97.

102. Bourdieu, *Logic of Practice*, 69.

103. "To have acquired a practical sense is to have absorbed communally shared plausibility structures that constitute the world in certain ways—not just 'seeing' the world from a certain perspective but intending the world as an environment that call for certain responses and invites us to certain kinds of projects." Smith, *Imagining Kingdom*, 89.

104. Smith, *Imagining the Kingdom*, 89 (emphasis original).

105. Smith explains that "practical sense is a mode of understanding and orientation that operates without concepts." Smith, *Imagining the Kingdom*, 89.

106. Smith, *Imagining the Kingdom*, 90 (emphasis original).

acting.[107] Foot washing, like other ritual actions, defies logic. It is a logic of *doing*.[108]

When OFWBs practice foot washing, it is this logic of doing. OFWBs are not so much concerned about the concepts. For many, because Jesus said to do it means it should be done. Doing it is following Jesus and is living by doing. This logic, Smith contends, "Is inherently pragmatic, not in the sense of being cynically instrumentalizing, but in the sense of being primarily concerned with action."[109] OFWBs are not interested in speculating about foot washing. Their thinking connects to their doing.[110] To separate foot washing from its practice is difficult for them to conceive.[111] Foot washing is their identity.[112] It is part of their life and experience.[113] How foot washing works, while interesting, is less important. For OFWBs, foot washing is about what it does rather than how it works.[114]

107. Bourdieu suggests that this logic "can only be grasped in action." Bourdieu, *Logic of Practice*, 92.

108. Ritual action has a logic that challenges typical norms. Smith states, "Ritual logic defies conceptualization in a particularly intense way, almost to the extent that rites seem 'designed' to point up the limits of conceptual analysis and articulation. They are not 'expressing' what can be known by other means; rites affect what they do." Smith, *Imagining the Kingdom*, 91.

109. Smith, *Imagining the Kingdom*, 89–90.

110. For example, Bourdieu writes, "Rites take place because, and only because, they find their *raison d'être* in the conditions of existence and the dispositions of agents who cannot afford the luxury of logical speculation, mystical effusions or metaphysical *Angst*." Bourdieu, *Logic of Practice* 96.

111. A pastor puts it this way, "I have tried to emphasize in my churches for the people that don't know it, it's really not necessarily washing the feet for cleansing. That's what we practice now in person, but I think we practice it for the purpose of teaching us what it means [to be a] fellow Christian. You're their servant, you are to serve with them." Interview with OFWB pastor (I), February 2, 2015.

112. "I think it should be part of our identity as the Christian community. But particularly as OFWB I do see as part of our identity, a cherished part of our identity." Interview with OFWB pastor (C), February 4, 2015.

113. Describing his identity, a pastor observes, "I don't know if I [was] a Christian in another church, another tradition that did not practice washing of the saints' feet that I would actually be as communally minded and service minded, and socially minded as I am. In our articles of faith and our symbols for our denomination actually has the basin and the towel on it. . . . For me that speaks volumes of what the Christian experience is supposed to be. We take up our cross like we're supposed to and go into the world to serve. It's in serving others that we serve Christ. To me my whole theology is shaped by OFWB doctrine with what is washing of the saints feet is supposed. I can't really tell you how it changed my theology. I guess maybe it's actually formed, it's shaped, formed, whatever word you want to use." Interview with OFWB pastor (G), February 6, 2015.

114. "By cutting practices off from their real conditions of existence, in order to credit them with alien intentions, out of a false generosity conducive to stylistic effects,

Thinking and speculating requires separating our own self. This is difficult when a practice has always been a part of your life. It was almost impossible for OFWBs to think of their lives without foot washing.[115] Foot washing has always been there. How can you conceive of your life using a perspective other than your own? Their perspective comes from the body. OFWBs believe through the body.[116] Foot washing embodies that reality.

Foot washing reminds us that there is no escape from the body.[117] Formation does not end, but rather begins with the body. The body is the lens through which we see the world. We learn through acting, touching, motion, and repetition. Learning does not begin with propositions but by *doing*.[118] By living into the practice, we being to understand what practice means. Foot washing keeps OFWBs connected to the body. The body is not a thing to ignore or abandon. Instead, OFWBs come to embrace the body of others, and through that body, their own. By crossing that boundary of intimacy, OFWBs are effectively saying that spirituality is a bodily experience. That is, doing the will of Christ is enacting that will physically. Loving, serving, and forgiveness happen through the body. For OFWBs, foot washing demonstrates that we cannot do these concepts in abstract. This is not propositional knowledge. It is bodily knowledge.

Being-with and habitus work together to shape individuals into community. Both influence and modify the interactions between people. Being-with brings together individuals, moving being-singular to

---

the exaltation of lost wisdom dispossesses them of everything that constitutes their reason and their *raison d'etre*, and locks them in the eternal essence of a 'mentality.'" Bourdieu, *Logic of Practice*, 96.

115. For most, the experience of foot washing is not instantly transformative. Rather it is a gradual change that adds to your Christian experience. OFWB pastors and members describe foot washing's effects as gradual and subtle. For many, it is hard to describe how foot washing has changed their Christian experience. A pastor shares, "I don't know because it's always been a part of my life. So it's not like I've ever known the Christian walk without foot washing." Interview with OFWB pastor (F), March 5, 2015.

116. Smith puts it this way, "Ritual is the way we (learn to) believe with our bodies." Smith, *Imagining the Kingdom*, 92.

117. Drawing from Wittgenstein, Fergus Kerr states, "What constitutes us as human beings is the regular and patterned reactions that we have to one another. It is in our dealings with each other—in how we *act*—that human life is founded. . . . Community is built into human action from the beginning." Kerr, *Theology after Wittgenstein*, 65.

118. D.Z. Phillips suggests that "the child does not believe in the existence of chairs and tables because it has been taught that material objects exist. It is taught to sit on a chair or at a table, and that, one might say, is what shows one's belief in the existence of material objects. A child comes to know people in its dealings with them—its mother, father, brothers, sisters, friends, the butcher, the milkman, the grocer. . . . The belief is not the presupposition of its actions, but shows itself, has its sense, in those actions." Phillips, *Faith After Foundationalism*, 41.

being-singular-plural. It demonstrates that existence is connection. Existence is shared existence, and habitus lives in this shared existence. Thus, being-with is also acting-with. Action is shared action and therefore it influences behavior within communities. This shared action creates long lasting effects of being-with, and being-with builds the *habitus* thereby creating a new way of being, *being-community*. Being-community is the long-term result of being-with and habitus working together.

Through foot washing, OFWBs live as being-with and act in a *habitus*. They are connecting and living that connection with one another. Their experience of foot washing is complete and total. When washing feet, OFWBs are connecting the present and the future. Thus, being-with is forever. Sharing existence means living and acting in both the present and future. Foot washing symbolizes that eternal connection.[119] Through foot washing, OFWBs give a resounding *yes* to each other. They give each other the *yes* of acceptance, the *yes* of affirmation, and the *yes* of existence. OFWBs accept one another, which is the message that each person matters and is important. Through affirmation, they build and strengthen one another. OFWBs accept and affirm every existence as important and equal.[120] They do this through foot washing. Foot washing is both a being-with and habitus. Being-with is a commitment to each other, while habitus is the living out of that commitment.

BODY AND SPACE

Foot washing also produces social space. Being-with and habitus work together to produce a space of relationship.[121] Through physical gesture, a

119. Foot washing makes that connection between one another and Christ more real. A layperson explains, "I would say that symbolically [foot washing] is a cleansing. Spiritual cleansing, cleansing our hearts and minds and consciences. Which is liberating knowing that through Christ's example we can, it makes it more real, makes it more tangible for us." Interview with OFWB member (A), March 3, 2015.

120. A pastor explains, "Yeah, I think it changes my outlook on servant leadership because it reminds me that just because I'm in a leadership position within a congregation, that doesn't mean that I'm any better than anyone else and that we're all on an equal playing field in God's eyes. Just because I may be in the full time ministry doesn't mean that I'm going to receive special rewards at the end of time or anything. That we're all equal and that it's not, my role is not to be a dictator it's not to sit around and tell everyone else what to do while everyone else is doing the work. My role is to minister along with the people." Interview with OFWB pastor (F), March 5, 2015.

121. According to Lefebvre, "Humans as social beings are said to produce their own life, their own consciousness, their own world. There is nothing in history or in society, which does not have to be achieved and produced." Lefebvre, *Production of Space*, 68.

body of relations is created among OFWBs.[122] Physical action, continually re-enacted and re-presented, produces a way of being that is physically present. Relationship acquires physical form.[123] Foot washing brings relationship into the physical plane, whereby they can touch and see relationship. Relationship becomes more than emotion. It becomes matter, and all of this physical activity is collective and purpose driven. Therefore, these collective physical actions are moving toward a specific goal.[124] Relationship and action work together in order to achieve the same purpose. In the case of foot washing, this is to develop a Christ-like community. That is a community built upon humility, service, forgiveness, and love. Relationship and action, both singular and corporate, work together toward achieving this goal.

This working together, or bridging, is neither intentional nor planned. Production does not imply creation. Action and relationship are not creating but are a point of origin.[125] Production is an origin, and what is happening within those actions and relationships is immensely important. They are neither creating nor pointing to something outside themselves. Instead, it brings to light an experience that was always present between them. Between relationship and action, both singular and plural, is what Henri Lefebvre calls *space*.

Space is not a thing. Space is social. This social space is interrelationship and connection. In space lives the old and new, the fresh and expected, and the allowed and prohibited.[126] Social space is the outcome of action and

122. This pastor explains, "I think for me the individuals, [in the past] I've had the opportunity to share in that practice, it does deepen one's relationship. As a pastor, I think it would be safe to say that for me; overall, I was closer to the men with whom I participated in foot washing as opposed to those who didn't practice it or didn't attend those services. Not that there weren't friendships there, I think it made a difference in the connections that I had with members of the congregation." Interview with OFWB pastor (J), February 26, 2015.

123. "Relations based on an order to be followed—that is to say, on simultaneity and synchronicity—are thus set up, by means of intellectual activity, between the component elements of the action undertaken on the physical plane." Lefebvre, *Production of Space*, 71.

124. Lefebvre explains that "form is inseparable from orientation towards a goal—and thus also from functionality (the end and meaning of the action, the energy utilized for the satisfaction of a 'need') and form the structure set in motion (know-how, skills, gestures and co-operation in work, etc.)." Lefebvre, *Production of Space*, 71.

125. Space's rationality, according to Lefebvre, "Is not the outcome of a quality or property of human action in general, or human labour as such, of 'man', or of social organization. On the contrary, it is itself the origin and source—not distantly but immediately, or rather inherently—of the rationality of activity." Lefebvre, *Production of Space*, 71–72.

126. "(Social) space is not a thing among other things, nor a product among other products: rather it subsumes things produced, and encompasses their interrelationships

relationship. This outcome suggests what can happen, what should happen, and what should not happen. In this, it is similar to the habitus. However, social space suggests another level of depth, one of relation, action, and information.

This space is a network of relationships.[127] Lefebvre states that social space "is not a thing but rather a set of relations between things."[128] Space is not something we can point to and find. It appears through a network of relationship and interaction. Therefore, social space is a social experience comprised of individuals and the social exchanges that occur between them. Social space is the lived expression of exchange between the individuals who both live in and comprise it.[129] Accumulated actions and behaviors by a community or group produce social space. As a result, space does not exist without the relations that exist between persons. These relationships form a network that manifest social space. Its appearance in relationships points to its complexity and *both/and* nature.[130] It is both natural and cultural. Social space is already there, but it needs cultivation to produce fruit.

OFWBs produce social space through foot washing. Through their relationships, a way of being emerges. It is their lived expression of humility, service, forgiveness, and love.[131] This social space is something they produce and live out. Accumulated layers of acting and behavior form in their bonds

---

in their coexistence and simultaneity—their (relative) order and/or (relative) disorder. . . . Itself the outcome of past actions, social space is what permits fresh actions to occur, while suggesting others and prohibiting yet others." Lefebvre, *Production of Space*, 73.

127. Lefebvre explains that this social space "contains a great diversity of objects, both natural and social, including the networks and pathways which facilitate the exchange of material things and information. Such 'objects' are thus not only things but also relations." Lefebvre, *Production of Space*, 77.

128. Lefebvre, *Production of Space*, 83.

129. Society is situated in social spaces according to Lefebvre. He writes that "the space of society, of social life . . . all 'subjects' are situated in a space in which they must either recognize themselves or lose themselves, a space which they may enjoy and modify." Lefebvre, *Production of Space*, 35.

130. There is nothing simple about relationship. For example, Lefebvre writes, "Is that space natural or cultural? Is it immediate or mediated—and, if the latter, mediated by whom and to what purpose? Is it a given or is it artificial? The answer to such questions must be: 'Both.' The answer is ambiguous because the questions are too simple: between 'nature' and 'culture', as between work and product, complex relationships (mediations) already obtain." Lefebvre, *Production of Space*, 83–84.

131. It demonstrates the OFWB character. A pastor tells how "[foot washing] is indicative of those who don't mind serving. I think we see that. We have an outreach center. We do a lot of service in our community every day. We are open every day to do that. To feed people and that sort of thing. We have a lot of people involved. . . . It works for us. I hope it's an indicator." Interview with OFWB pastor (A), April 7, 2015.

they make with each other. Space takes on a physical and tangible expression, not as something identifiable, but something lived. This space is not their own creation.[132] They are not the producers of humility and love. Such things do not belong to them. Instead, OFWBs work as the producers and caretakers of these realities. In foot washing, OFWB relationships cultivate things such as love and forgiveness by giving them a space to grow. It is a space to grow closer to Jesus, the first to establish such a space. Therefore, when OFWBs live in this space of foot washing, they are living the same space of their parents and grandparents. It is the space of their forefathers and foremothers. Ultimately, and most importantly, it is the space of Jesus.

Foot washing provides an opportunity for the future growth and development of humility, love, and service. It makes sure that future generations experience these things. Social space is therefore dynamic. Dynamic in that people are the means of production. It is not a tool they use and discard. Lefebvre explains, "Though a product to be used, to be consumed, it is also a means of production. . . . Production, produced as such cannot be separated either from the productive forces."[133] The means of its production are just as important as the product.[134] OFWBs do not practice foot washing to receive. They expect to give rather than receive. The product is natural outcome of giving. The production of humility requires people willing to give. The results of foot washing can be very meaningful but are not guaranteed. Foot washing depends on actions, attitudes, and behaviors of people. The potential for humility, love, and forgiveness may be present, but these are unable to arrive without human mediation.

Thus, social space becomes the means of production. In turn, the means of production becomes bound to what it produces.[135] The outcomes of foot washing, the social space it produces, become the means for its practice. Humility is not just a result of what happens when OFWBs wash feet. It enables the process. OFWBs stress that washing feet requires a humble,

---

132. "Space is never produced in the sense that a kilogram of sugar or a yard of cloth is produced. Nor is it an aggregate of the places or locations of such products as sugar, wheat or cloth. . . . It would be more accurate to say that it is at once a precondition and a result of social superstructures." Lefebvre, *Production of Space*, 83.

133. Lefebvre, *Production of Space*, 85.

134. "Thus this means of production, produced as such, cannot be separated either from the productive forces, including technology and knowledge, or from the social division of labour which shapes it, or from the state and the superstructures of society." Lefebvre, *Production of Space*, 85.

135. "As it develops, then, the concept of social space becomes broader. It infiltrates, even invades the concept of production, becoming part—perhaps the essential part—of its content." Lefebvre, *Production of Space*, 85.

servant attitude. We cannot expect to experience humility, forgiveness, or love without first experiencing those from others.

The Movement of Space

Social space takes place in networks of living relationships, and these relationships form an infinite number of spaces. Social space exists alongside other social spaces.[136] These social spaces continually connect and interpenetrate one another.[137] These can include for example, small communities, groups, and churches. Movements, big and small, continually collide with one another. As social spaces, we cannot separate these movements from their larger context. Like small ripples in a large pond, these spaces penetrate, affect, and adjust to one another.[138] Spaces, no matter how small, are constantly affecting and penetrating. Social spaces, Lefebvre explains, "may be intercalated, combined, superimposed—they may even sometimes collide."[139] Social space is complex and dynamic. Each space is constantly pushing and pulling against other spaces. Social space does not exist as fixed points. It is not clear where one space ends and another begins.[140]

Foot washing creates a social space, but not in isolation. Each participant brings his or her own social space. The church exists as one of many social spaces within the community, and as OFWBs wash feet, these social spaces are interacting and colliding. Nothing requires OFWBs to leave behind their identity. Instead, OFWBs bring their whole selves, both the good and the bad, into foot washing. In addition, OFWBs bring their everyday life and experience. For example, men talk about sports, crops, work, or other mundane topics. All these things form a unique blend of spaces. Foot washing is among these things, all of which are discussed in the doing. The

---

136. Social space does not exist in isolation. Instead, we are confronted by several spaces. All individuals, Lefebvre states, "Are confronted not by one social space but by many—indeed, by an unlimited multiplicity or uncountable set of social spaces which we refer to generically as 'social space.'" Lefebvre, *Production of Space*, 86.

137. Lefebvre writes, "*Social spaces interpenetrate one another and/or superimpose themselves upon one another.*" Lefebvre, *Production of Space*, 86 (emphasis original).

138. Drawing from hydrodynamics, Lefebvre proposes, "A much more fruitful analogy, it seems to me, may be found in hydrodynamics, where the principle of the superimposition of small movements teaches us the importance of the roles played by scale, dimension and rhythm. Great movements, vast rhythms, immense waves—these all collide and 'interfere' with one another; lesser movements, on the other hand interpenetrate." Lefebvre, *Production of Space*, 87.

139. Lefebvre, Lefebvre, *Production of Space*, 88.

140. "They are not things, which have mutually limiting boundaries and which collide because of their contours or as a result of inertia." Lefebvre, *Production of Space*, 87.

experience accepts and incorporates these other spaces. Foot washing inter-penetrates these other spaces. Foot washing enters into daily life and experience. It is not something foreign but engages and enhances what it means to be Christian. Once assimilated, the lessons of foot washing become natural.

Social space is not an empty container waiting to be filled with meaning. The space is already *full.* Lefebvre writes that "space is neither a mere 'frame', after the fashion of the frame of a painting, nor a form or container of a virtually neutral kind, designed simply to receive whatever is poured into it. Space is social morphology."[141] It is a lived experience. There is no space to fill because it is already full.

Social space is an encounter. It is a dynamic movement of and the things that comprise it.[142] Social space is not an escape from life; it is an embrace of life. Foot washing, as social space, is an extension of everyday life. The strangeness of the action, washing feet, does not preclude its intense familiarity. When OFWBs wash feet, they extend everyday life into the moment and action of foot washing. Washing feet is a symbol[143] of their daily identity.[144] This space is grounded in their history.[145] This space reflects who they are every day and with everyone.[146] To understand OFWB social space is to encounter their practice. Social space connects to everyday practice.[147]

141. Lefebvre, *Production of Space*, 93–94.

142. Social space's form "is encounter, assembly, simultaneity . . . everything that there is in *space*, everything that is produced either by nature or by society, either through their co-operation or through their conflicts. Everything: living beings, things, objects, works, signs and symbols." Lefebvre, *Production of Space*, 101 (emphasis original).

143. "To say that something is symbolic is to enrich it with meaning not impoverished it. We have to use symbol when literal language is no longer adequate to describe what we're dealing with. So when I say that the elements of Holy Communion are symbolic of the presence of Christ they are reminders of the fact that Christ is present in, though, and around the elements. He is present as he promised to be. . . . I would say that in the same way we affirm the real presence of Christ as we gather about the table, I am willing to make the same affirmation about gathering about with the basin and the towel. We need to recognize the spirit of God who is particularly present." Interview with OFWB pastor (C), February 4, 2015.

144. A layperson explains this symbolic effect. She explains, "To actually kneel before someone and to wash their feet. To take on that attitude of heart that belongs to a servant and recognizing that is the attitude Jesus wants us to have. To be able to serve others. To minister to them, whatever their need is. That's just an example, a model for us." Interview with OFWB member (A), March 3, 2015.

145. "Every social space has a history, one invariably grounded in nature." Lefebvre, *Production of Space*, 110.

146. "Social space *per se* is at once *work* and *product*—a materialization of 'social being.'" Lefebvre, *Production of Space*, 102 (emphasis original).

147. "Nothing can be taken for granted in space, because what are involved are

Interpretation continually unfolds, and social space blends with daily life. It feels so natural, thus Lefebvre claims that, "Interpretation comes later, almost as an afterthought. . . . The 'reading' is thus merely a secondary and practically irrelevant upshot, a rather superfluous reward to the individual for blind, spontaneous and lived obedience."[148] For OFWBs, foot washing is just part of who they are. Separating this practice for purposes of interpretation seems superfluous.[149] The attitudes expressed during foot washing are the same as in everyday life. Foot washing becomes part of their everyday life and experience. They use this practice as a reminder of how to live every day. Foot washing exists to be lived, not analyzed. Space, Lefebvre suggests, "was produced before being read; nor was it produced in order to be read and grasped, but rather in order to be lived by people with bodies and lives in their own particular urban [or rural] context."[150] Space connects with everyday life. What happens in space is real, not theoretical.[151] OFWBs practice foot washing as a real action.

SPACE AND TACTICS

Ritual action works is a tactical action. Michel de Certeau writes, "A *tactic* is a calculated action determined by the absence of a proper locus."[152] Tactical action is subversive, meaning that it must work in the context it finds itself. These actions have no control over their wider environment. Tactics lives in the space of the other. As such, it maneuvers in an imposed context.[153] Certeau describes tactics as "an art of the weak."[154]

---

real or possible acts and not mental states or more or less well-told stories." Lefebvre, *Production of Space*, 144.

148. Lefebvre, *Production of Space*, 143.

149. For many, it is hard to describe how foot washing has added to their Christian experience. A pastor states, "I don't know because it's always been a part of my life. So, it's not like I've ever known the Christian walk without foot washing." Interview with OFWB pastor (F), March 5, 2015.

150. Lefebvre, *Production of Space*, 143.

151. "Nothing can be taken for granted in space, because what are involved are real or possible acts, and not mental states or more or less well-told stories. In produced space, acts reproduce 'meanings' even if no 'one' gives an account of them." Lefebvre, *Production of Space*, 144.

152. Certeau, *Practice of Everyday Life*, 37 (emphasis original).

153. For this reason, Certeau notes that, "The space of a tactic is the space of the other. Thus it must play on and with a terrain imposed on it and organized by the law of a foreign power." Certeau, *Practice of Everyday Life*, 37.

154. Certeau, *Practice of Everyday Life*, 37.

Foot washing is tactical action, a weak action, and an unusual action.[155] It exists on the fringes of normal action. Its unusual nature does not fit into any established context. Foot washing must be subtle. Unlike baptism or communion, it is practiced subtly in small and intimate contexts, typically in the evening toward the end of service. Foot washing does not *call* to others. It is a gentle *nudging* of the heart. Its effects are going to be gentle and subtle, and OFWBs understand that washing feet does not fit in the contemporary context. OFWBs quietly practice foot washing with the hope that their actions will speak louder than words. Foot washing is a weak action. It does not enjoy the privilege of power. As an everyday practice, OFWBs live and act foot washing as a countercultural model. Foot washing represents their message to the surrounding culture and environment.[156]

Foot Washing and Walking

As a tactical action, OFWBs live this message of foot washing through walking. They write this message by walking it each day.[157] OFWBs walk the message of washing feet.[158] It is how foot washing comes to life. Foot washing represents their way of proceeding.[159] It subtly suggests this connection between walking and living the message. Feet are for walking, and OFWBs prepare for walking by washing feet. Foot washing gives the message, which is then lived in everyday life.[160] It prepares each individual to walk in his or

155. Explaining its unusual nature, a pastor explains, "The stigma is I'm not going to wash somebody's feet. It's nasty. Then when you explain it and you read the scripture and you see it done it means a lot more than just somebody getting dirt off your feet. It means humility and obedience and those things. That makes it special." Interview with OFWB pastor (H), February 3, 2015.

156. Describing everyday tactical action, Certeau writes, "Dwelling, moving about, speaking, reading, shopping, and cooking are activities that seem to correspond to the characteristics of tactical ruses and surprises: clever tricks of the 'weak' within the order established by the 'strong,' an art of putting one over on the adversary on his [or her] own turf." Certeau, *Practice of Everyday Life*, 40.

157. Walking creates a system or way of acting. Like the speech act, walking is conveys a message. According to Certeau, "The act of walking is to the urban system what this speech act is to language or to the statements uttered." Certeau, *Practice of Everyday Life*, 97.

158. "They walk . . . whose bodies follow the thicks and thins of an urban 'text' they write without being able to read it. These practitioners make use of spaces that cannot be seen." Certeau, *Practice of Everyday Life*, 93.

159. "These practices of space refer to a specific form of *operations* ('ways of operating')." Certeau, *Practice of Everyday Life*, 93.

160. Explaining how foot washing carries into everyday life a pastor explains, "I think it sets an example of loving your fellow Christian and reaching out to them in

her own context. OFWBs take this experience and demonstrate humility, service, and love. With washed feet, OFWBs are expected to walk a walk of humility, service, forgiveness, and love. Pastors as well as lay people, are all prepared to walk. OFWBs are ready to walk the walk of Jesus.[161]

Walking acts out possibilities. Walking is, following Certeau, "a space of enunciation."[162] Through walking, we speak. Walking is a way of creating, organizing, and enacting new actions or ways of behavior.[163] Thus, walking establishes identity. Walking chooses which possibilities to actualize or create. We choose what actions are important, but walking is also an act of transformation. Walkers choose which possibilities to actualize. A city walker may opt to take the side street, plot a new course, discover a new short cut, or stop to shop. The walker is writing a new story each time he or she goes to work, searches for something to eat, or visits a friend. Walking is a way of living out the story of the day. It is a way of transforming our own space.[164]

OFWBs wash, walk, and transform their spaces. Pastors transform what it means to be a leader through servant leadership, and laypeople transform what it means to live as church through service. Foot washing transforms through improvisation. OFWB's have no set pattern. They wash feet, and what follows simply happens. OFWBs, whether they are laughing,

---

good times, but especially in bad times. When they're going through difficult times. We can reach out to them a little ways. In fact, I think it was [name], he preached a sermon one night at the ministers' conference on washing feet without using water. That's what he was talking about. Letting the imagery of washing the saints' feet play out in everyday life. As you love and respect your fellow man." Interview with OFWB pastor (E), March 27, 2015.

161. Foot washing prepares OFWBs to walk the walk of Jesus. A pastor says, "Because when he was in the upper room . . . that is that process that takes place and that's the real purpose in our having the ordinances of our church so people can understand why you're doing this and what the love of Christ has done. Why he choose to give himself to us that he was willing to humble himself and wash his disciples feet. And he set that example for us to do." Interview with OFWB pastor (B), March 26, 2015.

162. Certeau, *Practice of Everyday Life*, 98.

163. "In that way, he [or she] makes them exist as well as emerge. But he also moves them about and he invents others, since the crossing, drifting away, or improvisation of walking privilege, transform or abandon spatial elements." Certeau, *Practice of Everyday Life*, 98.

164. "In the same, the walker transforms each spatial signifier into something else. And if on the one hand he [or she] actualizes only a few of the possibilities fixed by the constructed order (he [or she] goes only here and not there), on the other he [or she] increases the number of possibilities (for example, by creating shortcuts and detours) and prohibitions. . . . He [or she] thus makes a selection. 'The user of a city picks out certain fragments of the statement in order to actualize them in secret." Certeau, *Practice of Everyday Life*, 98.

crying, singing, or sitting in silence, are transforming one another. Their walking speaks, and through foot washing, the OFWB trajectory steps through everyday life.[165] Foot washing, at least for OFWBs, is about how you walk. It is about how you live. Walking is meant to be surprising.[166] Like life, walking is unpredictable. Foot washing demonstrates this unpredictability. We never know what will happen.

Because foot washing walks, it walks from space to space. To walk is to be on the move. Walking, Certeau writes, "is the indefinite process of being absent and in search of a proper . . . an immense social experience of lacking a place."[167] In the country or city, people walk along back and forth in a way that seems endless. People need to be somewhere they are not. People are always on the go, unsatisfied with where they currently are. There is always somewhere to go. Walking, like life, is always on the go. In the same way, foot washing is on the go. It does not have a space of its own. Therefore, when OFWBs wash feet, it occurs in spaces designated for other functions. Practitioners make their own space for washing feet. Sunday school rooms, fellowship halls, and choir rooms represent the transitory nature of foot washing. It occupies spaces belonging to others.[168] Foot washing prepares us for walking. It reflects a life on the go, where meaning is meant to be lived. A space for foot washing would suggest that it is becoming static. Instead, foot washing acts in the walking. For OFWBs, walking is where foot washing comes to life.

Enacted Stories

The stories of foot washing demonstrate life on the go. Their stories dwell in the uncelebrated moments of daily life.[169] These are the stories of celebrat-

165. "Walking affirms, suspects, tries out, transgresses, respects, etc., the trajectories it 'speaks.' All the modalities sing a part in this chorus, changing from step to step, stepping in through proportions, sequences, and intensities which vary according to the time, the path taken and the walker." Certeau, *Practice of Everyday Life*, 99.

166. Walking "is like a peddler, carrying something surprising, transverse or attractive compared with the usual choice." Certeau, *Practice of Everyday Life*, 101.

167. Certeau, *Practice of Everyday Life*, 103.

168. Walking lives in "a universe of rented spaces haunted by a nowhere or by dreamed of paces." Certeau, *Practice of Everyday Life*, 103.

169. It is the stories that connect practitioners with the meanings of foot washing. Stories make it meaningful. Without stories the practice would be empty. The stories bring us back to the event, and the present is filled with the past. Explaining how stories bring meaning, a layperson shares, "I did go to one [service] where I did go back that night and they had brought coolers of warm water into each of the rooms to use for washing feet. There's nothing wrong with that but I just thought, I remembered how I

ing with a potluck dinner. These are the stories of men working together to build handicap ramps for members in the community.[170] Foot washing lives wherever OFWBs serve. For OFWBs, their actions relate to foot washing. It is their spatial story. Foot washing connects their story with everyday life.[171] People carry on these stories through practice.[172] Foot washing works in the lives of practicing OFWBs. Foot washing is a life long journey.[173] We do not think about walking. Once learned, walking comes naturally, and we create stories by walking. The narrative tapestry of everyday life is comprised of where we go, how we walk, who we walk with, and so on.[174]

---

felt as young person when that cold water hit my feet. I remember the chills that that cold water did to me. I remember almost like that when the cold water when washing feet, as a child. I remember that. Then I thought, I guess when I felt that warm water, there's nothing wrong with that, but it was like, I don't know how to explain it. It was almost like we had . . . I can't explain it." Interview with OFWB member (B), March 31, 2015.

170. A pastor describes the wider impact foot washing has on the community. He recalls, "I had a guy who came from a Methodist church . . . he said 'I think [foot washing] is something that is supposed to teach me humility. If that's the case, it's not coming to that because [before becoming OFWB] I would never be caught touching someone else's foot.' He actually saw a connection between washing the saints' feet and the wider community, service to the wider community. He's been one of our best deacons, one of our best Sunday school teachers. His helped us to lead projects in our community. Like I said, replacing roofs for widows and building accessibility ramps for handicap. All kinds of service in the wider community. A lot of times it's not necessarily Christians, a lot times it's not people a part of our church. Sometimes it's not Christians at all, sometimes it's someone from another church down the road. It doesn't matter who it is. If they're in need we try to help. I think that kind of affected his life to some degree, maybe not completely, but some degree he saw the connection." Interview with OFWB pastor (G), February 6, 2015.

171. "To go to work or come home, one takes a 'metaphor'—a bus or a train. Stories could also take this noble name: everyday, they traverse and organize places; they select and link them together; they make sentences and itineraries out of them. They are spatial trajectories." Certeau, *Practice of Everyday Life*, 115.

172. "Every story is a travel story—a spatial practice. For this reason spatial practices concern everyday tactics, are part of them, from the alphabet of spatial indication." Certeau, *Practice of Everyday Life*, 116.

173. Speaking of the journey, a layperson reflects, "I think [foot washing is] a process of getting me to where I am today. It's taken all those people, it's taken all of that learning of service. It [has] taken learning more about who Jesus is and what he did and how he taught the disciples. There are so many things that I look at differently, so much differently. It's all built. I'm not the same person I was then. I think that the washing of the saints' feet is something that's very special in our denomination. Other people talk about it. I get teased sometimes. I can remember that in college years and young years about being teased about washing feet. I have never been ashamed of it. I just always felt it had such a special part in our lives and within our denomination." Interview with OFWB member (B), March 31, 2015.

174. Certeau makes it clear that "narrated adventures, simultaneously producing

OFWBs transform space as they live foot washing. They actualize their stories into physical encounters.[175] Thus, the story attaches itself to the bodies of OFWBs. OFWBs become the story; therefore, their story goes with them wherever they go.[176] The OFWB story of foot washing lives in its participants, and thus finds validity.[177] They are living signs of foot washing's meanings.[178] Foot washing prepares OFWBs to reflect those characteristics of humility, love, service, and forgiveness. More importantly, for OFWBs, they live the story of Jesus.[179] His story becomes their story.[180]

THE OFWB STORY CONTINUES

From being-with to everyday life, the OFWB story of washing feet continues through its participants. Foot washing establishes relationship (being-with), it prescribes action (habitus), contains networks of relationship (social space), and finally lives in the everyday lives of participants (tactical action). Foot washing is not only something that OFWBs do. Foot washing is who they are. It is a lived practice. As a result, interpretation plays a secondary role. The goal cannot be to explain why or how OFWBs practice washing

geographies of actions and drifting into the commonplaces of an order, do not merely constitute a 'supplement' to pedestrian enunciations and rhetorics. . . . In reality, they organize walks. They make the journey, before or during the time the feet perform it." Certeau, *Practice of Everyday Life*, 116.

175. "Space is a practiced place." Certeau, *Practice of Everyday Life*, 117.

176. "Normative discourse 'operates' only if it has already become a story, a text articulated on something real and speaking in its name, i.e. a law made into a story and historicized . . . recounted by bodies." Certeau, *Practice of Everyday Life*, 149.

177. "Every social orthodoxy makes use of instruments to give itself the form of a story and to produce the credibility attached to a discourse articulated by bodies." Certeau, *Practice of Everyday Life*, 149.

178. The story, "leads living beings to become signs, to find in a discourse the means of transforming themselves into a unit of meaning, into an identity." Certeau, *Practice of Everyday Life*, 149.

179. A pastor describes how they strive to be like Jesus, "Here's what comes to our mind. Number one, that if you want to be like Jesus and follow his example like he asked us to, his promise was that we would be happy or blessed if we did, if you want to be like our Lord that would be one way to do that. Number two, if you want to show your love for others that's a perfect way to do so. When you're down on your knees at the foot of someone, and you're looking up at their eyes and they realize what you're doing. I think that says volumes about how much I love you and I love you with the love of Christ." Interview with OFWB pastor (E), March 27, 2015.

180. Their story connects to Jesus' story. A pastor explains, "When we wash feet I am reminded as I get down that this is where the Lord was, this is where he expects me to be." Interview with OFWB pastor (A), April 7, 2015.

feet. This cannot show why it is important to OFWBs, nor why they continue to do it. Doing, not interpretation, is the pathway toward understanding.

Chapter Five

Love and Community

ESTRANGED EXISTENCE

THEOLOGY DOES NOT SIGNAL the end of a process or method. It is the opportunity to further the conversation and keep it open.[1] And as the conversation with foot washing continues, the goal is not to interpret OFWB foot washing theologically. The goal is to listen and further the conversation. Theology prepares us for a conversation that overcomes estrangement and renews our hope for connection with one another.

Being lives in a state of estrangement. Existence does not automatically begin in co-existence. Our existence begins with an existence of the self. Separation is the universal fact of humanity.[2] Human beings know that they are separated from one another. Their separation is three-fold, Tillich writes that there is "separation among individual lives, separation of a man from himself, and separation of all men from the Ground of Being."[3] Estrangement thus affects existence on multiple levels. It is not something we can avoid. We live in estrangement for all of our lives. We enter alone and leave this world in much the same way. Humanity shares a collective estrangement that carries on to subsequent generations.[4] Such separation is unavoidable. It lives at the core of our being.

1. Theology works through the multiple meanings of Christianity and human experience. It does so not to simplify things. Theology instead embraces and furthers this complicated mix of meanings to further the conversation. As David Tracy puts it, "contemporary Christian theology is best understood as philosophical reflection upon the meanings present in common human experience and the meanings present in the Christian tradition." Tracy, *Blessed Rage for Order*, 34.

2. Tillich, "You Are Accepted," 156.

3. Tillich, "You Are Accepted," 156.

4. Tillich writes, "Such separation is prepared in the mother's womb, and before

The difficultly of separation is the knowledge that we are separated. Existence, the knowledge of being, taunts us with this knowledge. The human life, Erich Fromm writes, is *"life being aware of itself."*[5] Life is strangely aware of other life. We are acutely aware of being alone and separated from all that we love and hold dear. This knowledge can create a prison of existence.[6] The knowledge of existence, of our own separation, traps us within the self. Existence becomes claustrophobic.

The feeling of separation can be worse than the state of separation. To know and feel separation is to suffer anxiety. It is the anxiety of being helpless before a world over which we have no control. Consequently, the world, our environment, appears as a hostile invader.[7] Separation makes the world a stranger. Thus, we shun the world in a desperate attempt to escape and gain some control. It is us alone against the world. And yet, this conflict only furthers our anxiety. The conflict reminds us of what we are missing. We feel a longing for the very connection we are fighting against.

Separation evokes a longing for connection. In separation, we feel a call toward unity and togetherness. Separation evokes within us a longing toward something perhaps undefined and unknown.[8] In this sense, separation is also a calling. The gulf between individuality and plurality calls to each of us. Estrangement refuses to remain silent. We *know* that we are estranged, and this knowledge reveals itself each day.[9] Every moment is a reminder of the shared estrangement that exists between individuals.

---

that time, in every preceding generation. It is manifest in the special actions of our conscious life. It reaches beyond our graves into all the succeeding generations." Tillich, "You Are Accepted," 157.

5. Fromm, *Art of Loving*, 8 (emphasis original).

6. "This awareness of himself as a separate entity, the awareness of his own short life span, of the fact that without his will he is born and against his will he will die before those whom he loves, or they before him, the awareness of his helplessness before the forces of nature and of society, all this makes separate, disunited existence an unbearable prison." Fromm, *Art of Loving*, 8.

7. "Being separate means being cut off, without any capacity to use my human powers. Hence to be separate means to be helpless, unable to grasp the world—things and people—actively; it means that the world can invade me without my ability to react." Fromm, *Art of Loving*, 8.

8. Tillich suggests that *"we* as men [and women] know that we are separated. We not only suffer with all other creatures because of the self-destructive consequences of our separation, but also know *why* we suffer. We know that we are estranged from something to which we really belong, and with which we *should* be united." Tillich, "You Are Accepted," 157 (emphasis original).

9. Separation "is not merely a natural event like a flash of sudden lightning, but that it is an experience in which we actively participate, in which our whole personality is involved." Tillich, "You Are Accepted," 157.

Estrangement lives at the core of existence. Existence, Tillich declares, "*Is separation!*"[10] It does that affect only a misfortunate few but us all.

The State of Sin

This state of estrangement, or separation, is the state of sin. According to Tillich, "To be in the state of sin is to be in the state of separation."[11] Rather than immoral acts, sin points to something fundamentally deeper about the human condition. The problem is not that human beings commit sins or immoral acts, but that the human condition exists in a state of sin, also known as estrangement. Sin is not a category that divides the good from the bad or sinners from the righteous.[12] Sin is separation.

The state of sin is life in isolation.[13] It is a voluntary isolation where each individual chooses being-singular over being-singular-plural. The individual lives for the self, thus ignoring the needs of others. It is not that the singular is against the plural. Others may matter, but it is each individual living for his or her own needs. In place of unity there is a collective individuality.[14] Bonhoeffer writes, "Whereas the primal relationship of [human] to [human] is a giving one, in the state of sin it is purely demanding."[15] In separation, existence takes away from existence. We place our will over and against the other.

All individuals are separated from one another. No one can, Tillich writes, "penetrate the hidden centre of another individual; nor can that individual pass beyond the shroud that covers our own being. Even the greatest love cannot break through the walls of the self."[16] The self remains alone even amid others, perhaps even more so. Amid many people we are reminded of

---

10. Tillich, "You Are Accepted," 157 (emphasis original).

11. Tillich, "You Are Accepted," 156.

12. Tillich calls for a radical redefinition of sin. He asks, "Do we, still realize that sin does *not* mean an immoral act, that 'sin' should never be used in the plural, and that not our sins, but rather our *sin* is the great, all-pervading problem of our life? Do we still know that it is arrogant and erroneous to divide men [and women] by calling some 'sinners' and others 'righteous?'" Tillich, "You Are Accepted," 156 (emphasis in the original).

13. "Thus, the state of our whole life is estrangement from others and ourselves." Tillich, "You Are Accepted," 161.

14. "Every man [or woman] exists in a state of complete voluntary isolation; each lives his own life, instead of all living the same God-life." Bonhoeffer, *Sanctorum Communio*, 71.

15. Bonhoeffer, *Sanctorum Communio*, 71.

16. Tillich, "You Are Accepted," 158–59.

our loneliness. Thus, in the company of others we realize that we will never be able to see life through anyone else's eyes. Nor will we ever experience thoughts and feelings other than our own. People live as a stranger to one other.[17] And life lives in strangeness to life.[18] We all share in this strangeness. Consequently, this strangeness creates the illusion that it is the normal state of things, but the state of sin is a shared state of being alone. Separation is most felt in the collective separation from and with others.[19] Therefore we struggle to move our own perspectives outward, and we inevitably turns inward instead. Bonhoeffer writes, that "even in the awareness of the closest belonging together the ontic and ethical separateness of individual persons on account of sin can never cease. . . . There is no overleaping the limits of the I."[20] Strangeness persists still.

Estrangement makes life strange. Life bumps into life, and life retreats from life. Being-singular is not a unified existence. Rather, as Tillich maintains, "the depth of our separation lies in just the fact that we are not capable of a great and merciful divine love toward ourselves. On the contrary, in each of us there is an instinct of self-destruction, which is as strong as our instinct of self-preservation."[21] Singular existence is split existence. There is something within each of us that is uncomfortable with being-singular. There is the knowledge that we need others. We know that our own fulfill-ment is connected to the fulfillment of others. When trapped in existence, we become destructive to both ourselves and the other.[22] The personal life can only occur through encounter.[23] Without such an encounter, the split

17. "Feeling of our separation from the rest of life is most acute when we are surrounded by it in noise and talk. We realize then much more than in moments of solitude how strange we are to each other, how estranged life is from life." Tillich, "You Are Accepted," 158.

18. Tillich explains that the "strangeness of life to life" is evident in the way nations and groups of people treat one another. Strangeness is also found in human apathy. Human beings rarely show concern for issues and problems outside their immediate context. Tillich, "You Are Accepted," 159–60.

19. Bonhoeffer writes that "the qualitative nature of sin, that the misery caused by sin is infinitely great; this means that it must have not only an individual but also a supra-individual significance. . . . Thus the perception that *in sin* one is to the highest degree alone leads to the other perception that one's sin is to the widest extent shared." Bonhoeffer, *Sanctorum Communio*, 72.

20. Bonhoeffer, *Sanctorum Communio*, 80.

21. Tillich, "You Are Accepted," 160.

22. In estrangement there is a "tendency to abuse and to destroy others. Cruelty toward others is always also cruelty toward ourselves. Nothing is more obvious than the split in both our unconscious life and conscious personality." Tillich, "You Are Accepted," 160.

23. "Personal life emerges in the encounter of person with person and in no other

within the self and others only grows larger. Consequently, there is no full actualization of our personhood. We remain forever caught in the external and internal split of estrangement. Consequently, estrangement is also a split within our own aim in life. When split both internally and externally, life becomes a mystery to itself.[24] We become estranged from the depth of our existence. This estrangement leads to despair, the feeling "that there is no escape."[25] According to Tillich, when there are no escapes, life spirals into "feelings of meaningless, emptiness, doubt, and cynicism—all expressions of despair, of our separation from the roots and the meaning of our life. Sin in its most profound sense, sin, as despair, abounds amongst us."[26] Sin is selfish. It does not release its hold easily. Sin prefers that we remain in isolation and despair. It is content with separation. Thus, in separation sin increases its hold.[27] Sin convinces us that the separation is normal, that we do not need anyone else for fulfillment.[28] Estrangement makes us blind to the world outside ourselves. Being-singular becomes both the beginning and end of existence, and this self-imposed blindness only furthers our shame. It blinds us to the true source of our shame, and we are therefore damned twice. We are damned in estrangement and blind to that estrangement. The cure to that estrangement can only begin when we acknowledge it. Acknowledgement puts us on the path of love. It puts us on the path of reunion.[29]

---

way. If one can imagine a living being with the psychosomatic structure of man, completely outside any human community, such a being could not actualize its potential spirit." Tillich, *Systematic Theology, Volume 3*, 40.

24. For example, Tillich says that "our whole life is estrangement from others and ourselves, because we are estranged from the Ground of our being, because we are estranged from the origin and aim of our life. And we do not know where we have come from, or where we are going. We are separated from the mystery, the depth, and the greatness of our existence." "You Are Accepted," 161.

25. Tillich, "You Are Accepted," 161. Also see Sartre, *No Exit and Three Other Plays*.

26. Tillich, "You Are Accepted," 162.

27. "Sin demands to have a man [or woman] by himself [or herself]. It withdraws him [or her] from the community. The more isolated a person is the more destructive will be the power of sin over him [or her], and the more deeply he [or she] becomes involved in it, the more disastrous is his [or her] isolation. Sin wants to remain unknown. . . . It poisons the whole being of a person." Bonhoeffer, *Life Together*, 118.

28. Bonhoeffer writes that the "root of all sin is pride, *superbia*. I want to be my own law." Bonhoeffer, *Life Together*, 113.

29. "*The awareness of human separation, without reunion by love—is the source of shame. It is at the same time the source of guilt and anxiety.*" Fromm, *Art of Loving*, 9 (emphasis original).

LOVE

Love as Reunion

Existence is separation, but it does not have to remain that way. We know the feeling of separation, but we also know the longing toward unity. Being-singular is driven toward being-with and plurality. This drive toward the other is love. The action of life is animated by love.[30] And love "is the drive towards the unity of the separated."[31] Being-singular is an awareness of that which fulfills our existence. Like star-crossed lovers, being calls to being. This call is not toward the unknown, but rather toward what we once knew. Life may be strange, but it was not always so.[32] In strangeness we recognize the familiar. Life calls out to life because we know that we belong to the one other.[33] Estrangement cannot exist without the knowledge of unity. We know our estrangement because the memory of our unity has not been completely wiped away.[34] Like a still small voice, the memory reminds us that things were not always this way. We know that something is wrong even if it cannot be named. We struggle against this voice in order to forget it, but the memory will not fade away.[35]

Love is the reminder of the way things were. Love nags at our existence, pushing us to look outward instead of inward. It unites our self-centered self with another self-centered self. That is love brings together what is already

---

30. "Life is being in actuality and love is the moving power of life. In these two sentence the ontological nature of love is expressed." Tillich, *Love, Power, and Justice*, 25.

31. Tillich, *Love, Power, and Justice*, 25.

32. The ultimate tragedy of the Fall is not that Adam and Eve disobeyed God. The story of the Fall is tragic because Adam and Eve were separated from each other and God. They no longer enjoyed the unity they previously experienced. Original sin is not inherited and passed on through procreation. It is the state of being separated both externally and internally. Gen 3:1–24 (NRSV).

33. Tillich describes this phenomena as belongingness. He writes, "Unity embraces itself and non-being. It is impossible to unite that which is essentially separated. Without an ultimate belongingness no union of one thing with another can be conceived. The absolutely strange cannot enter into a communion. But the estranged is striving for reunion." Tillich, *Love, Power, and Justice*, 25.

34. "Estrangement presupposes original oneness." Tillich, *Love, Power, and Justice*, 25.

35. "We are separated from the mystery, the depth, and the greatness of our existence. We hear the voice of that depth; but our ears are closed. We feel that something radical, total, and unconditioned is demanded of us; but we rebel against it, try to escape its urgency, and will not accept its promise." Tillich, "You Are Accepted," 161.

complete.[36] Estrangement cannot exist without unity, and love cannot exist without separation. In love what was radically separated and self-centered comes together.[37] Though complete, being-singular desires reunion. We are driven by love. Therefore, the individual, "Strives to reunite himself [or herself] with that to which he [or she] belongs and from which he [or she] is separated."[38]

In love we strive to participate with the other. We are striving against the greatest barrier of all, the barrier between individuals. We strive to participate in the life of the other. It is a desire for closeness and intimacy. It is the hope that, with enough effort, we will be able to participate in the life of another. The ultimate desire of being is to know another being fully and completely. Love moves us toward this goal despite the knowledge that it is unattainable. In love we participate in the life of the other, but this participation is also separation.[39] We endure this separation because it is only through participation that a person becomes a person. Therefore, participation is the place of encounter.[40] In this place of encounter where we are affirmed as both singular and plural. Accordingly, we strive toward the other in a courageous act to be both one and in part.[41] The courage to be is the courage to encounter the other. Love is both the drive and the result. Separation and reunion is a cycle of love seeking love.

Love as Knowing

Love seeks to know the other. To fully know the other is to love the other.[42] Knowing and love go hand in hand. Love drives the reunion between the

36. Tillich explains, "Love reunites that which is self-centered and individual. The power of love is not something which is added to an otherwise finished process, but life has love in itself as one of its constitutive elements." Tillich, *Love, Power, and Justice*, 26.

37. In love, Tillich states, "Separation is overcome. But without the separation there is no love and no life. It is the superiority of the person-to-person relationship that it preserves the separation of the self-centered self, and nevertheless actualizes their reunion in love." Tillich, *Love, Power, and Justice*, 27.

38. Tillich, *Love, Power, and Justice*, 29.

39. Tillich writes that participation is "being a part of something from which one is, at the same time, separated. Literally participation means 'taking part.'" Tillich, *Courage to Be*, 88.

40. "Only in the continuous encounter with other persons does the person become and remain a person. The place of this encounter is community." Tillich, *Courage to Be*, 91.

41. The courage to be "is essentially always the courage to be as a part and the courage to be as oneself, in interdependence." Tillich, *Courage to Be*, 89–90.

42. Or as Tillich puts it, "Full knowledge presupposes full love." Tillich, "Knowledge

separated so that they may finally know one another and see face-to-face. As a result, the act of knowing is an act of love. Knowledge cannot exist without love, nor can love exist without knowledge. In love, the self penetrates the life of the other, and vice versa. In that act of penetration, we discover ourselves in the life of the other. We come to know ourselves by knowing the other.[43]

Love's knowledge goes beyond knowing *about* another person. We can know a person without actually *knowing* him or her. For example, we may know *about* a certain celebrity. We can know his or her likes or dislikes, political opinions, and habits. Yet we do not really *know* that individual. The same can be said of co-workers, acquaintances, and some friends. At what level does knowing *about* become *knowing*? Love penetrates that barrier between knowing *about* and *knowing*. Fromm makes the case that love "is the daring plunge into the experience of union."[44] Love holds nothing back. We will only *know* the other when we love the other. Love and knowledge are inseparable.

In love and knowledge, we can *see* into the life of another. We see the other as the other sees himself or herself. It is thus a face-to-face encounter into the life of another.[45] This love, Tillich describes, "Is a seeing love, a knowing love, a love that looks through into the depth of our hearts."[46] Separation is a longing for knowing the other, but it is also a longing to be known. The loneliness of the heart can only be satisfied when it is known. It is the voice of existence calling out, wishing and waiting for another voice to respond. We want to be heard, to be seen, and to be known. To be known is fundamentally important for our own being. Existence needs acknowledgement, and our existence cries out for love.[47]

In theory, separation is impossible to overcome. But love bridges that gap between the seemingly impossible and the possible. Love is a bond that bridges these opposites. Tillich writes, "Full knowledge does not admit a difference between itself and love, or between theory and practice.

Through Love," 114.

43. "In the act of loving, of giving myself, in the act of penetrating the other person, I find myself, I discover myself, I discover us both, I discover [humanity]." Fromm, *Act of Loving*, 31.

44. Fromm, *Act of Loving*, 31.

45. Therefore, "in love, the seeing face to face and the knowledge of the centre of the other I are implied." Tillich, "Knowledge Through Love," 114.

46. Tillich, "Knowledge Through Love," 114.

47. "The 'thou' demands by his [or her] very existence to be acknowledged as a 'thou' for an 'ego' and as an 'ego' for himself [or herself]. This is the claim which is implied in his being." Tillich, *Love, Power, and Justice*, 78.

Love overcomes the seeming opposition between theory and practice; it is knowing and doing at the same time."[48] It is *being* singular-plural and *doing* singular-plural. It is full knowledge, it is both a state and an action. Love is the overcoming of estrangement, but it is also the act of doing so.

LOVE, DESIRE, AND DEFEAT

Love is both the state and action of overcoming estrangement. As both a state and action, love is a coming to know the other. It does so at great cost and effort. Love is the greatest risk a human being can take. To love is to reach out with a daring passion for the other. Love sets aside what it knows for the sake of the unknown. It is this unknown that makes love such a risk for both us and the other. The participation and pull between the separated consists of risks and potential pitfalls. Nothing about love is easy. It is just as likely to fail as it is to succeed.

Love is blind, or so the saying goes. It is neither stable nor predictable. This is partly due to estrangement. Estrangement blinds us in its fog making it difficult to see beyond. However, *love is blind* is more than just estrangement. Love is an embrace of the unknown, unpredictable, and unexpected. Love *leaps* into the unknown of the other. Our own certainty can never account for the other's unknown. In love, we face the unknown fate of the other. We give ourselves up to the unknown chasm of love's fate. Zygmunt Bauman writes that "love means opening up to that fate, that most sublime of all human conditions, one in which fear blends with joy into an alloy that no longer allows its ingredients to separate."[49] Love charts a course toward the unknown, yet this journey is not for the self alone. In love, two or more share this unknown and uncharted journey. The self and the other sail toward one another on a mutual journey of discovery and exploration. Therefore, this journey into the unknown requires both humility and courage.[50] Humility begins the journey, but it takes courage to stay on it. Love is both the state of openness and the will or action to remain so.

Love takes courage because it is always on the brink of defeat, therefore it is forced to plunge ahead into the unknown depths of estrangement and isolation. Love, Bauman writes, "Leaves no fortified trenches behind

---

48. Tillich, "Knowledge Through Love," 115.

49. Bauman, *Liquid Love*, 7

50. "Without humility and courage, no love. Both are required, in huge and constantly replenished supplies, whenever one enters an unexplored and unmapped land, and when love happens between two or more human beings it ushers them into such a territory." Bauman, *Liquid Love*, 7.

to which it could retreat, running for shelter in case of trouble."[51] Love has nowhere to go but forward. It has no safe zone or space to escape in case things go wrong. It must bet everything, its very existence on the future. Love invests in the future rather than the past.[52]

The courage to love is also the courage against desire. Love and desire, while similar, have different goals. Desire seeks to consume the other. It sees the other as something there for its own pleasure.[53] Desire does not truly wish for connection. Its reach is one of consumerism and consumables. The other is something to be used and discarded once desire is fulfilled. Desire is drawn to the other's consumable nature but is equally repelled once done.[54] Thus, desire is the will of the *I*. It roams about searching for more to consume and yet is never satisfied. Desire eventually faces its own self-destruction. It eventually consumes itself when there is no one left. The path of desire is the path of the *I*. Eventually there is nowhere left to retreat to. It must consume itself, thus passing away into a black hole of nothingness. We enters the event horizon never to return.

Love is an escape from the black hole of the self. It seeks the other for the sake of the other. That is love looks at the other as something to care for.[55] Unlike desire, love looks to the other for its own existence. Love bonds the other to the itself in a symbiotic relationship. In love, the self and the other increase one another. Each existence, the self and the other, expand through love's embrace.[56] This expansion differentiates love from desire. Bauman describes love as "being-in-service."[57] Being-in-service means that love not only seeks the other, but love seeks to care for that other.

---

51. Bauman, *Liquid Love*, 8.

52. Bauman describes love as an investment into an uncertain future. He writes that love "will never gain confidence strong enough to disperse the clouds and stifle anxiety. Love is a mortgage loan drawn on an uncertain, and inscrutable, future." Bauman, *Liquid Love*, 8.

53. "Desire is an impulse to strip alterity of its otherness; thereby, to disempower." Bauman, *Liquid Love*, 9.

54. "Consumables attract; waste repels. After desire comes waste and disposal. It is, it seems, the squeezing of alienness out of alterity and the dumping of the desiccated carapace that congeal into the joy of satisfaction, bound to dissipate as soon as the job is done. Desire is the urge of destruction." Bauman, *Liquid Love*, 9.

55. Bauman explains that love is "the wish to care, and to preserve the object of the care." Bauman, *Liquid Love*, 9.

56 , "Love is about adding to the world—each addition being the living trace of the loving self; in love, the self is, bit by bit, transplanted onto the world. *The loving self expands through giving itself away to the loved object.*" Bauman, *Liquid Love*, 9 (emphasis original).

57. Bauman, *Liquid Love*, 10.

Desire seeks to consume, whereas love seeks to add. Desire is temporary, but love builds for eternity.[58]

Love needs to continually fight the urge to control and bind the other,[59] whereby love becomes a twisted version of itself where it controls the other. Love struggles against itself in an internal conflict between service and preservation. It struggles against the fear of estrangement and the separation of anxiety. We alone cannot overcome estrangement, yet we can convince ourselves that we can. As such, this resistance of estrangement becomes a version of estrangement itself. Love entraps the other and isolates it. The other is irrevocably bound in our gaze. The other neither grows nor diminishes but remains frozen in time.[60] The fear of separation replaces love.

Love's greatest enemy is fear, not desire. Desire is clear about what it wants. It wants the other for its own sake. Fear, on the other hand, masquerades as love. It believes it has the other's best interests at heart. It fears the potential loss of love. Love, Bauman writes, is "suspending the answer, or refraining from asking the question. . . . It means consent to the future's indefiniteness."[61] Love resists fear and remains open to the future and all its possible outcomes. It accepts the possibilities of both success and failure. Love is not a guarantee but a hope for the future.

Love's Crossing

Love bridges theory and practice. There is a special relationship between love and thinking. Love lies at the heart of all thinking, and thinking is an act of love. Jean-Luc Nancy writes, "Love does not call for a certain kind of thinking, or for a thinking of love, but for thinking in essence and in its totality. And this is because thinking, most properly speaking, is love."[62]

58. Or as Bauman describes it, "Love is a net cast on eternity, desire is a stratagem to be spared the chores of net weaving. True to their nature, love would strive to perpetuate the desire. Desire, on the other hand, would shun love's shackles." Bauman, *Liquid Love*, 10.

59. Love "takes captive and puts the apprehended in custody; it makes an arrest, for the prisoner's protection." Bauman, *Liquid Love*, 10.

60. "Lovers want to smother, extirpate and cleanse the vexing, irritating alterity that separates them from the beloved; separation from the beloved is the lover's most gruesome fear, and many a lover would go to any lengths to starve off the spectre of leave-taking once and for all. . . . Wherever I go, you go; whatever I do, you do; whatever I accept, you accept; whatever I resent, you resent. If you are not and cannot be my Siamese twin, be my clone!" Bauman, *Liquid Love*, 17.

61. Bauman, *Liquid Love*, 20.

62. Nancy, "Shattered Love," 84.

In both philosophy and theology there is a thinking love. In thinking love, philosophy and theology move toward an acceptance of all the possibilities. That is both disciplines remain open to love in all its forms.[63] Without love "the exercise of the intellect or of reason would be utterly worthless."[64]

Neither philosophy nor theology achieve a thinking love, despite it being at the center of both.[65] Thus, love becomes an achievement rather than an experience. It is a means toward an end.[66] Love becomes a means toward a certain goal or fulfillment.[67] Love is turned into a thing to be used instead of an experience. Philosophy and theology hold all the power when love is used, but love cannot be neatly organized. It is unpredictable and messy.[68] As such, love is not something we use to overcome estrangement. It is a presence that grasps.

As a presence, love occurs over and over. Its work is never complete. Love is a continually encounter that operates in the cycle between the self and other, and thus returns over and over again.[69] Love's transcendence enables this encounter to take place.[70] However, this is a special kind of transcendence. It is not the transcendence of the singular self. Love's transcendence is the all-encompassing experience that comes from the outside. It is the outside *itself*.[71] This means that love is not linear. It does not simply

63. Nancy explains that "all, of love, is possible and necessary, that all the loves possible are in fact the possibilities of love, its voices or its characteristics, which are impossible to confuse and yet ineluctably entangles: charity and pleasure, emotion and pornography, the neighbor and the infant, the love of lovers and the love of God, fraternal love and the love of art, the kiss, passion, friendship. . . . To think love would thus demand a boundless generosity toward all these possibilities." Nancy, "Shattered Love," 83.

64. Nancy, "Shattered Love," 84.

65. "Philosophy never arrives at this thinking—that 'thinking is love'—even though it is inscribed at the head of its program, or as the general epigraph to all its treaties." Nancy, "Shattered Love," 86.

66. According to Nancy, "Philosophy always thinks love as an accomplishment, arriving at a final and definitive completion." Nancy, "Shattered Love," 86.

67. Nancy, "Shattered Love," 87.

68. Nancy writes that in the hands of philosophy and theology love "operates in an identical manner between all the terms in play: The access and the end, the incomplete being and the complete being, the self and the beyond the self, the one and the other, the identical and the different. The contradiction of the contradiction and of the non-contradiction organizes love infinitely and in each of its meanings." Nancy, "Shattered Love," 87.

69. "We will have to admit that the rendezvous, our rendezvous with love, takes place not once, but an indefinite number of times." Nancy, "Shattered Love," 93.

70. "Love is the act of a transcendence." Nancy, "Shattered Love," 97.

71. Nancy describes it as something that "does not pass through the outside, because

move us from the singular to the singular. Love encompasses both as the other.[72] It encompasses the singular and the plural. Thus, it is both an arrival and a departure in an endless coming and going. According to Nancy, "Love arrives, it comes, or else it is not love. But it is thus that it endlessly goes elsewhere than to 'me' who would receive it: its coming is only a departure for the other, its departure only the coming of the other."[73] In both coming and going love endeavors to bring together the separated. It brings us, being-singular, into relationship with the other. Love, for being-singular, is an experience of both departure and arrival, loss and gain. We must lose ourselves for the other in order to experience the gain of the other. Reunion is both a giving and receiving.

Love cuts our being, exposing finitude, and thus creates a space for the other.[74] This cut breaks the self, being-singular in its completeness, to make the heart.[75] Without this break there is no room for the other. The singular must be broken for the plural. The *I* is broken so that the *we* can exist. Being-singular-plural remains a coming together of total centered selves. In the being-singular, love opens the smallest of cracks. Love makes room from the other so that the other is not just an addition to being. Love incorporates the other into being, and a broken heart becomes a loving heart. It is a heart that embraces finitude, thus exposing the truth of finitude. It is the truth that we must be broken in order to be whole.[76]

The cut of love never rests. It renews that break so that the fissure is never sealed. It never pushes the other away. Thus, it will move across that first cut to keep the separation at bay.[77] But being-singular wants to pull

---

it comes from it. . . . Love does not stop, as long as love lasts, coming from the outside. It does not remain outside; it *is* this outside itself, the other." Nancy, "Shattered Love," 97.

72. In this movement, Nancy writes, "the transcendence of love does not go from the singular being toward the other, toward the outside. It is not the singular being that puts itself outside itself: it is the other, and in the other it is not the subject's identity that operates this movement or this touch." Nancy, "Shattered Love," 97.

73. Nancy, "Shattered Love," 98.

74. "Because the singular being is finite, the other cuts across it (and never does the other 'penetrate' the singular being or 'unite itself' with it or 'commune'). Love unveils finitude." Nancy, "Shattered Love," 98.

75. Nancy suggests that it is the "break itself that makes the heart." Nancy, "Shattered Love," 98.

76. "Love cuts across finitude, always from the other to the other, which never returns to the same—and all loves, so humbly alike, are superbly singular. Love offers finitude in its truth; it is finitude's dazzling presentation." Nancy, "Shattered Love," 99.

77. "Love does not simply cut across, it cuts itself across itself, it arrives and arrives at itself as that by which nothing arrives, except that there is 'arriving,' arrival and departure: of the other, always of the other, so much *other* that it is never *made*, or done." Nancy, "Shattered Love," 102 (emphasis original).

away. It wants to flee the other and return to the self. Like two repelling magnets, love must pull them together, for separation desires its own return. The state of sin is not easily defeated. As such, love's cut can never end. It cannot because love is a constant challenge between the self and the other.[78] Love's pull and cut will return again and again so that the other can remain. Love, Nancy writes, "Comes *across* and never simply *comes* to its place or to term, that it comes across itself and overtakes itself, being the finite touch of the infinite crossing of the other."[79] No separation is too great for the cut of love.

Love Is Giving

Love's cut is also an act of giving. It is the action of giving yourself to the other. As such, nothing about love is passive. Love is first and foremost an action of giving.[80] In love, we give and receives. Thus, love requires two. We cannot give to our own self. Certainly, we can give our self a gift, but in such a case nothing is lost. We gain without loss. Giving, as love, is a giving of plurality. It is the act of giving our own self to another.

Life is a gift that we can share with another. The act of love is the act of enriching the other with the gift of the self. Love is the gift of life. We take what is most alive in ourselves, our uniqueness, and share that with another. The gift of love is comprised of our hopes, dreams, and passions. Giving, however, is more than that. We can share our own joy with little loss to the self. The gift of love must be the gift of the total self. As such, when we give, we are also giving those things that we hide away. Giving is also the gift of our sadness, fears, neuroses, and secrets to the other. Giving gives all that is alive.[81]

Giving enriches others. Love gives to share in one another's mutual *aliveness*. In mutual *aliveness*, the categories of giver and receiver are blurred. Giving love becomes receiving love. Giving, Fromm explains, "enhances the other's sense of aliveness by enhancing [one's] own sense of aliveness."[82]

---

78. Fromm describes love as a challenge. He writes that love "is a constant challenge; it is not a resting place, but a moving, growing, working together." Fromm, *Art of Loving*, 103.

79. Nancy, "Shattered Love," 102 (emphasis original).

80. Fromm describes love as an activity. He explains that "the active character of love can be described by stating that love is primarily *giving*, not receiving. Fromm, *Art of Loving*, 22.

81. Fromm, *Art of Loving*, 24.

82. Fromm, *Art of Loving*, 24–25.

Giving also gives to the receiver.[83] This is why giving love is never truly a loss.[84] The self does give itself away to the other. The self passes away for the sake of enhancing the other with its own life, its own *aliveness*. What the self loses pales in comparison to what is gained. In mutual *aliveness* the giver and receiver celebrate their shared joy. The giving of love is the giving of life.[85]

We cannot compel or demand love. Love remains first and foremost a gift.[86] It must be a gift, for any other way carries the risk of imposing a law. For love does not wish to be defined, structured, or named. It lives in the surplus of being as a gift. As such, love remains a surprise to sin. No one can prepare for love, nor can anyone predict it. It is a mystery to sin and therefore has the element of surprise.

Love as the Essence of Life

Love is a reunion between the separated. It is an event that grasps individuals and moves them from *being-singular* to *being-singular-plural*. Love is the essence of life. It is also, Karl Barth writes, "the essence of Christian living."[87] Love and Christian living have a special unity. The Christian life is a life grasped by love, and the Christian life begins and ends with love. Christian action is the action of love.[88] The Christian life does not create love. There is, Barth asserts, "nothing in the Christian life which can precede love, the love of God for [humanity] must first precede the Christian life."[89]

---

83. Rahner writes, "God's self-communication is given not only as gift, but also as the necessary condition which makes possible an acceptance of the gift which can allow the gift really to be God, and can prevent the gift in its acceptance from being changed from God into a finite and created gift which only represents God, but is not God [Godself]." Rahner, *Foundations of Christian Faith*, 128.

84. For example, Fromm makes the case that "in giving he [or she] cannot help bringing something to life in the other person, and this which is brought to life reflects back to him [or her]; in truly giving, he [or she] cannot help receiving that which is given back to him [or her]." Fromm, *Art of Loving*, 25.

85. "*Love is the active concern for the life and the growth of that which we love.*" Fromm, *Art of Loving*, 26 (emphasis original).

86. Love is "neither unique nor necessary. It comes, it is offered; it is not established as a structure of being or as its principle, and even less as its subjectivity." Nancy, "Shattered Love," 273.

87. Barth, *Doctrine of Word*, 372.

88. "The Christian Life begins with love. It also ends with love, so far as it has an end as human life in time. There is nothing that we can or must be or do as a Christian, or to become a Christian, prior to love. Barth, *Doctrine of Word*, 371.

89. Barth, *Doctrine of Word*, 372.

By itself, the Christian life has no power to overcome estrangement. Christian living, separate from love, is impossible.

The Christian identity begins in love. In love we are grasped and transformed by love's cut across our being. In love we experience the presence of God. A presence that, Barth writes, "opens our eyes and ears and therefore kindles our faith. When that occurs, the Christian life begins."[90] Love recreates human reality in the event of human action. Love's cut moves through action, thus giving love a physical reality.[91] Love does not change action into another substance. Love is not a replacement of the physical.[92] Love does not sweep away human action as if it does not have value. Nor is action replaced as something inferior and worthless. Physical action is already meaningful, but love brings out the physical's full potential. In love we find the subject of our action.[93] We discover the true purpose of human action in love.

Love speaks and reminds us that "God's love for us is an overwhelming, overflowing, free love."[94] Love is free, and its outpouring is neither solicited nor necessary. Love's movement is the free mercy and kindness of God's very self. It is this self, as love, which we encounter.[95] Our love grows in love itself. It is not that we are incapable of love. We already believe that we have a knowledge of what love is.[96] Unfortunately this love is a love that exists in separation, and it is a pale shadow of love's full potential. This limited love longs for union, but it does not understand how to achieve that.

90. Barth, *Doctrine of Word*, 372.

91. "A creaturely reality, let us say, which as such, as human self-determination, is re-created by [Godself] in the sphere or light of the divine predetermination, thus being transformed, becoming love instead of non-love, but not ceasing on that account to be human self-determination and therefore a creaturely reality." Barth, *Doctrine of Word*, 373.

92. "We cannot therefore say that it is the product of a transformation of the creaturely into divine reality, nor can we say that in it the divine reality has taken the place of the creaturely." Barth, *Doctrine of Word*, 373–74.

93. Barth uses the example of Christ. He writes, "In strict analogy with the incarnation of the Word in Jesus Christ, what takes place in [humanity] by the revelation of God is this: his [or her] humanity is not impaired, but in the Word of God heard and believed by him [or her] he [or she] find the Lord, indeed in the strict and proper sense he [or she] find the subject of his humanity." Barth, *Doctrine of Word*, 374.

94. Barth, *Doctrine of Word*, 377.

95. "How then can we for our part declare it to be necessary that we should be loved by [God]? It is, in fact, the free mercy and kindness of God which meets us in [God's] love. Barth, *Doctrine of Word*, 379.

96. Barth remarks, "We cannot deny or hide the fact that in one way or another we all think we know already about human loving, and we continue to do so even when confronted by the fact of the love of God to us." Barth, *Doctrine of Word*, 380.

Our own love lacks the strength to overcome separation. This is because being-singular's love only knows strength. Being-singular has nothing of its own to offer. It cannot be the work of the self. Instead, we must accept love. It must work on our behalf.[97] We must move beyond our own love. That is, our own love, including self-love, can only grow when it accepts the love of the other.[98] We must give up our claim to love.[99]

In love we encounter a genuine partner. Describing this love, Barth writes, "Only of love to God can it be said that it has a genuine partner, for it is only in love to God that there is love to one's neighbor. For that reason only the love of God can be called real love."[100] To be grasped by love is to be grasped by the genuine other. In the love between a genuine partner and the other, we discover the true meaning and purpose of love. Being-singular encounters one who wills to be loved.[101] The genuine other does not demand or command love. The genuine other, our true partner, comes fully. Love does not hold itself back. It is a complete giving of the self. Therefore, the experience of love is an experience of the other's totality. The experience of love is neither theoretical nor philosophical. Love goes where one's own knowledge cannot. It takes us into a full knowledge of the other. Love takes us into the nature and being of the other. Love is a complete knowledge.[102]

In this knowledge, we set aside the old self. The selfish self, being-singular, is left behind to embrace the true other.[103] Being-singular was never

---

97. "We cannot offer a love which is the work of our own hands or heart. We have to recognize that that [God] intercedes for us and represents us, that what is our own, even our own love for [God], can never be anything but our shame and our curse." Barth, *Doctrine of Word*, 384.

98. "Self-love is built out of the love offered to us by others. . . . Others must love us first, so that we can begin to love ourselves." Bauman, *Liquid Love*, 80.

99. "The love with which we reply to the love of God for us can begin and grow only when we go beyond what we can claim as our own love, when we recognize that we the unloving are beloved by [God]." Barth, *Doctrine of Word*, 384.

100. Barth, *Doctrine of Word*, 388.

101. As such, "it is the Lord who wills to be loved as the other." Barth, *Doctrine of Word*, 388.

102. "The knowledge of the uniqueness of God is not the result of a philosophical consideration of the nature of God. It is the answer to [God's] revelation as the Lord. The philosophical consideration of the nature of God can never lead us beyond the dialectic of the concepts of monotheism and polytheism, pantheism and atheism." Barth, *Doctrine of Word*, 389.

103. Barth writes, "It is only in the revelation of God as the Lord that the decision is made: I am the Lord thy God—I: not the idea of the unity of God, not the beings which want to be gods, not anything or everything which can be divine, not thou thyself in thine own divinity, but I—thou shalt have none other gods but me." Barth, *Doctrine of Word*, 389.

meant to be our true self. Being-singular is the self of separation. Instead to love, Barth writes, "means to become what we already are, those who are loved by [God]."[104] In love's grasp we become what we already are, a living embodiment of love for the other. It is the passage from immature love to mature love. We love freely and not out of compulsion.[105]

Love accepts the future. Being-singular has no future. It can only live within the self. As such, being-singular is trapped within itself. The self needs to embrace the other to grow. Our future lies outside the self, and this is the paradox of the self, that we do not have control over our own destiny. To discover our true self, we must search outside the self. Being-singular must seek the plural. It needs to live as being-with to have a future.[106] To love the other is to live in the reality of God.[107] The reality of God is a reality that puts others before the self. It is a reality that accepts love's grasp and the cut it places on the heart. The love for the other is the love of God.[108] *The reality of God is being-singular-plural.*

THE PRACTICE OF LOVE

Foot washing is a movement of love. Love is at the center of everything that occurs during foot washing. Humility, service, and forgiveness all originate in love. Love is the driving motivation for OFWBs.[109] Foot washing has no greater purpose or drive than love. So, when OFWBs wash feet, they are physically enacting this love. What cannot be said in words is said in action. What they say in action cannot be said in any other way. The love of OFWBs

104. Barth, *Doctrine of Word*, 389.

105. Fromm clarifies the distinction between infantile/immature love and mature love. He writes, "Infantile love follows the principle: '*I love because I am loved.*' Mature love follows the principle: '*I am loved because I love.*' Immature love says: '*I love you because I need you.*' Mature love says: '*I need you because I love you.*'" Fromm, *Art of Loving*, 40–41 (emphasis original).

106. According to Barth, "In every case, therefore, love is an accepting, confirming and grasping of our future." Barth, *Doctrine of Word*, 389.

107. Barth suggests that accepting "this future is identical with the reality of God, who in the most pregnant sense of the word is 'for us.' It is therefore an accepting, confirming and grasping of the God who is our future." Barth, *Doctrine of Word*, 389–90.

108. "If love, as distinct from the illusion of self-love, is love for another, and if this other is God the Lord, then our loving must be defined as the nature and attitude of [humanity]." Barth, *Doctrine of Word*, 390.

109. Reflecting on his experience, a pastor explains, "What more beautiful metaphor of that is there than the servitude of bowing at a brother or sister's feet and saying, 'I love you in Christ and it's my privilege to serve you by washing feet.'" Interview with OFWB pastor (G), February 6, 2015.

is the love that seeks to challenge estrangement. Their love moves to over-come separation. Their love pushes against the power of sin. For OFWBs, the act of foot washing is love.[110]

Through this, OFWBs recognize something fundamentally important about the human condition. They recognize the real separation that exists between us all. Foot washing is a way of connection. It is a way of overcom-ing the sin of separation. In this act, OFWBs are saying "No" to estrange-ment. As such, despite its simplicity (or maybe because of it) foot washing works at a deep level. In this act, OFWBs are acting out the overcoming of estrangement.[111] It represents the conflict between loneliness and con-nection, despair and joy, and sin and love. OFWBs are crossing barriers when they practice foot washing. They cross the barriers that separate one another. Physically they do this through touch, but more importantly, they do this emotionally. Their touch conveys more than a physical connection. That touch, at least briefly, overcomes sin. Isolation and despair, the fruits of sin, diminish. And in their place emerge service and forgiveness. The self, being-singular, finally moves outward toward being-with. The needs of the other replace the needs of the self.

Foot washing is a strange act, and yet life is strange. Life is discon-nected, disjointed, and fragmented. It is fitting that a strange act, foot wash-ing, finds it place in a strange world. For only a strange act can overcome a strange world. OFWBs embrace this strangeness through foot washing. They know that foot washing is going to make others hesitant. Foot wash-ing does not fit into what others consider *acceptable* behavior.[112] Therefore,

110. A youth pastor explains what she has experienced concerning love. She says, "Because if there's someone that you're not, maybe you had a disagreement with or maybe you aren't seeing eye to eye on something or maybe not even talking with. If they're in the same room what better way to try to make amends then offering to wash their feet, and that's one reason why, like my husband's church, they actually, all go around after they've washed feet and hug each other and say, 'I love you brother, I love you sister.' When you've had that kind of contact and interaction with another person it's kind of hard to sit there and argue at business meeting with each other." Interview with OFWB pastor (F), March 5, 2015.

111. This overcoming of estrangement brings a renewed intimacy. A member describes this intimacy stating, "Intimacy is a closeness with my Christian family . . . because you are bearing part of yourself that you don't normally bear to just anybody." Interview with OFWB member (D), February 5, 2015.

112. A member shares that she realizes others consider foot washing strange. She shares, "I've always heard cleaning other people's feet as if it's some bizarre thing. It gives us a testimony that people are still doing that, and people are taking the time to do it. And are not embarrassed to do it or ashamed to do it." Interview with OFWB member (G), January 29, 2015.

foot washing is not something we are naturally inclined to do.[113] It pushes and challenges the boundaries of the self. The boundaries that we desire to keep. Life bumps against life, but the self is defensive. Being-singular remains defensive even though it can feel the call toward the other. It is reminded each day of what unity and togetherness looks like. Estrangement desires that the strangeness remains. Estrangement convinces us that we do not need others, that estrangement is *normal*. Kneeling and washing another's foot challenges estrangement.[114] Foot washing challenges strangeness through strangeness. It uses what is strange to remind us that estrangement is strange. Thus, foot washing is an embrace of uncomfortableness. It embraces the uncomfortable to make it normal.

Love brings together the strange. Knowing the other overcomes strangeness. When OFWBs practice foot washing, there is a deep desire to know the other person. OFWBs come to know one other through touching, washing, drying, and embracing. Foot washing is knowledge of life beyond estrangement. It is a knowledge of reunion between the separated. In their love, OFWBs catch a glimpse of life without separation. They glimpse a life where estrangement does not the rule. They witness the reunion of being. In foot washing, at least for the moment, the cry of existence is satisfied. Foot washing is more than an embrace of the foot. It is an embrace of the total self.

Foot washing cuts the heart. It is an exposure of the self. Foot washing must be, otherwise the action is impossible. Without love's cut, being-singular has no room for the other. OFWBs understand this. They understand that without love's cut their own being has no room for anyone else. The separation is too strong. We cannot cross the chasm that exists between ourselves and the other under our own strength. We cannot force being. Therefore, it is necessary to be cut, exposed, and broken. Foot washing breaks OFWBs. Kneeling and washing another's feet breaks them. Love breaks their hearts,

113. A pastor shares that in his experience "People shy away from it. Especially people who did not grow up Free Will Baptist and joined our church, because they think it's a little demeaning in some ways. I think we all do, but some do, and we do at [church name] we have our communion in the morning service and feet washing at night. When you say you're going to have a feet washing service your numbers are not going to be as large as you would on a normal Sunday night even though Sunday nights are not greatly attended but anyway. People have a little stigma about it." Interview with OFWB pastor (H), February 3, 2015.

114. Explaining the effect of kneeling and washing, a pastor shares, "I realized what an honor it is to be able to reach out to your brother, usually a brother in your church that you've served together with, being able to knell down in front of him and doing something you would think to be so lowly, but in reality it represents all what Christ is all about. Even if it means stooping low. You love one another, doing whatever it takes to love one another I guess." Interview with OFWB pastor (E), March 27, 2015.

and yet they rise as renewed people. They rise not as being-singular, but as being-singular-plural. OFWBs rise *together*.

Foot washing breaks down the things that being-singular considers important. Things such as class, race, status, job, and age are cut and broken, and these things are replaced by humility, service, and forgiveness. Foot washing is their reminder that love's cut should never close.[115] It is their check against power and selfishness. Power and selfishness, the fruits of sin, are pushed away so that love can grasp them.

GRACE AS ACCEPTANCE

Love for the other, a love that models the reality of God, is the love of acceptance. It is love that accepts the other totally and completely. Living in the reality of God is living in the state of grace. Grace, Tillich writes, "Is the reunion of life with life, the reconciliation of the self with itself. Grace is the acceptance of that which is rejected."[116] Love is a reunion, but it is more than that. Love is an acceptance of the rejected. Separation is a rejection. In being-singular, a self rejects the other. Being-singular pushes back against the other and retreats inward. Consequently, there is thus a mutual rejection of being. Life lived in the singular is a life lived in rejection, rejection of the other and the self. However, in grace rejection becomes acceptance.

Grace accepts in spite of sin. Grace is the *in-spite-of* element that loves even when love seems to be impossible.[117] Grace appears when sin, separation, is at its strongest. Grace appears when the gulf of separation appears insurmountable. Grace does not diminish in the presence of sin, instead it increases.[118] Grace cannot exist without sin, thus to live in grace is to live in the knowledge of separation. Continually, we are pulled toward separation. Grace reminds us of our acceptance. In a life of acceptance, despair and loneliness never have the last word. The temptation to retreat inward

115. Love should continue to grow. Love never ceases its transformation upon the individual. A pastor shares, "I think the experience of washing feet too is an experience of growing in Christ and growing in love for your fellow believers. It teaches us how we love unconditionally sometimes. . . . I think that's what it would teach." Interview with OFWB pastor (H), February 3, 2015.

116. Tillich, "You Are Accepted," 158.

117. "There is something triumphant in the word 'grace': in spite of the abounding of sin grace abounds much more." Tillich, "You Are Accepted," 158.

118. Tillich uses the example of Christ. He writes that in Christ's "separation from other [people], from himself and God, he found himself accepted in spite of his being rejected. And when he found that he was accepted, he was able to accept himself and to be reconciled to others." Tillich, "You Are Accepted," 162.

never disappears. Despair and loneliness live at the edge of existence await-
ing their return.

Being-singular-plural is impossible without grace. We cannot accept
another without first experiencing acceptance. We cannot force ourselves to
accept ourselves.[119] This is the trap of sin, and it leads us to believe that we
can never be accepted or accept others. Being-singular has no strength of its
own to overcome loneliness and despair.[120] Grace needs to act first. Grace
comes before love's grasp, before love's cut across the heart, and before reunion. It is the source of love.

The grasp of grace comes when we least expect it. Grace "strikes us
when we are in great pain and restlessness. It strikes us when we walk
through the dark valley of a meaningless and empty life. It strikes us when
we feel that our separation is deeper than usual."[121] In those dark moments,
according to Tillich, the light of grace appears in order to tell you that "*You
are accepted*, accepted by that which is greater than you, and the name of
which you do not know."[122]

Grace makes relation with others possible. It is the foundation of
being-singular-plural. Grace is the experience of relationship. It truly is, as
Tillich explains, the "reunion of life with life."[123] Therefore grace is never a
singular experience. It is not a feeling of enlightenment, personal transcendence, or wisdom. Grace does not come to serve the *I*. It comes to build the
we. This is the miracle of grace. It is the miracle of finally coming to understand the other and knowing he or she fully. In grace we come to know the
whole person, both the good and bad. Accordingly, we come to understand
the other in his or her complexity.[124]

The experience of grace is the experience of hope. It is the hope for a
better world. A world built on being-with rather than being-singular. Grace

119. For Rahner, "[One] experiences [oneself] at the same time as a subject who experiences the event of God's absolute self-communication, as a subject who has already
responded in freedom with a 'yes' or 'no' to this event, and who can never bring the
concrete and real mode of [one's] response to the level of reflection completely." Rahner,
Foundations of Christian Faith, 133.

120. "We cannot transform our lives, unless we allow them to be transformed by
that stroke of grace. It happens; or it does not happen. And certainly it does not happen
if we try to force it upon ourselves, just as it shall not happen so long as we think, in our
self-complacency, that we have no need of it." Tillich, "You Are Accepted," 163.

121. Tillich, "You Are Accepted," 163.

122. Tillich, "You Are Accepted," 163 (emphasis original).

123. Tillich, "You Are Accepted," 164.

124. According to Tillich, "We experience the grace of understanding each other's
words. We understand not merely the literal meaning of the words, but also that which
lies behind them, even when they are harsh or angry." Tillich, "You Are Accepted," 164.

is the hope for reunion of life to life. It is the experience, Tillich writes, "which is able to overcome the tragic separation of the sexes, of the generations, of the nations, of the races, and even the utter strangeness between [humanity] and nature."[125] In grace we are finally able to say *yes* to the other and *yes* to ourselves. We accept and are accepted.[126] In acceptance, grace points us toward life in community.

THE GRACE IN PRACTICE

There is nothing mystical or magical about washing feet. It does not connect us to a heavenly reality, nor does it solicit a spiritual presence. The practice does not physically or spiritually change matter. For all intents and purposes, though strange, foot washing is utterly mundane. Foot washing, at least for those OFWBs who practice it, is about acceptance. OFWBs say *yes* to one another when washing feet. It is all about the *yes* of acceptance. Hence, foot washing is emotional for OFWBs. It is the feeling of another's acceptance.

The *yes* of acceptance is the OFWB experience of grace. Foot washing prepares OFWBs for the reality of grace. It does not solicit or control grace. Grace comes, or it does not. However, foot washing does prepare us to experience the *yes* of grace.[127] Not all OFWBs experience the grasp of grace. Often the experience of foot washing depends on what you bring to it.[128] You must have the right attitude.[129] It is easy to retreat into the singular self. The strangeness and intimacy of foot washing prevents many from participating. Even still, the actions do not always facilitate an overcoming

125. Tillich, "You Are Accepted," 164.

126. "But sometimes it happens that we receive the power to say 'yes' to ourselves, that peace enters into us and makes us whole, that self-hate and self-contempt disappear, and that our self is reunited with itself. Then we can say grace has come upon us." Tillich, "You Are Accepted," 165.

127. Foot washing is an act of grace. A member shares, "It's driven me to my knees more. It makes appreciate more what Christ did for us. It also makes me thankful. It's not something that I'm proud of. I'm just thankful and I think there's a difference. It took me awhile to learn that. I'll be candid with you. It also makes me feel very blessed, very blessed and wholly inadequate. It's nothing that I did for my salvation." Interview with OFWB member (C), June 30, 2015.

128. A member suggests that one must "do it with an open spirit with an open heart." Interview with OFWB member (D), February 5, 2015.

129. This same member goes on to state, "You have to do it. Yeah. I think it's not just okay going and sitting and watching. You have to be willing to wash someone's feet, but more than that you have to be willing to have your feet washed." Interview with OFWB member (D), February 5, 2015.

of separation. Washing feet does not guarantee an experience of humility, service, and forgiveness. Love can fail to cut across the heart, and without that cut, the heart fails to make room for the other. Being-singular can do the actions and remain being-singular. Foot washing is not magic.

It does not mean that meaning is absent from the practice. Foot washing carries the hope of grace. Foot washing is a practice filled with potential. Its meaning is present within the practice. In foot washing, the *yes* of acceptance is already there. Unfortunately, the state of sin distorts our perspective. We cannot see the other beyond the self. Sin prevents us from seeing across that chasm. Therefore, unless we can see the other, the *yes* will never come. Foot washing puts us before the other. We encounter the other face-to-face and touch-to-touch. As such, this encounter prepares us for grace. Through physical touch we hope for grace's grasp.

Foot washing opens OFWBs to the experience of grace and to one another. OFWBs know that foot washing's influence is subtle. It is not easy to overcome estrangement. Loneliness and despair are powerful enemies, but foot washing carries the hope of grace. It carries the hope that estrangement is not forever. It carries the hope that the other will not always remain a stranger. Foot washing hopes for community. The *yes* of acceptance is also the *yes* of community. By washing feet, OFWBs hope that grace will lead to love, that love will lead to acceptance, and acceptance will lead to community.

TOWARD COMMUNITY

The outcome of love and grace is community; however, community is both a birth and death. Community is birthed from death, and the *I* must die for it to begin. According to Nancy, "Community is revealed in the death of others; hence it is always revealed to others. Community is what takes place always through others and for others."[130] Community cannot begin in the *I*. Community reveals itself through others. Specifically, it is born out of the death of others. Community does begin as a coming together of the *I*'s. If it were, the *I* would have nothing to lose. The *I* keeps itself and gains the *we*. Nancy writes that community "is not a project of fusion."[131]

Community begins with the other. It is born out of the death of the *I*. Community does the impossible. It brings life out of death.[132] Total fu-

130. Nancy, *Inoperative Community*, 15.

131. Nancy, *Inoperative Community*, 15.

132. "Community occurs in order to acknowledge this impossibility, or more exactly—for there is neither function nor finality here—the impossibility of making

sion between individuals is impossible. The *I* can never cross the barrier that separates it from the other. The *I* needs to lose itself by embracing its finitude. This creates an impossible predicament for the *I*, for the *I* must face its own death if it is to ever be anything else. The *I* has no future on its own. It is not eternal. Accordingly, Nancy insists that the *I* must face "the finitude and the irredeemable excess that make up finite being: its death, but also its birth, and only the community can present me my birth."[133] The death of the *I* is not the end. In its death the other is found. Community opens and expands our world toward new possibilities and experiences.[134]

Community wears its finitude proudly. It holds it and cherishes it, because community is finitude. Community does not pretend to be something it is not. It does not replace finitude with the infinite. Because community is not embarrassed of its finitude. It does not brush aside the finite or attempt to replace it with something else. Finitude is the human experience in all of its ambiguities, contradictions, and shortcoming. Thus, our denial of these things is a denial of our humanity. Therefore, "finitude alone is communitarian."[135] Finitude communicates, reaches out, precisely because of its limited nature. To survive, finitude depends on others. As opposed to the infinite, finitude cannot be self-sufficient. Finitude needs the other. On the other hand, the individual believes itself to be infinite.[136] Therefore the infinite is closed and requires nothing from the other. Community, wishing to remain open, is unsurprised by its finitude and limitations. Instead, limitations are incorporated into the community itself.[137] The individual, as infinite, cannot live in community. Only the singular being, being-as-finitude, can live in community. A singular being lives as the embodiment of finitude, its limitations and shortcomings. The singular being is not the individual. The individual lives under the illusion that it is infinite. Even in contact with the other, the individual lives for itself. The singular being, on

---

a work out of death is inscribe and acknowledge as 'community.'" Nancy, *Inoperative Community*, 15.

133. Nancy, *Inoperative Community*, 15.

134. "What community reveals to me, in presenting to me my birth and my death, is my existence outside myself." Nancy, *Inoperative Community*, 26.

135. Nancy, *Inoperative Community*, 27

136. "As an individual, I am closed off from all community, and it would not be an exaggeration to say that the individual—if an absolutely individual being could ever exist—is infinite." Nancy, *Inoperative Community*, 27.

137. For example, Nancy explains that the "limit of the individual, fundamentally, does not concern [community], it simply surrounds it." Nancy, *Inoperative Community*, 27.

the other hand, comes into itself in the presence of another being.[138] The singular being appears in the presence of the other. It appears as finitude itself and shares that finitude with the other. Singular being shares its finitude, therefore, community is the sharing of finitude. It is the realm of the singular being's journey toward being-in-common.[139]

Community cannot exist without sharing finitude, and community cannot exist without the other.[140] It cannot be a community of individuals, otherwise it would be a farce. A community of *I*'s is a mock community. The community of the *I* rejects the other in preference for itself. Community cannot be based on rejection, even if that is a shared rejection.

True community is the community of mutual exposure. Thus, singular beings extend themselves in a mutual sharing of exposure. Singular beings expose themselves to the outside, in the reality of the other.[141] Community is based on this exposure of our finitude. Therefore, community is not a creation or product. It is an experience. If community were a creation, it would belong to individuals. Community could be claimed.[142]

Community does not belong to the group. Its origin does not come from the self. The origin of the community is "the tracing of the borders upon which or along which singular beings are exposed."[143] Community arises out of the exposure of being-to-being. It comes out of the limits of being, not from being-itself. The singular being, has no claim upon community. It does not belong to a *he, she,* or *it.* Instead community's origin comes from the way in which the singular is broken. Broken for whom? The singular is broken for the other. Therefore, community originates in the ways that the singular experiences the other. Community begins when

138. "A singular being *appears,* as finitude itself: at the end (or at the beginning), with the contact of the skin (or the heart) of another singular being." Nancy, *Inoperative Community*, 27–28.

139. Being-in-common, according to Nancy, "does not mean a higher form of substance or subject taking charge of the limits of separate individualities." Nancy, *Inoperative Community*, 27.

140. "Community means, consequently, that there is not singular being without another singular being." Nancy, *Inoperative Community*, 28.

141. "This outside is in its turn nothing other than the exposition of another areality, of another singularity—the same other." Nancy, *Inoperative Community*, 29.

142. "Community is not the work of singular beings, nor can it claim them as its works, just as communication is not a work or even an operation of singular beings, for community is simply their being—their being suspended upon its limit." Nancy, *Inoperative Community*, 31.

143. Nancy, *Inoperative Community*, 33.

the singular and other can share identity.[144] It begins when all singulars become others.

Community lives in the resistance of being-to-being. In this sense community is difficult. There is nothing easy about shared identity. The singular actively works against community and may even create its own version of it. The singular resists the immanence of the other. Community does not do away with resistance, nor does it overcome it. Community is resistance.[145] The sharing of identity is not about transcending resistance. There will always be that urge to escape from other, even in the closest of communities.[146] Community struggles within the resistance, because the work of community is never complete. It struggles against itself repeatedly. Therefore, community is never complete because community cannot exist apart from resistance. A community without resistance would represent something false or imaginary. It would create the illusion of unity. A unity without resistance is no true unity for there is nothing to overcome. Community ought to have that *in spite of* element in order to exist. It requires courage, but not the courage of strength. It is the courage of letting go. That is of letting go of the self, the *I*, in favor of the other.

COMMUNITY IN PRACTICE

The ideal community is neither the unattainable community nor the perfect community. The ideal community is the *un*-ideal community. The *un*-ideal community is the imperfect community, the work-in-progress community. But work-in-progress toward what? It is certainly not perfection, nor is it transcendence. The goal of community is not to run away toward some perfect transcendent ideal. The community, Nancy declares, "Is the sacred . . . but the sacred stripped of the sacred."[147] This community, the *un*-ideal community, is anything but sacred. For if by sacred we mean *set apart*, then the sacred must be rejected. If by sacred we mean the *shared* community, then, call the community sacred.[148]

144. Nancy defines community as "that singular ontological order in which the other and the same are alike (*sont le semblable*): that is to say, in the sharing of identity." Nancy, *Inoperative Community*, 34.

145. Or as Nancy puts it, "Community is, in a sense, resistance itself: namely, resistance to immanence." Nancy, *Inoperative Community*, 35.

146. This resistance to immanence, Nancy explains, is "resistance to the communion of everyone or to the exclusive passion of one or several: to all the forms and all the violences of subjectivity." Nancy, *Inoperative Community*, 35.

147. Nancy, *Inoperative Community*, 35.

148. Nancy writes, "For the sacred—the separated, the set apart—no longer proves

The sacred community is *not* the set apart community. The goal of community is not perfection but the living presence of a continually face-to-face encounter with the other. The OFWB community is not a model of the perfect community. The OFWBs make no claim that their community is anymore special or set apart than other Christian communities. Foot washing does *not* set apart OFWBs, nor should it. What purpose is there to set apart the OFWBs? If the goal of foot washing was setting apart, separation, then it would be a practice in vanity. Foot washing would be a farce, a mockery of itself. What OFWBs do is unique and unusual, but in no way is it meant to set them apart.

OFWBs are uncomfortable with the idea of being unique or special because of foot washing.[149] They lack a clear consensus on what this practice means for their identity. This is not due to a lack of OFWB reflection on foot washing. Foot washing is an important part of their OFWB history and heritage. It is something they value, but it does not set them apart. OFWBs do see foot washing as something they *share*. Foot washing is *shared* with all.[150] It is a future shared in imperfection.

Foot washing is an embrace of the imperfection all beings share. It does not shy away from what makes us uncomfortable. Foot washing thrusts us toward an encounter with the imperfect, the flawed, and the damaged. Foot washing typifies what it means to be human. It points to what is real about individuals, not the personas we wear for others. Washing feet is a collision of finitude. It is hard to hide our imperfections and blemishes when washing another's feet. The exposure of feet is an exposure of the self. It is placing our finitude into the hands of another. The giving of the foot is a giving of finitude. It tells the other that one is indeed *human*. We give humanity and the other accepts it. The *I* gives itself to the *we*.

---

to be the haunting idea of an unattainable communion, but is rather made up of nothing other than the sharing of community." Nancy, *Inoperative Community*, 35.

149. A pastor speaks about the OFWB and its identity as related to foot washing. He says, "Well we're not the only denomination that washes feet. But many times, when you say your Free Will Baptist they say you're that foot washing group or something. I don't think it should make us unique, I think it should make us glad that we're children of God and love others like he loved us, and we love ourselves." Interview with OFWB pastor (E), March 27, 2015.

150. Speaking of this shared experience, a pastor explains, "It's a shared experience. . . . Afterwards there's an embrace that brings [everyone] together and there's a literal conversation of 'Thank you brother I appreciate all you do. You meant this much to me.' It's a unifying thing once you let it in." Interview with OFWB pastor (H), February 3, 2015.

This is what OFWBs give to one another. In reality, the feet are secondary.[151] It was never about the feet. The feet are the conduct and means for something much more important. Foot washing is about the sharing of imperfection and finitude. OFWBs share the same insecurities about their feet and bodies as many others do, but the feet do not that matter. What matters is the sharing of the self. The practice feels real and genuine because it embodies and shares finitude. The OFWB readily admit that they fight and disagree and hold grudges against one another. Yet, they also laugh and have fun. This is especially true around homecomings and potlucks. OFWBs fight, but they also learn how to forgive. They learn how to show humility and love to one another. For many, this originates in foot washing.[152] In foot washing, OFWBs learn how to share their finitude.

Sharing finitude is not easy for OFWBs. There is resistance, but this resistance makes community. The struggles and joys that typify communal existence are on full display during foot washing. Foot washing brings to light the communal imperfection. It does not hide them away, rather it brings them to light. Foot washing is the catalyst toward a shared community. Shared imperfection and finitude points toward a shared identity. OFWBs share in their finitude. They share imperfection. Consequently, the OFWB identity is not an identity based on what could be. The OFWB identity is based on what *is*. Foot washing is an encounter with the real. It is this reality, the reality of Christ, which is the basis of OFWB community.

The reality of Christ is the reality of the other. In this there should be no difference between the secular and Christian community. Both are a yearning and struggle for the other. In community, the other is a source of strength. They share the same future. Community, if it is to exist, requires a foundation built upon the experience of the other. It needs a foundation of shared finitude; therefore community places its future in the *we* rather than the *I*. Through foot washing, the OFWB practice a community based on the

---

151. "It's our feet, but it's still a symbol of the heart being purified. Because it's just a humble significance of what Jesus did to his disciples and he said 'do as I have done you.' Again, I don't necessarily think the actual act of feet washing is, it's being a servant. We're to serve, not wait for somebody to pat us on the back and say what a good singer you are or good preacher you are or good deacon you are. That's not what our job is. Our job is to set an example of humbleness and servitude." Interview with OFWB member (F), March 17, 2015.

152. And ultimately to Jesus. OFWBs learn through the love and service. OFWBs love through service. As a pastor puts it, [Foot washing] reminds [us] of what it means to truly believe in Christ and to be the body of Christ in our world. Because it teaches us about the humility of Christ and that we need to humble ourselves, and it teaches us again that Jesus came into the world to serve and not be served and that's what he's calling us to do. It's not serving ourselves it is serving people, not only the church but the other community." Interview with OFWB pastor (I), February 2, 2015.

we. In foot washing the *I* forgoes itself for the sake of the *we*. Foot washing builds for the future. It builds for a future of shared imperfection, finitude, and identity.

Christ the Other, Christ the Community

Bonhoeffer writes that "Christianity means community through Jesus Christ and in Jesus Christ. . . . We belong to one another only through and in Jesus Christ."[153] Christ becomes the source of connection between the self and the other, though it is much more than that. Christ does not simply connect one to the other. Christ is the urge of love that drives the self, the *I*, toward the other.[154] Christ becomes the other that directs one outside the self. As a result, the self sees the other as the source of one's salvation. For the Christian, Christ becomes the living embodiment of the other.[155] Christ and the other are one and the same. In seeking the other, we are also seeking Christ. Each other, all persons, become an *Other-in-Christ*. Because, Bonhoeffer writes, Christ took "our being, our nature, ourselves. . . . Now we are in him. Where he is, there we are too, in the incarnation, on the Cross, and in his resurrection. We belong to him because we are in him."[156]

The other becomes Christ, and Christ is the other. The other becomes the foundation of community precisely because the other is Christ. In opening the self toward others, we are by implication opening ourselves toward Christ. The other strives for the other, Christ strives for Christ, and community is born. Community is thus born and subsists through the person of Christ.[157] In turn, the other ceases to be the other and becomes a brother or sister.[158] In community the other loses *otherness*. We cease to be defined

153. Bonhoeffer, *Life Together*, 21.

154. According to Bonhoeffer, a community in and through Christ means "first, that a Christian needs others because of Jesus Christ. It means, second, that a Christian comes to others only through Jesus Christ. It means, third, that in Jesus Christ we have been chosen from eternity, accepted in time, and united for eternity." Bonhoeffer, *Life Together*, 21.

155. "Christian is the man [or woman] who no longer seeks his [or her] salvation, his [or her] deliverance, his [or her] justification in himself [or herself], but in Jesus Christ alone." Bonhoeffer, *Life Together*, 21–22.

156. Bonhoeffer, *Life Together*, 24.

157. Community is founded on the work of Christ. Bonhoeffer states that "community with one another consists solely in what Christ has done to both of us." Bonhoeffer, *Life Together*, 25.

158. "One is a brother [or sister] to another only through Jesus Christ. I am a brother to another person through what Jesus Christ did for me and to me; the other person has become a brother [or sister] to me through what Jesus Christ did for him [or

as the other, as different. In Christ, *togetherness* replaces *otherness*. Repeated exposure to the other furthers strengthens the bond between the self and the other, but estrangement cannot be overcome completely. There still exists a barrier between individuals. As the other ceases to be other, not once but repeatedly, that barrier becomes less challenging. The deeper the bond the easier it is for individuals to transverse the barrier. The journey becomes a well-trodden path. Christ makes that path clearer and more familiar.[159]

The bridge between others is built on Christ and his work. Christ, the quintessential other, forms the path between us and the other. Christ takes on *otherness*, which frees us from the burden of estrangement. The feeling of *togetherness* replaces *otherness* through the work of Christ. Christ not only becomes the bridge, Christ is the light to the other side. Christ allows us to see the other, to touch and feel the other, precisely because Christ is that other. Christ replaces the *I*, being-singular, so that we can be being-with.

Christ is the foundation of community, and every other becomes bound by the work of Christ as one community. It is a foundation that has already been prepared.[160] There is a way out of estrangement, otherwise all would despair. The way out is not easy to see, especially if we go it alone. The status of estrangement convinces us that the way out is a matter of personal fortitude, but being-singular demands connection. It makes demands of the other. The individual, as being-singular, traverses estrangement with its own idea and vision. Being-singular attempts to establish community under its own name. Its community is founded on the self rather than the other. A community of the self cannot be a community of Christ. Christ-the-other is *Christ-the-community*. A community built on the selfish desire of the individual, being-singular, is doomed to fail.

her]. Bonhoeffer, *Life Together*, 25.

159. Community helps to ease the burden between the self and the other. Bonhoeffer writes that the "more genuine and the deeper our community becomes, the more will everything else between us recede, the more clearly and purely will Jesus Christ and his work become the one and only thing that is vital between us." Bonhoeffer, *Life Together*, 26.

160. "God has already laid the only foundation of our fellowship, because God has bound us together in one body with other Christians in Jesus Christ, long before we entered into common life with them, we enter into that common life not as demander but as thankful recipients." Bonhoeffer, *Life Together*, 28.

Community is a gift. It cannot be claimed as our own.[161] As a gift, community must be received to grow.[162] It is not something we can take for granted. Genuine connection with the other is not something we can take lightly. Community is a daily gift. It is a reminder that we are not alone. This gift is a reminder of the reality that calls all beings to participate. This is a reality "created by God in Christ in which we may participate."[163] It is the reality of the other and for the other. This is the reality of Christ that invites all people. It is the reality of ultimate openness. As such, it excludes no one. It is a reality where no other remains *other* because Christ became *other* for all.

Service is the foundation of the community of the other. True community sees hope in the other rather than the self. The community of the other loves the other for the sake of the other. True community loves others for the sake of Christ.[164] That is they love others for the other's own sake. The love of truth replaces the love of desire.[165] Truth here does not mean a proposition or law, nor is it a cold and disconnected propositional truth. The truth of the community is not from above, it comes from within. It is the truth that others matter more than the self. It is the truth that each person is valuable, and that value directly affects each person in a shared existence. It is the truth that being-singular-plural, being-with, is the destiny of every person. *Desire takes but truth gives.*

The community of Christ-the-other, is the community of *all* others. A community of exclusion is a community that excludes Christ. We cannot control the identity or status of the other. A genuine encounter with the other, a true encounter, is an encounter that places no conditions on who can be that other.[166] For who can put preconditions on the other and expect a community of truth, a community of Christ? The other must be unexpected. Unfortunately, sameness may replace otherness, whereby an

161. One can make the claim that any community, Christian or otherwise, is a gift. Any genuine community is a gift. Bonhoeffer declares, "Christian community is like the Christian's sanctification. It is a gift of God which we cannot claim." Bonhoeffer, *Life Together*, 30.

162. For example, Bonhoeffer writes that the "more thankfully we daily receive what is given to use, the more surely and steadily will fellowship increase and grow from day to day as God pleases." Bonhoeffer, *Life Together*, 30.

163. Bonhoeffer, *Life Together*, 30.

164. "Human love is directed to the other person for his [or her] own sake, spiritual love loves him [or her] for Christ's sake." Bonhoeffer, *Life Together*, 34.

165. "Human love lives by uncontrolled and uncontrollable dark *desires*; spiritual love lives in the clear light of service ordered by the *truth*." Bonhoeffer, *Life Together*, 37.

166. "The exclusion of the week and insignificant, the seemingly useless people, from a Christian community may actually mean the exclusion of Christ; in the poor brother [or sister] Christ is knocking at the door." Bonhoeffer, *Life Together*, 38.

encounter with the other must meet some criteria or standard. No demands should be placed on the other, for this is tantamount to putting demands on Christ. An excluding community excludes Christ-the-other. For without Christ community cannot exist. Therefore, a community that excludes is not a true community because it excludes its very foundation. Without Christ, community has no future.

THE OTHER AND THE COMMUNITY OF GOD

Christ-the-other is the reality of God. Bonhoeffer writes, "The *subject matter of a Christian ethic is God's reality revealed in Christ becoming real among God's creatures.*"[167] The reality of the other reveals the reality of God. God becomes real in the presence of others rather than the self. The experience of God is based upon an experience of the *we*. In the other (Christ) we experience the good (God). We cannot abstract the good from reality, for it is only in reality that we can find the good.[168] The reality of the good is the reality of God.[169] They are one and the same. To find the good we need to find the *other*. Therefore, the journey toward God is a journey toward the other (Christ). According to Bonhoeffer, "Only by participating in reality do we also share in the good."[170]

The individual and society are only be separated in abstraction.[171] The reality of the situation is that the individual cannot be split from society. Estrangement convinces us that our estrangement is in fact real. More importantly, estrangement blinds us to reality. In estrangement we can only see the self. Sin separates us from the reality of the other and therefore the reality of God. God is not found in the self, the *I*. This abstracts God from the lived conditions of life. We find God in the reality of the other.

The good is the reality of God. It is a reality that we cannot separate from human existence. Thus, the good encompasses all aspects of human behavior and action. Humans "with their motives and their works, with their fellow humans, with the creation that surrounds them . . . reality as a

167. Bonhoeffer, *Ethics*, 49 (emphasis original).

168. "Good is the real itself." Bonhoeffer, *Ethics*, 50.

169. Good, according to Bonhoeffer, is "not the abstractly real that is separated from the reality of God, but the real that has its reality only in God. Good is never without this reality." Bonhoeffer, *Ethics*, 50.

170. Bonhoeffer, *Ethics*, 51.

171. "The split between individual and society that is expressed here [referring to Reinhold Niebuhr's concepts of the moral human and immoral society] is just as abstract as that between person and work. What is inseparable is here torn apart, and each part, which by itself is dead, is examined separately." Bonhoeffer, *Ethics*, 51.

whole held in the hands of God—that is what is embraced by the question of the good."[172] The good is not separated from human action. This is not to say that works predicate the good. Works does not create the good for that would be tantamount to creating the reality of God. Rather, human action, behavior, and experience is where the good resides. The good resides in the other and God resides in the reality of the other. The good is experienced in the experience of others. As such, the good relates to the whole person, the whole other. This embrace of other is the embrace of the whole and indivisible person. Human beings are complete indivisible wholes both individually and in community.[173] God establishes this wholeness.[174]

Good relates to the whole person. Good relates to what occurs in the everyday experience of individuals working together and toward community. The good is found in the struggle, the resistance, between being-singular and being-singular-plural. The resistance includes all aspects of being human. The struggle between the self and the social is the struggle. Therefore, the good is part of the struggle. How do we experience the good? The good is experienced in the reality and resistance of the other. The good is the shared struggle with the other. It is the shared struggle in the reality of Christ.

The good is the participation of the whole self into the reality of God.[175] The good participates in the reality of God, and the reality of God is the good. They are one and the same. This good, the reality of God, is not abstracted from the reality of humanity. Both realities interpenetrate one another so that the reality of God is found in the reality of humanity. Therefore, the reality of humanity is the reality of God. The good is found neither above nor below it, but rather within it. As Bonhoeffer explains, "Good here does not consist of an impossible 'realization,' i.e., making real something that is unreal; it is not a realization of ethical ideas. Rather, reality itself teaches what is good."[176] Good only understood as an ideal or an ethic is the good of the self. Being-singular strives to create ideals or ethics. It seeks the source of the good within the self. The good becomes a matter of the *I* rather

172. Bonhoeffer, *Ethics*, 53.

173. "*Human beings are indivisible wholes, not only as individuals in both their person and work*, but *also as members of the human and created community* to which they belong." Bonhoeffer, *Ethics*, 53 (emphasis original).

174. "It is this indivisible whole, that is, this reality grounded and recognized in God, that the question of good has in view." Bonhoeffer, *Ethics*, 53.

175. "*To participate in the indivisible whole of God's reality is the meaning of the Christian question about the good.*" Bonhoeffer, *Ethics*, 53 (emphasis original).

176. Bonhoeffer, *Ethics*, 54.

than the *we*. It is a created good. The good cannot be created or destroyed because it is the reality of God. The reality of God is the reality of humanity.

Nowhere is this more evident than in the life of Christ. Christ is the physical manifestation of this interpenetration between the reality of God and the reality of humanity. Because Christ entered the reality of humanity, God (the good) and humanity are forever bound to one another. And Christ is the bond between these two realities. They are held together through and by Christ.[177] Christ is the reality of God and the reality of humanity together as one. Bonhoeffer states, "All concepts of reality that ignore Jesus Christ are abstractions."[178] There is no reality of God outside the reality of humanity, and there is no reality of humanity without the reality of the good. In Christ we participate in both.[179]

We cannot see how reality (humanity and God) function on their own. As such, the actions of God and humanity are bound to each other. We cannot look at human action, ritual or otherwise, without also looking at the action of God. There is neither a human nor divine ethic on its own. There is an only the ethic of Christ. The work of Christ is the work of God and humanity together. This God-humanity reality is the ultimate realization of being-singular-plural. And in Christ these realities are reconciled to one another. Because of this reconciliation, the question moving forward is no longer how one reality works with the other. Instead, the most pertinent question is how does this God-humanity reality work today? The work of Christ is the work of the here and now. It is the experience of both realities working as one.[180] Through Christ, contemporary problems, concerns, actions, and work are the concerns of both God and humanity.

The reality of God and the reality of humanity (God-humanity) should not be split. A division between God and humanity creates the unhelpful distinction of sacred and profane realities, with the sacred dominating the profane. Thus, the profane becomes inferior to the sacred. It becomes a

177. According to Bonhoeffer, "*In Jesus Christ the reality of God has entered into the reality of this world.* The place where the questions about the reality of God and about the reality of the world are answered at the same time is characterized solely by the name: Jesus Christ. God and the world are enclosed in this name." Bonhoeffer, *Ethics*, 54 (emphasis original).

178. Bonhoeffer, *Ethics*, 54.

179. Or as Bonhoeffer describes it, "In Christ we are invited to participate in the reality of God and the reality of the world at the same time, the one not without the other." Bonhoeffer, *Ethics*, 55.

180. "What matters is *participating in the reality of God and the world in Jesus Christ today*, and doing so in such a way that I never experience the reality of God without the reality of the world, nor the reality of the world without the reality of God." Bonhoeffer, *Ethics*, 55 (emphasis original).

relationship built on the wrong type of resistance. It is a resistance of the strong over the weak. The sacred and the profane are isolated from one another. As such, we are then called to make a choice between one and the other. We may choose to abandon the world for the sake of the sacred or choose to forsake the sacred for the profane. We may attempt to stay in both through our own strength. However, the *I* is then torn apart by eternal conflict.[181]

The God-humanity reality is one. This one reality is the Christ-reality. In Christ we move beyond the static distinctions between God and the world. Instead, in Christ, there is one dynamic reality that includes all the work of God in and through Christ. The sacred and profane lose all meaning as both are incorporated into one Christ-reality, a true being-with or being-singular-plural.[182] Being-singular no longer has the ability to stand on its own in such a reality. The Christ-reality is the reality of acceptance. It is the reality where the sacred and profane are both accepted as one through Christ.[183] In this reality, the work of God is fulfilled in the actions of human beings.[184] Therefore there is unity rather than opposition.[185] The sacred and the profane cease to be in the Christ-reality. The Christ-reality is one reality, and so it embraces the world. We cannot escape the reality of humanity by running toward the reality of God. Yet this is exactly the type of scenario created when these realities are positioned as static opposites. The Christianity of static opposition is a Christian that flees from the world. Such a Christianity, "falls prey to unnaturalness, irrationality, triumphalism, and arbitrariness."[186] The danger of separate realms is that it only furthers estrangement between God and humanity.

---

181. When reality is split "either we place ourselves in one of the two realms, wanting Christ without the world or the world without Christ—and in both cases we deceive ourselves. Or we try to stand in the two realms and the same time, thereby becoming people in eternal conflict." Bonhoeffer, *Ethics*, 58.

182. "Things work out quite differently when the reality of God and the reality of the world are recognized in Christ. In that way, the world, the natural, the profane, and reason are seen as included in God from the beginning." Bonhoeffer, *Ethics*, 59.

183. "It has its reality nowhere else than in the reality of God in Christ. It belongs to the real concept of the world that is at all times seen in the movement of the world's both having been accepted and becoming by God in Christ." Bonhoeffer, *Ethics*, 59.

184. That is this work, Bonhoeffer explains, "Realizes itself again and again in human beings." Bonhoeffer, *Ethics*, 59.

185. Meaning that, as Bonhoeffer puts it, "This unity is preserved by the fact that the worldly and the Christian, etc. mutually prohibit every static independence of the one over against the other, that they behave toward each other polemically." Bonhoeffer, *Ethics*, 59.

186. Bonhoeffer, *Ethics*, 61.

To live in Christ is to live in one reality. Life in the Christ-reality is not a life of separation or split realities. Christ does not further estrangement. Instead, to be in Christ is to also be in the world.[187] The Christ-reality points to wholeness both within and outside yourself. Both are necessary for overcoming estrangement. The Christ-reality is a life of accepting others and accepting yourself. Therefore, there is one realm, one space in the Christ-reality.

The one realm or one space of the Christ-reality calls for a *church-of-the-world*. The church is not a space of escape. It is not a refuge from the outside world nor does it live in a vacuum. The church cannot escape, even if it wanted, for there is nowhere to escape. A church that flees the world, flees its own purpose. More importantly, a church that flees ultimately flees from Christ. The church has no space to flee, nor does it have a space to call its own. It lives in the rented spaces of others.[188] Having no place to call its own, the church exists for the sake of others.[189] Though it has no place of its own, the church has not been abandoned. Christ has not left the church completely alone. In the Christ-reality, the church does have a space to live and work. Its space is the *world*.[190] Therefore, living in the spaces of others, the church lives in its work for others. Its actions, its existence, is tied to the existence of others. The church needs to be *being-with* to be the church, and in *being-with* it does the work of Christ. Once it ceases to do that it ceases to be the church.

The church does not fight for its own space. It fights for the spaces of others. The church fights for the excluded, marginalized, and forgotten. It does no action for itself. Therefore, the action of the church directly connects to others. In the church we should see the end of realms or separated realities. The reality of the church is the reality of the world, of Christ. Consequently, the church's work is the world's work. The church works and acts for Christ, therefore, all the church does exists in the world. The church does

187. "As reality is *one* in Christ, so the person who belongs to this Christ-reality is also a whole. Worldliness does not separate one from Christ, and being Christian does not separate one from the world. Belonging completely to Christ, one stands at the same time completely in the world." Bonhoeffer, *Ethics*, 62 (emphasis original).

188. The church lives in what Michel de Certeau describes as "a universe of rented spaces haunted by a nowhere or by dreamed-of places." Certeau, *Practice of Everyday Life*, 103.

189. Bonhoeffer writes that "the space of the church does not, therefore, exist just for itself, but its existence is already something that reaches far beyond it." Bonhoeffer, *Ethics*, 63.

190. "The space of the church is not there in order to fight with the world for a piece of its territory, but precisely to testify to the world that it is still the world, namely, the world that is loved and reconciled by God." Bonhoeffer, *Ethics*, 63.

not make space for Christ. Christ has already made space for the church through Christ's own redemptive action.[191] The church's work has already been done. The church is not the bridge between realms. It does not carry that burden. The church exists in the same state of estrangement shared by the world. In truth, the church shares in the general *otherness* of existence. The church itself is also *other*.

The church is not against the world. In *otherness*, the church shares itself for the world. The church shares in the *otherness*, not to fight against it, but to embrace it. The church does not embrace the world, the other, through its own will. It embraces the other because Christ already embraces all others.[192] Christ has already accepted both the church and the world. As such, there is no need for the church to reconcile the world. That is not the church's job. The work has already been done. Instead the church works in the world to show that Christ accepts the world. The church shares in the world so that the world may know that it is accepted. The actions of the church make that reality, the Christ-reality, visible.[193] The church does not create this reality, it merely exposes it. It uncovers it from the veil of estrangement so that it can proclaim Christ to one unified reality.[194]

PRACTICE AS PROCLAMATION

Foot washing proclaims one unified reality in Christ.[195] In foot washing, the church accepts and demonstrates its position as other. It accepts its *other-*

191. So, for example, Bonhoeffer writes that when one "wants to speak of the space of the church, one must be aware that this space has already been broken through, abolished, and overcome in every moment by the witness of the church to Jesus Christ." Bonhoeffer, *Ethics*, 64.

192. "There is no part of the world, no matter how lost, not matter how godless, that has not been accepted by God in Jesus Christ and reconciled to God." Bonhoeffer, *Ethics*, 67.

193. Bonhoeffer suggests that the church "expresses just this—that in the body of Christ all humanity is accepted, included, and borne, and that the church-community of believers is to make this known to the world by word and life." Bonhoeffer, *Ethics*, 67.

194. "It is the task and the essence of the church-community to proclaim precisely to this world its reconciliation with God, and to disclose to it the reality of the love of God, against which the world so blindly rages." Bonhoeffer, *Ethics*, 66.

195. This is a reality in which the words of Christ become real. The example of Christ is brought to others. A pastor explains his perspective, "I would say basically it's just following the example of Christ. And by following that example we are to likewise. If you look at the attitude in the upper room that night. Peter's response was 'Lord you'll never wash my feet.' The Lord told him if 'I don't wash your feet you'll have no part of me.' Peter's response was 'not just my feet, all of me.' To me that's an aspect that, the humility must come in. As Christians a lot of time we look at ourselves, and maybe we

ness so that the other might feel accepted and included. Thus, it opens a space for *all* others. Foot washing is an acceptance of one reality, the reality of the everyday. This reality is the reality of all others; therefore, the church is neither excludes nor is excluded. Unlike baptism or communion, you do not need to declare your faith before joining.[196] In this manner, foot washing is not set apart like baptism and communion. Whereas baptism and communion can be described as sacred, at least in the traditional sense, foot washing is not. Foot washing is not a sacred moment if the sacred consists of a escape from reality, the one Christ-reality. We cannot accept the everyday while remaining apart from it. Therefore, OFWBs choose the everyday. Foot washing signifies their choice. In foot washing, OFWBs choose the other. They choose Christ.

Foot washing is authentic in a way that baptism and communion are not. This is not to suggest that the actions of baptism and communion are in any way fake or false. Rather, separateness is fundamental to their being in a way that is not for foot washing. Certainly, anyone can be baptized without a profession of faith, but the action is not valid without a profession. An act of choice, "I choose Christ," makes the action real. Communion is contingent on the choice made in baptism. As such, only those who have made that choice can participate. Foot washing requires no such choice or commitment, at least for most OFWBs. If one is willing, he or she may participate in foot washing without making a profession of faith. Foot washing is not dependent on any prior choice. As long as you are other, and all are, you are invited.

Even the place of practice signifies foot washing's embrace of the everyday. Typically, OFWBs practice foot washing in a place other than the sanctuary.[197] Whether it is the fellowship hall, choir room, or a classroom,

---

see ourselves different than others, I know a lot times we see ourselves different then the way maybe Christ sees us. A lot of time it is hard to humble you. I take foot washing in the same aspect as the altar. You look at a lot of people; a lot of people will not go to the altar on a Sunday morning service. You don't understand why because you've basically taken your burdens to Christ, sharing your burdens with Christ, and he already knows about your burden. He told us to cast our cares upon him and to trust him. Foot washing [is] within the same perspective, when we're willing to do that we're not just taking a part of what Christ said but we are taking all of what Christ said." Interview with OFWB pastor (K), February 12, 2015.

196. At least based on the OFWB *Articles of Faith*. Practices vary from church to church, but there is no written rule preventing an unbaptized individual from participating.

197. Explaining how it is typically done, a pastor reflects how "it was at [church name], that church still divided the men and the women. At the time when we were there, they had a petition, say roughly 30 inches high that went down the center aisle of the church. And the ladies sat on one side and the men sat on the other. When they did

foot washing points to places other than the sanctuary.[198] Foot washing moves us from the sacred to the mundane. It gives special significance to the places we assume as regular or typical. Of course, this movement into other areas of the church is primarily for practical reasons such as space and modesty.[199] However, even in its practicality foot washing demonstrates something remarkable. Foot washing is not for sacred spaces. Instead it lives where people congregate and interact, like fellowship halls. Through and through, foot washing is mundane. Therefore, foot washing fits the OFWB character. The OFWB are practical people. They are very much, *what you see is what you get* type of people. Foot washing *works* because the people *work*. They *work* together in their *otherness*. Foot washing is thus their way of expressing their *otherness* and *acceptance* of one another.

Foot washing exposes the Christ-reality, thus uncovering it from the veil of estrangement. When practiced, the action of foot washing does not proclaim itself. Neither are the OFWBs proclaiming themselves. When OFWBs practice foot washing, they proclaim the reality of the *now*. Foot washing is not about connecting with a metaphysical or spiritual realm. It is a face-to-face encounter with the other. Foot washing is nothing less than up close and personal.[200] We cannot escape this reality because this reality is staring us in the face. There is no higher plane to escape to. This is the reality of touch, intimacy, and uncomfortableness. Foot washing is the *stuff* of the everyday. It is the *stuff* that is neither quantifiable nor predictable. Quite frankly, foot washing does not make sense. Yet this is why foot wash-

---

feet washing they did one at the time in what we would refer to now as a Sunday school room. One on each side, one lady at the time or two ladies rather. Two went in and two came out. They didn't do it collectively like we do now. The same thing with the men. It was that way as well. Of course now, the ladies go to their appropriate place and the men go to theirs. Everybody's either singing or doing feet washing all together taking turns basically speaking of taking care of each other." Interview with OFWB pastor (D), March 30, 2015.

198. Foot washing does and can occur in the sanctuary as well. In such case it usually occurs in the pews rather than the altar. Even in the sanctuary foot washing moves away from the places traditional considered as sacred.

199. This is not a perfect example of one reality in Christ. There is no perfect way of demonstrating the Christ-reality. OFWBs usually divide men and women in foot washing. This is done for modesty rather than signifying some ontological divide between men and women. The practice is meant to be equal for both men and women. Ideally men and women would wash one another's feet to demonstrate the oneness of their fellowship.

200. A pastor describes foot washing's personal nature, He says, "I feel like it's tied to the fact that we are incarnate, we're in the flesh. I think it's a very incarnational type of act for our church. I view it as a sacramental thing. It reminds us that we are incarnate. It leads to the incarnation of Christ. He came in the flesh to minister to people who are in the flesh." Interview with OFWB pastor, February 6, 2015.

ing works so well. It proclaims the unpredictable nature of life. It proclaims our humanity, the *otherness* of reality. It proclaims a reality that Christ has accepted and made his own.

TRUE LOVE

The Christ-reality is the reality of love. It is *one* reality, *one* acceptance, and *one* love in Christ. Therefore, the Christ-reality can also be called the *reality of love*. To love is to live in this reality. Love does not escape or separate itself from this realm. Love does not seek a higher plane of existence. It does idealize a reality hidden from human eyes. Love is the reality of Christ and, as Bonhoeffer writes, "Our living as real human beings, and loving the real people next to us is, again, grounded only in God's becoming human, in the unfathomable love of God for us human beings."[201] Love is grounded in Christ's love for the other as the ultimate other. Participation in the reality of the other is a participation in the reality of Christ. It is allowing ourselves to be formed and molded into the Christ reality, which is the reality of love. Christ, *who is love*, forms human beings.[202] And only love can form us into love.[203] Love molds us into itself. We do not add love to our own being. Love is never an addition to being. To be formed by love is to become love. Love is total, or it is not at all. Love forms us into its own form.[204]

The church, Bonhoeffer asserts, "Is not a religious community of those who revere Christ, but Christ who has taken form among human beings."[205] The church takes on this form, the form of love, in order share this love with all the world. The church is no greater than anyone else. It is neither special nor unique.[206] It lives in estrangement and *otherness*. It is not the church that acts, but Christ who acts through the church. The church does not proclaim a religion, instead the church proclaims the Christ-reality to all.[207]

201. Bonhoeffer, *Ethics*, 87.

202. "Formation occurs only by being drawn into the form of Jesus Christ, by *being conformed to the unique form of the one who became human, was crucified, and is risen*." Bonhoeffer, *Ethics*, 93 (emphasis original).

203. "Christ remains the only one who forms. Christian people do not form the world with their ideas." Bonhoeffer, *Ethics*, 93.

204. "Christ forms human beings to a form the same as Christ's own." Bonhoeffer, *Ethics*, 93

205. Bonhoeffer, *Ethics*, 96.

206. "The church is nothing but that piece of humanity where Christ really has taken form. . . . The church is the human being who has become human, has been judged, and has been awakened to new life in Christ." Bonhoeffer, *Ethics*, 97.

207. The "church's concern is not a religion, but the form of Christ and its taking

The church acts for human beings. The church does not act for a theory or a philosophy. The church acts for people, for all reality, or it does not act at all.[208] As an action of the church, foot washing is an act for people, so that all may know the Christ-reality. Ultimately, this is why OFWBs do foot washing. OFWBs practice foot washing for people.[209] They are the embodiment of Christ for others.[210] It is a *real love for real people.*

---

form among a band of people." Bonhoeffer, *Ethics*, 97.

208. Bonhoeffer makes it very clear that Christ acts for people rather than ideas. Christ became human. Christ did not become an idea. He states that "Christ was not concerned about whether 'the maxim of an action' could become 'a principle of universal law,' but whether my action now helps my neighbor to be a human being before God. God did not become an idea, a principle, a program, a universally valid belief, or a law; God became human." Bonhoeffer, *Ethics*, 99.

209. "It's a vibrant part of us as a denomination. To me it is a major part of who I am as an OFWB." Interview with OFWB pastor (D), March 30, 2015.

210. "*The church is the place where Jesus Christ's taking form is proclaimed and where it happens.*" Bonhoeffer, *Ethics*, 102 (emphasis original).

CHAPTER SIX

Toward a Relational Practical Theology

THE SILENT LANGUAGE

INTERPRETATION RUNS THE RISK of saying too much. Sometimes we need to step back and appreciate the silence. Silence is an appreciation of what we cannot say, hear, and predict in interpretation.[1] The early Wittgenstein suggests that "what can be said at all can be said clearly, and what we cannot talk about we must pass over in silence."[2] Certain limits should be respected in interpretation. Interpretation includes the known and the limits of what we cannot know.[3] The goal is balancing between language (the said or known) and silence (what we cannot say or know). Interpretation does not work to organize and categorize. Silence is not a mystery we need to solve or explain. Instead, interpretation is a matter of respecting silence and mystery.[4] Silence represents what we cannot put into words.[5]

---

1. It is not only important but necessary. Silence keeps our minds open. Franke writes, "The idea or ideal of the whole greater than what we can apprehend, of the whole that is yet to come, is actually necessary to keep us from closing the circle of our own little utopia around those who think like us, thereby ignoring the demand of universality." Franke, *Philosophy*, 46.

2. Wittgenstein, *Tractatus Logico-Philosophicus*, 3.

3. Wittgenstein writes that "in order to be able to draw a limit to thought, we should have to find both sides of the limit thinkable (i.e. we should have to be able to think what cannot be thought)." Wittgenstein, *Tractatus Logico-Philosophicus*, 3.

4. Sometimes what is most fundamental and true is what cannot be said. Franke states, "Truth is not what we grasp and deliver in the end as our final discourse, but what escapes all our formulations and remains in the silence after all is said and done." Franke, *Philosophy*, 53.

5. "There are, indeed, things that cannot be put into words. They make themselves

Silence is pregnant with meaning,[6] and meaning is birthed from silence.[7] Meaning, linguistic or otherwise, is not *ex nihilo*. Language may
begin in the mind, but as Martin Buber explains, "Speech does not abide in
man, but man takes his stand in speech and talks from there."[8] Language is
not its own creator, rather it begins in the unformed state of silence. Silence
is a place of openness, holding the unformed words yet to come. Augustine
recognized the value of silence, "Therefore, my God, my confession before
you is made both in silence and not in silence. It is silent in that it is not
audible sound; but in love it cries aloud."[9] Silence is not devoid of meaning,
instead silence speaks.

Silence challenges language.[10] Silence reminds language that it is not
alone. Language needs challenging for we *talk too much*.[11] Language comes
easy, and expression is not ending anytime soon.[12] The Teacher recognized
this long ago writing, "Of making many books there is no end."[13] While si-

---

manifest. They are what is mystical." Wittgenstein, *Tractatus Logico-Philosophicus*, 89.

6. "What we most strongly and deeply think and believe, what we passionately love
or ardently desire, inevitably escapes adequate articulation. It is always more, if not
completely other, than what we are able to say. This common human experience of butt-
ing up against the limits of language is experienced paradigmatically in the disciplines
of philosophy, theology, and poetry." Franke, *Philosophy*, 23.

7. "Nothing is pregnant with Everything—albeit a new, wild everything set free
from the nets and webs of language and so no longer corralled by Logos." Franke, *Philosophy*, 68.

8. Buber, *I and Thou*, 39.

9. Augustine, *Confessions*, 179.

10. Language is challenge by the unsayable. Sometimes a helpful skepticism about
language can help to make what can be said more understandable. Franke explains,
"The apophatic sage is skeptical about all this is known—all that is accessible to language—in order to be fascinated by the mystery that language does not deliver and
cannot master. In this way, when apophatic writers deprecate language, they have already presupposed its potency to gesture toward what it is insufficient to articulate but
nevertheless indicates as lying beyond itself." Franke, *Philosophy*, 64.

11. "The surprising thing, therefore, is not our difficulty in speaking of God but
indeed our difficulty in keeping silent. For in fact, with regard to God, overwhelm-
ingly, we speak. In a sense we speak only about that, and much too much, with neither
modesty nor precaution." Marion, *God Without Being*, 55.

12. Perhaps this indicates that there is still something that cannot be said. Human
beings are still searching for the right words to express the inexpressible. Franke argues
that this process will continue indefinitely. He writes that "what motivates never-ending
human saying of things could only be something that never can be said. The very fact
that we go on speaking indicates that something—something that concerns us enough
to make us keep on speaking—still remains unsaid. And since there is no built-in limit
to the continuation of our speaking, this something unsaid proves, in effect, to be unsayable, at least for as long as we go on speaking." Franke, *Philosophy*, 24.

13. Ecc 12:12 (NRSV).

lence is uncomfortable, language is oppressive. Language oppresses silence by telling it keep *silent*.[14] In a manner of speaking, silence is not allowed to *speak*.[15]

We should respect silence.[16] In interpretation, silence can become an obstacle to meaning. Thus, we fight against silence hoping that its removal will pave the way toward clarity. However, to fight against silence is to fight against interpretation itself. Silence exists within the foundation of language.[17] It marks the boundary and limit of language.[18] And instead of fighting silence, our interpretation must shift toward acknowledging its presence.

Silence is the flux, the unknown element. It is the unexpected within the expected. Once acknowledged, silence points toward the future. Marion writes, "This silence, and no other, knows where it is, whom it silences, and why it must, for yet a time, preserve a mute decency—to free itself from idolatry."[19] The silence must remain free to preserve the unexpected, waiting for its moment to emerge.[20] This hidden silence waits in all language,

---

14. Language can push silence away, and we are no longer able to *hear* the silence. Buber argues, "But truly though God surrounds us and dwells in us, we never have [God] in us. And we speak with [God] only when speech dies within us." Buber, *I and Thou*, 104.

15. There is discourse that "disqualifies or deconstructs the very notion of God; this discourse consists in speaking of God in order to silence [God], in not keeping silent in order to silence him." Marion, *God Without Being*, 55.

16. Marion explains, "More modestly, the silence suitable to [God] requires knowing how to remain silent, not out of agnosticism (the polite surname of impossible atheism) or out of humiliation, but simply out of respect." Marion, *God Without Being*, 107.

17. "We seek reassurance from language, from the stories it tells us, but words always essentially cancel themselves out because their meaning ultimately posits some absolute, unambiguous presence which can never be concretely given in the medium of language. It is the nature of the words as signs to indicate something absent from themselves, something they are not." Franke, *Philosophy*, 76.

18. "Silence, therefore, is not to be set in binary opposition to language, but is rather the margin that demarcates its center." Wolfson, *Language, Eros, Being*, 289.

19. Marion, *God Without Being*, 107.

20. Silence, the unsayable, reaches us at precisely the right moment. Franke writes, "The *what* that is said is but a vehicle for an undefined and indefinable, unspeakable but superlatively, pathetically significant . . . we cannot say what. We are confronted with this unspeakable again and again in the drama of human existence, and we are driven to all manners of shifts and evasions with words in our more or less transparent attempts to master it. It reaches us precisely at the moment when we perceive what cannot be said as the real and vital meaning or meaninglessness of all that actually is said." Franke, *Philosophy*, 78 (emphasis original).

including the body. The body hides what is to come. It hides the coming in-between, the unknown, and the unexpected.

It is necessary to find ways of appreciating and respecting silence.[21] This is especially important for interpreting ritual action. The natural tendency is to interpret and explain. As such, a respectful interpretation is one that respects and appreciates silence. It respects and appreciates what we cannot know.[22] Interpretation is that which respects silence and accepts it as boundary that we cannot across. This boundary is not a failure of knowledge or the absence of meaning. The boundary allow room for the unexpected to emerge.

SHIFTING TO RELATIONALITY

Engaging ritual action requires us to shift toward relationality. How this relationality will look remains a vexing problem. How do we approach ritual action without analyzing it like an object or a thing? Objectification of ritual action is challenging for the theologian, philosopher, and social theorist.[23] Over confidence remains a problem in ritual action. This is true for scholars and academics who still declare with total assurance, "See! This is what it means!" Scholars and academics would be better suited to follow the example of Paul who admits that even he does not understand his own actions.[24]

---

21. It requires a sensitivity to silence. Language does not have the final say. What cannot be said is as important as what can be said. Franke states, "Sensitivity to the apophatic means learning to interpret our own language somewhat more cannily in its inescapable relation to what it cannot say. This relation, though invisible and purely negative, determines our bearing toward all that we can and do say. . . . Perhaps we can learn to read them better by reading them together." Franke, *Philosophy*, 79.

22. "Discourses do not always—or perhaps ever—say what their deepest meaning and motivations are. To fathom this 'truth' we have to break with interpreting just the words, and yet, paradoxically, only the words [or actions] are there to guide us . . . beyond themselves." Franke, *Philosophy*, 79.

23. The temptation of objectification can never be removed. Human beings have a natural inclination toward knowing *how* things work. For the most part, this inclination serves humanity well. This works well in determining the nature of the universe or how a machine functions but is remarkably bad at determining human behavior. Human beings are notoriously illogical and unpredictable. Often, human beings do not know why they do the things they do. Humans are paradoxical in that pursue paths and courses of action that they know will fail. They continue practices they know are destructive to their own health and the health of those around them. Ascribing any meaning, globally or individual, to human practices appears as a futile endeavor. However, despite this, human beings continue to proclaim the meaning of things.

24. Consider Paul's classic formulation, "I do not understand my own actions. For I do not do what I want, but I do the very thing I hate." Rom 7:15 (NRSV).

Scholars and academics, theologically, philosophically, and socially, look from the outside in. While doing so, they determine the meaning of these actions. For them, meaning is coming from the outside in and ignores the meaning already present. It may not be the predicted meaning, but meaning was never absent. Ritual actions were already meaningful. The scholar only needs to converse with the meaning already present.[25]

Going forward, we require a *relational practical theology*. Using Martin Buber as a guide, let us take a glimpse at what a relational practical theology might look like. His seminal work, *I and Thou* can serve as a basis for future theological, philosophical, and social engagement with ritual action.

I, Thou, and It

Ritual action can be approached as a *thou* rather than an *It*. The mentality between a *Thou* and *It* is remarkably different. As Buber puts it, "Every *It* is bounded by others; *It* exists only through being bounded by others. But when *Thou* is spoken, there is no thing. *Thou* has no bounds."[26] *It* is under the control of others, existing for the will of others. *It* is used, manipulated, and regulated. *It* is the perfect scientific specimen, suitable for testing. All interaction with the *It* is one-sided, making true relationship impossible. The *It* exists for the *I*'s pleasure. Many of life's experiences are based on an *I-It* relationship.[27]

The *Thou* is characteristically different from the *It*. The *I* dominates the *It*, subduing "its actual presence and form so sternly that I recognise it only as an expression of law."[28] In contrast, an *I-Thou* relationship is a true relationship. In such a relationship, *I* does not control or objectify the *Thou*. Instead, it is a relationship of being bound. The *I* is bound in relationship to the *Thou*.

It is important to distinguish between experience and relationship, especially in person-to-person encounters. An experience is not necessarily a relationship. We can experience another person's existence without entering a relationship. An experience can be completely one-sided and impersonal. For example, the scientist experiences an object under his or her control when testing a hypothesis. A relationship, on the other hand, is a standing

25. This meaning, or meanings, may be unpredictable and unclear. Nevertheless, it is still meaning.

26. Buber, *I and Thou*, 4.

27. Buber writes, "As experience, the world belongs to the primary word *I-It*." Buber, *I and Thou*, 6.

28. Buber, *I and Thou*, 7.

before the other. The entire existence of the *I* stands before the *Thou*. Furthermore, it is not only that the *I* stands before the *Thou*. The *I* stands before the *Thou* in relationship.[29] A relationship with the *Thou* is, as Buber suggests, "the cradle of the Real Life."[30]

Relationship with the *Thou* comes as an act of grace.[31] It is meeting in the truest sense of the word. The *Thou* meets the *I* and in return the *I* enters into a direct relationship with the *Thou*.[32] The *Thou* does not coerce the *I*, rather the *I* chooses the *Thou*. The *I* accepts the *Thou's* invitation of a direct relationship.[33] This direct relationship is one of becoming. The *I* meets the *Thou*, and in turn is shaped and molded by the *Thou*. Thus, the *I* becomes an *I* only in relation to the *Thou*.[34] We do not enter the *Thou* and remain the same. Distance prevents growth in the *I-It* experience, but the *I-Thou* relationship fosters change.

The *I-Thou* relationship, is in the *eternal now*.[35] It is a continual process. The *I-Thou* is never complete, and it is always in the indeterminate flux of the now.[36] Because the relationship is never fixed, either in time or space, there remains the possibility of change. Both the *Thou* and the *I* exist in an indeterminate state. In each moment of the now, there is the potential for the *Thou* to shape the *I* and vice versa. It is a mutual relationship of shared

29. Or as Buber describes it, "I do not experience the man [or woman] to whom I say *Thou*. But I take my stand in relation to him, in the sanctity of the primary word. Only when I step out of it do I experience him [or her] once more. In the act of experience *Thou* is far away." Buber, *I and Thou*, 9.

30. Buber, *I and Thou*, 9.

31. "The *Thou* meets me through grace—it is not found by seeking." Buber, *I and Thou*, 11.

32. "The *Thou* meets me. But I step into direct relation with it. Hence the relation means being chosen and choosing, suffering and action in one." Buber, *I and Thou*, 11.

33. "The relation to the *Thou is direct*." Buber, *I and Thou*, 11 (emphasis original).

34. "I become through my relation to the *Thou*; as I become the *I*, I say *Thou*. All real living is meeting." Buber, *I and Thou*, 11.

35. As opposed to the *I-It* experience, where the *I* meets its objects in the past. According to Buber, "True beings are lived in the present, the life of objects is in the past." Buber, *I and Thou*, 13. As Tillich puts it, "We accept the present and do not care that it is gone in the moment that we accept it. We live in in and it is renewed for us in every new 'present.' This is possible because every moment of time reaches into the eternal. It is the eternal that stops the flux of time for us. It is the eternal 'now' which provides for us a temporal 'now.'" Tillich, *Eternal Now*, 131.

36. Living in the present prevents the *I-Thou* from becoming fixed. Buber explains that the "present is not fugitive and transient, but continually present and enduring. The object is not duration, but cessation, suspension, a breaking off and cutting clear and hardening, absence of relation and of present being." Buber, *I and Thou*, 13.

flux and instability.[37] A relationship with the *Thou* has to be indeterminate and instable, otherwise it risks being turned into a *It*. Buber suggests that when "the relation has been worked out or has been permeated with a means, the *Thou* becomes an object among objects—perhaps the chief, but still one of them."[38] As soon as the *I-Thou* relationship is defined it ceases to be *I-Thou* and becomes *I-It*. At the removal of the mystery, only the cold analysis of objectification remains. This is the continual temptation of the *I*. The *I*, unsatisfied with the undefined *Thou*, attempts to define the *Thou*. Perhaps it is done in an act of respect, and thus the *I* goes too far in seeking to better understand the *Thou*. The *I*, in its hubris, fails to recognize its own limitations. It fails to respect the boundaries between what is known and unknown. The *I* believes it knows more than it actually does and creates a thing of the *Thou*.[39]

The *I-Thou* relationship is unpredictable. This is due to the constant changing nature of the relationship. Because the relationship lives in the present, it is always subject to change. The past does not determine it, nor is the future set. As such, between the *I* and *Thou*, there is a mutual giving leading to mutual change.[40] This changes our total being. Once we enter an *I-Thou* relationship, it forever changes all our future relationships. All other relationships are subsequently compared to *Thou*, creating within us a continual longing. An experience of the *Thou* is an experience of infinite possibility. In meeting the *Thou*, we meet the infinite new.[41] Its *now-ness* precludes the *I-Thou* relationship from being set in space and time.[42] It occurs in the ever-present moment of the now.[43]

37. Buber writes, "Relation is mutual. My *Thou* affects me, as I affect it. We are molded by our pupils and built up by our works. . . . We live our lives inscrutably included within the streaming mutual life of the universe." Buber, *I and Thou*, 15–16.

38. Buber, *I and Thou*, 17.

39. "Every *Thou* in the world is by its nature fated to become a thing, or continually to re-enter into the condition of things." Buber, *I and Thou*, 17.

40. "Between you and it there is mutual giving: you say *Thou* to it and give yourself to it, it says *Thou* to you and gives itself to you." Buber, *I and Thou*, 33.

41. "You cannot make yourself understood with others concerning it, you are alone with it. But it teaches you to meet others, and to hold your ground when you meet them. Through the graciousness of its comings and the solemn sadness of its going it leads you away to the *Thou* in which the parallel lines of relations meet. It does not help to sustain you in life, it only helps you to glimpse eternity." Buber, *I and Thou*, 33.

42. "The world of *It* is set in the context of space and time. The world of *Thou* is not set in the context of either of these." Buber, *I and Thou*, 33.

43. "The mystery is that we *have* a present; and even more, that we have *our* future also because we anticipate it in the present; and that we have *our* past also, because we remember it in the present. In the present our future and our past are *ours*." Tillich, *Eternal Now*, 130 (emphasis original).

The *I-Thou* is fundamentally important for understanding ritual action. There is a striking contrast between objectification (*I-It*) and relationship (*I-Thou*). The temptation for scholars is to approach ritual action from the position of the *I-It*. This is the position of distance. We may experience the ritual action, in terms of participating and being present, but scholarly distance keeps us in the role of an outsider. If we remain at a distance, objectification cannot be overcome. Ritual action remains a thing. Scholarly distance is still important. However, between the *I-It* and *I-Thou* there is fundamental difference in interpretation. In the *I-It*, meaning is thrust upon ritual action from the outside. In the *I-Thou* meaning is relational. We enter a relationship with the other and are bound to that other. An *I-Thou* relationship is one that changes the scholar and the participant. Both enter into a mutual relationship with one another.

The *I-Thou* relationship is twofold. In addition to the relationship between the scholar and action there is the relationship between participants. The *I-Thou* requires both a recognition of the *I* (the individual) and the *Thou* (individuals in relationship). To be clear, this relationship cannot last forever. Inevitably *I-Thou* returns to *I-It*. Once the relationship of the present becomes an experience of the past, the ritual action becomes yet again a thing. This is a natural progression of experience into knowledge. The goal is recognizing this continual back and forth between *I-Thou* and *I-It*. We do not seek to stay in the experience of the *I-It*. The hope is that we would return to the relationship of the *I-Thou*.

The Mutual Relation of I-Thou

The *I-It* and the *I-Thou* are distinguished by spirit. According to Buber, "Spirit in its human manifestation is a response of man to his *Thou*."[44] Inbetween the *I* and *Thou* is spirit. Spirit is not something that comes from outside this relationship. Instead, spirit denotes the relationship between the two. Spirit is what enables the *I* to enter a relationship with the *Thou*. Spirit "is not like the blood that circulates in you, but like the air in which you breathe."[45] By living in this spirit, breathing it in, the *I* enters the *Thou*. The *I-Thou* is thus a spiritual encounter whereas *I-It* is based on knowledge. The experience is not necessarily spiritual, but a relationship implies a connection that one may call spiritual.[46] Spirit suggests a continual openness, an

---

44. Buber, *I and Thou*, 39.

45. Buber, *I and Thou*, 39.

46. "Only in virtue of his [or her] power to enter into relation is he [or she] able to live in the spirit." Buber, *I and Thou*, 39.

ability to live in the now, while *I-It* fixes things in place to better describe it. *I-It* slows and stops the flux, while the spiritual nature of *I-Thou* lives in the unpredictable and instable now. In between the self and the other, the spirit teaches the *I* how to live in the presence of the *Thou*. Life in the spirit, in the presence of the *Thou*, is a relationship with the living.[47] What separates *I-It* from *I-Thou* is a life lived among the living. The *I-It* experience is that of the past. It codifies life and thus ends it. The *I-Thou*, on the other hand, lives into life.

The realm of the *I-It* is institutions. In contrast, the realm of *I-Thou* is life itself. The institution is where the *It* is poked and prodded. It is a place of knowledge.[48] The institution takes what was alive and immobilizes it for careful study. The institution provides a snapshot of the object. We can learn a lot from a snapshot, everything *about* the object, but not the *living* subject in question.

The goal of the institution is not relationship. Buber states that the "separated *It* of institutions is an animated clod without soul, and the separated *I* of feelings an uneasily fluttering soul-bird. Neither of them knows [humanity]."[49] The mutual relation of the *I-Thou* is outside the boundary of both. The *I-Thou* relationship requires more than increased study or personal fervor. The *I-Thou* relationship is a living mutual relationship.[50]

This living mutual relationship is thus the goal of both the *I-Thou* relationship and our own being. The goal of relation "is relation's own being, that is, contact with the *Thou*."[51] A relationship with the *Thou* is a sharing of being. Thus, an *I-Thou* relationship is truly an encounter with the other. The *I* encounters the other, not as a thing, but as unified whole. Unlike the *I-It*, where both parties remain unchanged, *I-Thou* signals a relationship built on change. This change is due to the sharing of being with the other. The other no longer remains on the outside of the *I*'s existence, nor is the other

47. "This life is present, then, to those who come later, to teach them not what is and must be, but how life is lived in the spirit, face to face with the *Thou*." Buber, *I and Thou*, 42.

48. Buber defines institutions as the place "where all sorts of aims are pursued, where a man [or woman] works, negotiates, bears influence, undertakes, concurs, organizes, conducts business, officiates, preaches. They are tolerably well-ordered and to some extent harmonious structure, in which, with the manifold help of men's [and women's] brains and hand, the process of affairs is fulfilled." Buber, *I and Thou*, 43.

49. Buber, *I and Thou*, 44.

50. "Living mutual relation includes feelings, but does not originate with them. The community is built up out of living mutual relation, but the builder is the living effective Centre." Buber, *I and Thou*, 45.

51. Buber, *I and Thou*, 63.

absorbed into the *I*. Instead the other becomes a *Thou*.[52] Consequently, in a mutual relationship, a sharing existence, the other becomes a *Thou*. Buber writes that the "more direct the contact with the *Thou*, the fuller is the sharing."[53] The sharing serves to further the relationship and connection with the *Thou*. In this connection, the *I* realizes its true being and purpose. In the *Thou*, the *I* discovers itself as a sharing being.[54] We begin to define ourselves in relation to others. The *Thou* enlightens our own being, thus saving us from our own individuality.[55]

The *I-Thou* represents the ideal of theological relationship. The goal of theological reflection is neither for the institution nor the individual. Instead, in theological reflection we enter a relationship with the *Thou*. This is a theology founded on the *I-Thou* rather than the *I-It*. The theology of the *I-It* is a theology that exists for itself. It sees the outside world as a thing to study or discover. Thus, theology masters the object and by implication imposes its own will and purpose on an unwilling other. This is the theology of the institution or the scholar. It is a theology that proclaims and passes judgment on all it sees. The *I-It* is the theology of the strong. It is the inability to enter into a relationship with the other. Fearing change, it is unwilling to submit itself into the hands of the other. The *I-It* is a theology of distance. It remains at a safe distance because it fears the possibility of change. The *I-It* theology is careful to keep itself on the side of power. It seeks change, but not change for itself. *I-It* theology seeks to change the *It* without changing itself.

I-It theology is experience but not a relationship. Experience does not equal relationship. We can experience the other without building a relationship. There is no easy way of defining the passage from experience to relationship. Relationships do not form overnight, though some experiences can create the illusion of relationship. Their sudden and overwhelming intensity can create a belief of relationship. Of course, experiences can lead into a relationship, but there is no guarantee that they will. Relationships can develop from the repeated exposure of experience. Our experiences of another's thoughts, feelings, opinions, and story help form the foundation of relationship.

52. "He [or she] who takes his [or her] stand in relation shares in a reality, that is, in a being that neither merely belongs to him [or her] nor merely lies outside him [or her]." Buber, *I and Thou*, 63.

53. Buber, *I and Thou*, 63.

54. "The person becomes conscious of himself [or herself] as sharing in being, as co-existing, and thus as being." Buber, *I and Thou*, 63.

55. "The more a man [or woman], humanity, is mastered by individuality, the deeper does the *I* sink into unreality." Buber, *I and Thou*, 65.

We must work at a relationship for it to develop. The *I-Thou* requires the involvement of both parties in mutual sharing. The *I-Thou* is a sharing of existence, whereas the *I-It* retains a mutual independence. Mutual sharing parallels the theological relationship. It suggests a theology that not only seeks to experience the other, but also enters the other's life. Such a theology would recognize that it is not enough to explore and experience the world.[56] Consequently, a relational practical theology would consider ritual action as an opportunity for growth and mutual sharing.[57] In this case, ritual action ceases to be a stranger and becomes a theological partner. Ritual action is a sharing of existence. Theology shares in the life of the community, and in turn, the community shares its life theologically. Mutual sharing blurs who is doing theology. Theology becomes something shared between the theologian and the community. Ritual action *speaks* its theology and shares itself with the theologian. It opens itself to the theologian, and in turn, the theologian is opened to the ritual action.

This relationship is constantly changing. There are times when the *I-Thou* reverts to an *I-It*. The theologian and the community inevitably separate. It is impossible to achieve a perfect union; one where mutual sharing can continue indefinitely. There is inevitably a break between the theologian and community. This is precisely why relationship is so difficult. We have to continually seek it. We seek relationship, the *Thou*, continually.

Thou, God, and Theology

A theology of sharing places us into an encounter with God. The *I-Thou* applies not only to a relationship between persons, but also a relationship with God.[58] The *Thou* is a personal and complete confrontation with the other. This is not a partial encounter, thus our total being comes face-to-face with the *Thou*. The *I-Thou* relationship is a direct relation between whole beings. Moving toward each other, the *Thou* offers the invitation, which the *I* either accepts or rejects. The *I* cannot partially accept the *Thou*. It must be

56. A theology that explains or seeks to justify its existence (or God's for that matter) remains paralyzed in the *I-It*. It is a theology of the *I* in a world of *Its*. A theology of the *I-Thou*, on the other hand, abandons itself. It abandons its desire to be for itself so that it might be for the other.

57. The implication being that theology would seek not only to study the other but enter into the life of the other.

58. "For he [or she] who speaks the word God and really has *Thou* in mind (whatever the illusion by which he [or she] is held), addresses the true *Thou* of his [or her] life, which cannot be limited by another *Thou*, and to which he [or she] stand in a relation that gathers up and includes all others." Buber, *I and Thou*, 76.

complete or not at all. The *I* steps toward the *Thou*, leaving nothing of itself behind. The *Thou* will accept nothing less.[59]

Confrontation with the *Thou* takes place in the world rather than some outside reality. When confronting the *Thou*, we encounter others in shared space. The space of the *Thou* is the same space of the *I*. The *I-Thou* is not an otherworldly relationship, instead it occurs in the unfolding present without a barrier of separation.[60] It suggests a real and present relationship that occurs in the face-to-face encounter within the *I-Thou*. We must be in a position to meet our *Thou*. This can only take place in present reality. Buber states that "the one thing that matters is visible, full acceptance of the present."[61] We must accept the present as a place of encounter to meet the *Thou*. If our gaze is elsewhere, we cannot help but miss the *Thou*. The search for a world outside of the present, such as the metaphysical, ignores the present *Thou*. It ignores the *Thou's* present work in individual persons and communities.

The temptation is to hold onto to these otherworldly realms. The metaphysical becomes a scholarly domains of control. They exist as realms of the *It*, places where theologians and philosophers can confidently dabble. These realms function as a sandbox of experimentation, an eternal playground of control where scholars are only limited by their imaginations. In such places the *Thou* cannot exist. The world outside the present is a world of control and manipulation. It is no wonder that theologians and philosophers would prefer this over the present.[62] The present represents the uncontrollable and unpredictable. Scholars keep order in the metaphysical, but the present moment is beyond their control. It is subject to no one. The irony is that theologians and philosophers flee the present to find God and Being. They seek truth, goodness, and beauty elsewhere. Buber writes that "if you deny

---

59. "*Thou* confronts me. But I step into direct relation with it. Hence the relation means being chosen and choosing, suffering, and action in one; just as any action of the whole being which means the suspension of all partial actions, and consequently of all sensations of actions grounded only in their particular limitation, is bound to resemble suffering." Buber, *I and Thou*, 76–77.

60. "There is no illusory world, there is only the world. . . . Only the barrier of separation has to be destroyed. Further, no 'going beyond sense-experience' is necessary; for every experience, even the most spiritual, could yield us only an *It*." Buber, *I and Thou*, 77.

61. Buber, *I and Thou*, 78.

62. "The *I* is as indispensable to this, the supreme, as to every relation, since relation is only possible between *I and Thou*. It is not the *I*, then, that is given up, but that false self-asserting instinct that makes a man [or woman] flee to the possessing of things before the unreliable, perilous world of relation which has neither destiny nor duration and cannot be surveyed." Buber, *I and Thou*, 78.

the life of things and of conditioned being you stand before nothingness, if you hallow this life you meet the living God."[63]

The *I* eternally seeks for another *It* to control. The *I* seeks to know, and therefore control what it does not understand. The *I* does this in its naiveté, without thinking. Of course, knowledge comes from seeking that which we do not know or understand. However, seeking does not help us reach God.[64] We ought to therefore give up, or *let go*, of the instinct to seek God. God is not a treasure hunt. A treasure map gives us a sense of control. If we follow the map, destiny is within our control. The expectation is that we will find what we seek. Concerning God, the treasure is a fool's gold. And we accept this fool's gold as the real thing. This fool's gold is comfortable, easy, and predictable. For those who seek it, the validity of the gold makes little difference. It looks like the real thing, and for some that is all that matters. This treasure brings a certain satisfaction. However, the real treasure never needed to be found. It was never lost, moreover what we sought was never there. The *Thou* does not exist as thing waiting to be found.[65] The real treasure is seeing the present in light of the *Thou*.

We do not seek the *Thou*.[66] Concerning God, Buber contends, "It is a finding without seeking, a discovering of the primal, of origin."[67] The *I-It* is based on control. Impatient, the *I* does not wait for the *It*. Unwilling to wait, the *I* goes forth in confidence and belief. The *I* will not be denied. The *I-Thou*, on the other hand, is built on the idea of waiting. The *I* waits to be found by the *Thou*. Through waiting, the *I* discovers, that "this finding is not the end, but only the eternal middle, of the way."[68] The *I-It* works toward completion, thus exhausting the *It* of all its mysteries. The *I-Thou*, on the other hand, is freeing. It is a relationship without limits. Each partner

---

63. Buber, *I and Thou*, 79.

64. "To look away from the world, or to stare at it, does not help a man [or woman] to reach God; but he [or she] who sees the world in [God] stand in [God's] presence. 'Here world, there God' is the language of *It*; 'God in the world' is another language of *It*; but to eliminate or leave behind nothing at all, to include the whole world in the *Thou*, to give the world its due and its truth, to include nothing beside God but everything in [God]—this is full and complete relation." Buber, *I and Thou*, 79.

65. Or as Buber maintains, "God cannot be inferred in anything—in nature, say, as its author, or in history as its master, or in the subject as the self that is thought in it." Buber, *I and Thou*, 80.

66. "Actually there is no such thing as seeking God, for there is nothing in which [God] could not be found." Buber, *I and Thou*, 80.

67. Buber, *I and Thou*, 80.

68. Buber, *I and Thou*, 80.

increases the freedom of the other. Both enjoy the possibilities, potentiality, and freedom opened by the other.[69]

The *I-Thou* is a dynamic relationship. As a dynamic relationship, the integrity of both parties is upheld. A dynamic relationship depends on both giving, sharing, and interacting.[70] Both parties confront each other, as such neither withdraws nor dominates the other. Instead, both live in the now, in the *presentness* of each other's being. As a result, the present moment is filled with meaning so that nothing beyond it holds the same seriousness.[71]

Reality is found in the present action. The now is what matters most, and action holds the full depth and breadth of meaning.[72] The now has a direct impact on the nature and shape of reality, thus molding what occurs in the present. It is not just action alone. Rather it is a mutual action that connects the *I* to the *Thou*.[73] What is done by one, directly impacts the other. Neither party can act on its own without direct and present consequences. Mutual action unites the *I-Thou* in a lived reality.[74] As a union, the *I-Thou* are united by their present action. Such action brings each closer to the other and present reality. Consequently, the *I-Thou* relationship pushes each party toward the world rather than away from it. As such, the *I-Thou* places itself in world, living in the meaningful moment of present mutual action.

69. "In pure relation you have felt yourself to be simply dependent, as you are able to feel in no other relation—and simply free, too, as in no other time or place: you have felt yourself to be both creaturely and creative. You had the one feeling then no longer limited by the other, but you had both of them limitlessly and together." Buber, *I and Thou*, 82.

70. "What the ecstatic man calls union is the enrapturing dynamic of relation, not a unity arisen in the moment of the world's time that dissolves the *I* and the *Thou*, but the dynamic of relation itself, which can put itself before its bearer as they steadily confront one another, and cover each from the feeling of the other enraptured one." Buber, *I and Thou*, 87.

71. "What does it help my soul that it can be withdrawn anew from this world here into unity, when this world itself has of necessity no part in the unity—what does all 'enjoyment of God' profit a life that is rent in two? If that abundantly rich heavenly moment has nothing to do with my poor earthly moment—what has it then to do with me, who have still to live, in all seriousness still to live, on earth?" Buber, *I and Thou*, 87.

72. "Reality exists only in effective action, its power and depth in power and depth of effective action." Buber, *I and Thou*, 89.

73. "The most powerful and the deepest reality exists where everything enters into the effective action, without reserve the whole man [or woman] and God the all-embracing—the united *I* and the boundless *Thou*." Buber, *I and Thou*, 89.

74. Buber describes the union stating, "The united *I*: for in lived reality there is (as I have already said) the becoming one of the soul, the concentration of power, the decisive moment for a man [or woman]. But this does not involve, like that absorption, disregard of the real person." Buber, *I and Thou*, 89.

The *I-Thou* relationship dwells in the world.[75] It embraces the world as part of its own being.[76] The *I-It* is also bound to it. This is part of the *I-Thou*'s irony. The *I*'s freedom is found in that which binds it.[77] The *I* is set free in the world by the power of the *Thou*. The *I* is free when it no longer sees the world as an *It*. The objectification, or *thingification*, of the world binds not only the object, but also the one who objectifies. The world remains other, thus becoming dead to the *I*. In return, the *I* is bound to its dead object. Therefore, the *I* is unable to move beyond its own objectifying. It sees no possibilities or openness, and thus remains closed to the world and itself. The *Thou* frees the *I* to see the possibilities that exist in the world. Through the *Thou*, the *I* sees its own self as part of that world. Instead of an object, the *I* sees a living reality. The *I* sees the world as the dwelling place of the *Thou*, and the world becomes the meeting place of God.[78]

The *I-Thou* relationship is a lived relationship. Buber writes that "the situation is that it is lived, and nothing but lived, continually, ever anew, without foresight, without forethought, without prescription, in the totality of its antinomy."[79] The *I-Thou* is neither occupied by the past nor concerned about the future. Instead, the *I-Thou* embraces the present. Thus, in mutual action, *I-Thou* lives in the reality of the moment. It is not that the past and the future are unimportant. The past and future serve as extensions of the present. The past founds the present, while the future holds the destiny of the present. Neither the past nor future exist without the present. What we perceive as the past and the future is the same present continually in motion.

The perception of the past, present, and future marks the difference between the world of the *It* and the *Thou*.[80] The *It* controls the past and sets the course for the future. The *Thou*, on the other hand, is content to remain present. The world of the *Thou*, is the everlasting new. The now remains

75. The *I-Thou* is a freeing relationship. It is a relationship that opens possibilities, both for one another and in the world.

76. "Certainly the world 'dwells' in me as an image, just as I dwell in it as a thing. But it is not for that reason in me, just as I am not in it. The world and I are mutually included, the one in the other." Buber, *I and Thou*, 93.

77. Buber explains the irony stating, "This contradiction in thought, inherent in the situation of *It*, is resolved in the situation of *Thou*, which sets me free from the world in order to bind me up in solidarity of connexion with it." Buber, *I and Thou*, 94.

78. "I know nothing of a 'world' and a 'life in the world' that might separate a man from God. What is thus described is actually life with an alienated world of *It*, which experiences and uses. He [or she] who truly goes out to meet the world goes out also to God." Buber, *I and Thou*, 95.

79. Buber, *I and Thou*, 95.

80. "The world of *It* is set in the context of space and time. The world of *Thou* is not set in the context of either of these." Buber, *I and Thou*, 100.

forever new. In the *Thou*, we learn to appreciate each moment. Life's diverse moments and exchanges are encompassed under the *Thou's* unity. The *Thou* does not dominate the present like a tyrant. The present is not forced upon the *I*. Instead, the *Thou* graciously guides the *I* into the ever unfolding present. The *Thou* invites the *I* into the totality of the present. The *I* enters this relationship without leaving anything behind, bringing all its spheres of relation into its relationship with the *Thou*.[81] Every moment, interaction, and relationship is brought into the presence of the eternal *Thou*. The *Thou* shines its light onto the life of the *I*, illuminating its entire being. So much so that it encounters the presence of the *Thou* everywhere. The *Thou* brings a sudden awareness of *presentness* of each moment. The *I-Thou* relationship is an immersive awareness of the *Thou's* eternal presence,[82] bringing the fragmented life into unity. All the alienated aspects of individual existence find a new unity in the *Thou*. The *I*, previously broken and estranged, finds a wholeness in the presence of the *Thou*.[83] In such a presence, "what confronts us has blossomed into the full reality of the *Thou*. Here alone, then, as reality that cannot be lost, are gazing and being gazed upon, knowing and being known, loving and being loved."[84]

The *I* gazes into the eyes of the *Thou*. In return, the *Thou* gazes back. But there is something familiar about this gaze. It is like recognizing someone across a crowded room. At first, we are unsure if the other really is someone we know. There is a moment of hesitation as we cross the room toward the other, unwilling to fully commit in fear of being wrong. We want to avoid embarrassment, but that fear begins to wash away as we move closer. All that fear is forgotten once we recognize our friend. The *I* and the *Thou* confront one another not as strangers, but as familiar friends. However, the gaze does not end at friendship. Under the gaze of the *Thou*, the *I* confronts its long lost lover. In love, the *I* meets God.[85]

81. There are three spheres of relation according to Buber. He writes, "First, our life with nature, in which the relation clings to the threshold of speech. Second, our life with [humanity], in which the relation takes on the form of speech. Third, our life with spiritual beings, where the relation, being without speech, yet begets it." Buber, *I and Thou*, 101.

82. "In every sphere in its own way, through each process of becoming that is present to us, we look out toward the fringe of the eternal *Thou*; in each we are aware of a breath from the eternal *Thou*; in each *Thou* we address the eternal *Thou*." Buber, *I and Thou*, 101.

83. "Through every sphere shines the one present." Buber, *I and Thou*, 101.

84. Buber, *I and Thou*, 103.

85. "The relation with [humanity] is the real simile of the relation with God; in it true address received true response; except that in God's response everything, the universe, is made manifest as language." Buber, *I and Thou*, 103.

Nothing about this meeting is simple. It is both easy and difficult at the same time. Describing this meeting, Buber writes, "At times it is like a light breath, at times like a wrestling-bout, but always—it *happens*."[86] The meeting between *I* and *Thou* is bound to happen. We cannot prevent or hide from this meeting. The *Thou* will confront the *I*, not as experience, but as relationship.[87] Invoking or creating this meeting is not the problem. We have no choice over when, where, and how this meeting will occur. The *I* is destined to encounter its *Thou*. However, this meeting is not always recognized. The *I-It* experience dominates perception, so that all meetings are placed in this framework. The relationship of *I-Thou* is mistakenly perceived as an *I-It*.

Being undefinable, *I-Thou* is difficult to discern. We know that there is a meeting but understanding that meeting is beyond our comprehension. We know that in meeting the *Thou*, something remarkable has happened. Meaning is there, under the surface, but it remains elusive. Our instinct is to search for this meaning objectively. In the *I-It*, we desire to know and understand the meaning of it all. All of our resources are deployed to find this meaning. And despite all that we do, this search for meaning is unsatisfying.[88] We search above and beyond for this meaning, but it escapes our grasp. The irony is that we never had to search for this meaning. The meaning was, or rather *is*, there already. This meaning is not above or beyond our lives. It is, in fact, already present in our lives. Meaning lives in the now, that is present action.[89] Meaning is already there in every person and action. This meaning waits patiently for its chance to be born into the world. We are the midwives of meaning.[90]

86. Buber, *I and Thou*, 109 (emphasis original).

87. This meeting, "is not an 'experience' that stirs in the receptive soul and grows to perfect blessedness; rather, in that moment something happens to the [person]." Buber, *I and Thou*, 109.

88. "You do not know how to exhibit and define the meaning of life, you have no formula or picture for it, and yet it has more certitude for you than the perceptions of your senses." Buber, *I and Thou*, 110.

89. One expects the search for meaning to be hard, and that is not to say it is not. Meaning is obviously difficult to discern. Yet, we make it all the more difficult by searching anywhere and everywhere for this meaning. Buber writes that "this meaning is not that of 'another life,' but that of this life of ours, not one of a world 'yonder' but that of this world of ours, and it desires its confirmation in the life and in relation with this world. This meaning can be received, but not experienced; it cannot be experience but it can be done, and this is its purpose with us." Buber, *I and Thou*, 111.

90. "The assurance I have of it does not wish to be sealed within me, but it wishes to be born by me into world." I Buber, *I and Thou*, 111.

Meaning is born in present, in the relationship of the *I-Thou*. Once born, this meaning stands before the *I*. Face-to-face with mystery, the *I* enters into this mystery, not to solve it, but to live in it. In mystery, Buber states, "We have come near to God, but not nearer to unveiling being or solving its riddle. We have felt release, but not discovered a 'solution.'"[91] This is the paradox of the *Thou*. Despite the closeness, we are no closer to solving the mystery. The *I-Thou* is inexpressible, undefinable, and unpredictable. This is frustrating for the *I*, which seeks to define and solve all mysteries.[92] It matters not that this is the mystery of the *Thou*, of God. The *I* desires to solve the *Thou* by whatever means possible, even if that means transforming God into an object. The *I* seeks to bring the *Thou* into space and time.[93]

The desire to objectify God is a misunderstanding of the encounter itself. The irony is that the more we define God, the further we move from God. This is because the *I* misunderstands the purpose of the search. The purpose of the search was never to find God. Instead, as Buber explains, "Meeting with God does not come to [humanity] in order that [we] may concern [ourselves] with God, but in order that [we] may confirm that there is meaning in the world."[94] We who searche for God will in fact miss God.[95] The search for God will inevitable make God into an object.[96]

The search for God is not a search at all. It is entering into a relationship with the present.[97] Consequently, we cannot find God, we encounter

91. Buber, *I and Thou*, 111.

92. Humanity is not content with mystery. Buber explains that one "is not content with the inexpressible confirmation of meaning, but wants to see this confirmation stretched out as something that can be continually taken up and handled, a continuum unbroken in space and time that insures [one's] life at every point and every moment." Buber, *I and Thou*, 113.

93. "[One] longs for extension in space, for the representation in which the community of the faithful is united with its God." Buber, *I and Thou*, 114.

94. Buber, *I and Thou*, 115.

95. Buber writes that "the man [or woman] who seeks God . . . instead of allowing the gift to work itself out, reflects about the Giver—misses both." Buber, *I and Thou*, 116.

96. "Reflexion, on the other hand, makes God into an object. Its apparent turning towards the primal source belongs in truth to the universal movement away from it." Buber, *I and Thou*, 116.

97. Richard Rohr states, "The belief that God is 'out there,' is the basic dualism that is tearing us all apart. That's why we have raped the earth, why we have such poor understanding of our bodies, our economy, and our health. That's why we live such distraught and divided lives. What is worse is that Jesus came precisely to put it all together. He said, 'This, the human, is good. The material, the physical can be trusted and enjoyed. This world is the hiding place of God and the revelation of God.' We believe, for example, in the resurrection of the *body*, which says material and physical

God in the presence of the other. The world is the place of encounter. The world is realm of the *I-Thou*, and therefore the realm of God.

THOU, THE PRESENT, AND RITUAL ACTION

Theology is a relationship. It exists as the dynamic mutual sharing of the *I-Thou*. In this manner it is unique. Theology cannot stand apart from the object of its study.[98] It cannot exist outside of its *Thou*, theology has no meaning outside the *I-Thou* relationship. It is unable to hold the other at a distance to better examine it as would a science. Theology cannot exist as a science or as a discipline with the ability to determine its own course and fate. The illusion that theology charts its own path is a tantamount to living in a delusion. Theology is done under the precept that is it something that it is not. It is doing philosophy by another name. Despite this theology is still considered a discipline, but its status as a discipline is questionable.[99] As a relationship, theology is less a discipline and more so a meeting with the *Thou*. Theology is an entering into relationship, and therefore its actions model relationship. This is not just any relationship. Theology is confronted by and enters into a relationship with the *Thou* that confronts us all. Theology lives in relationship with the now.

Theology lives in the reality of the present. By being in relationship with the *Thou*, theology is opened toward the present. The *Thou* opens the eyes of theology, thus helping it to see its true purpose. The gaze of theology is neither the past nor future. Its gaze is the present, where it neither seeks nor controls. Theology longs for the past, dreams of the future, but it misses the present. Only in the present is theology freed. The *Thou*, the other, sets theology free, and theology is set free to live in the present with its *Thou*.

---

realities are a part of the mystery. It is not just an accident or a mistake or a burden. This bodily self, this physical world, participates in whatever it is that God is doing." Rohr, *Everything Belongs*, 119.

98. Unlike other disciplines, say for example philosophy.

99. Pattison is critical of theology as a discipline. He suggests to "abolish free-standing, independent theology and religious studies departments. This will force those who are trained and interested in religious ideas, traditions and insights to work at them in the interdisciplinary market place of ideas." Pattison continues, "Wherever possible, avoid the use of the self-ghettoizing term 'theology.' Theology is a vague and pluralistic term anyway. Often it adds nothing to debate and its use may be ideologically obfuscating. The designation of discourse as theological allows people prematurely to ignore insights that they might otherwise find useful. 'Theology' has too much ideological and historical baggage attached to it. Those theologians who want their ideas to be taken seriously in the public arena should eschew pigeonholing themselves by using it." Pattison, *Challenge of Practical Theology*, 223–24.

In the presence of the *Thou* theology finally discovers how to *be*. Theology discovers how to *be* in its present moment of mutuality with its *Thou*. Theology learns how to *be* when it has ceased to be for *itself*. The *Thou* moves theology's gaze toward the other. *Thou* teaches theology to see the other. In the other, theology gazes upon its *Thou*. Theology discovers the God it has so passionately sought after.

The gaze of the *Thou* lives in the gaze of others. The present, the world of the other, is a place of meeting and activity. These others, whom theology has ignored, are finally seen as bearers of meaning. Their actions and behaviors are seen in a new light. People become the meeting place of the *Thou*, and the importance of their actions are finally recognized. Theology is renewed with a sense of purpose through people. It is renewed with a vision beyond the self. With the help of the *Thou*, theology learns to see others as partners rather than objects. A meeting of strangers becomes a meeting of lovers. Theology becomes a matter of falling in love with people.

Theology does not save the world. *Theology is saved by the world*. It is saved by the world in order to be for the world. This is what the *Thou* shows theology. Theology finds itself in the work it does for and with others. Theology must be a theology of the people or nothing at all. It should concern itself with the things that people do, their actions and behaviors. Doing theology is also being-with. Therefore, theology is a matter of acting, working, and being-with others.

Relationship thus makes ritual action immensely important to theology. Ritual action is the mutual action between the *I-Thou*, theology, and God. Ritual action serves as the dynamic flux, the instable element, in an *I-Thou* theology. Theology lives in the moment of mutual relationship and change between itself, the other, and God. Ritual action, the outward giving and receiving of relationship, serves as the catalyst of the now. Ritual action is the embodiment of the present. Ritual action keeps our wayward eyes from drifting too far beyond the now. Ritual action draws us toward the *Thou*. Theology's relationship is thus twofold. Ritual action draws the gaze of theology toward the other, the participants of ritual. This pull toward the other is also a pull toward the *Thou*. Ritual action is mutually dynamic and changing. This mutually dynamic relationship saves theology. Theology is saved to become the expression and embodiment of the *I-Thou*. As such, theology is saved for relationship to *become* relationship itself. Ritual action teaches theology to becoming the living, dynamic, and mutual embodiment of the *I-Thou*.

The present saves theology from the need to objectify. Theology no longer sees the past or the future. Instead, theology lives in the fullness of the present. When theology no longer sees the past or the future it is saved from turning people and actions into objects. No longer preoccupied with the past or future, theology can focus on the present moment. As a result, theology can help us know the other deeply and personally. When the other is no longer an object or a thing, theology can form personal relationships. Theology as relationship is only possible if it is a theology of the present. This is by necessity, for there is nothing to relate to beyond the present.

We cannot form a relationship with the ghost of the past or the potential of the future. That is not to say that the past and future are unimportant for theological understanding. Nevertheless, the temptation exists to either stay in one or the other. We can dwell comfortably in the past without much concern for the present. In addition, we can crave for a future that does not exist. Perhaps this future will exist, but not yet. Accordingly, to enter the present does not require us to throw away either the past or the future. Instead, the past and future are brought into the present. What has happened and what will happen become the domain of the present. The past and future enter the relationship with the present. People, their pasts and futures, meet and dwell in the present. The action of the present is simultaneously the action of the past and future. The present is not a vacuum, but the place of dynamic interaction of what has been and what is to come. In a matter of speaking, the past and future find fruition in the present. The heritage and destinies of people find their fulfillment in the present. People do not exist in either the past or the future. They exist in the now. Therefore, the fullness of their being, including their actions, is only possible in the present. We cannot *be* in either the past or future, nor can we act in either the past or future. We can only *be* and act in the present. *Presentness* is the fullness of being. We cannot *be* anymore than we are right now at this very moment.

Therefore, any theological relationship can only exist in the present. Such a theology can only engage with people in the here and now. Thus, theological relationship is contingent on entering the fullness of the present. Theology, if it is to be in any sense relational, should be rooted in the present moment. What is happening now is therefore a theological imperative. The imperative of the now is the imperative of action. Action defines the present. The present is always a matter of doing, and the present is ever unfolding. The present is incapable of remaining still. It continues to push forward into eternity. Our own personal present will inevitable end in death, but that eternal present remains forever. The present continues to act. A relational practical theology should therefore bind itself to the present. Theology binds itself to the present through personal relationship. Others and their actions become part of theology itself. That is theology is no longer seen as separate from the things people do. What people do, their actions and behaviors, becomes theology itself. The present becomes a theological present.

The theological present can only occur once theology abandons its *I-It* mentality. Theology will always be on the outside, an invader, as long as people and action are objectified. An outsider theology lives outside the present and is thus increasingly irrelevant. Theology does not belong in the world of the *I-It* and objectification. Even though this is where many theologians want to dwell. The *I-It* world is comfortable and easy, but it is also increasingly hostile. Theology does not belong in the *I-It* world. It is not a place where it can survive.[100]

A relational practical theology dwells in the theological present where it can thrive *with* rather than apart. As such, engaging ritual action becomes theology's gateway into the present. Ritual action becomes more than an object of study, it is a place of encounter and relationship. Ritual action embodies the present because it can only occur in the present. Ritual action cannot be done apart from it appointed moment. That is ritual action is unable to exist in either the past or the future. When ritual action occurs, it occurs in the now. As such it carries the very idea of *presentness*. Ritual action's *presentness* is the key to theology's own *presentness*. Theology learns to be relational by learning from the relational. Ritual action is an opportunity for meeting. Theology places itself before action itself, the present, to become the present. Becoming the present means engaging and learning from the present. This means a fundament shift in theological perspective. Rather than investigating ritual action, theology learns from it. There is a reversal of roles in the present. Ritual action is the teacher and theology is the learner. Entering the present means letting go of what we know.

Living in the present means that theologians must learn from the participants of ritual. And therefore, theologians must also lose their privileged status as experts. The present means doing away with experts and objects. Ritual action is no longer something studied. It loses the stigma of being an object or thing. Ritual action helps to move theologians into the present. Ritual action beckons us to enter its world. It calls the theologian to experience its reality. Moreover, it calls for the theologian to go beyond experience. The reality of the present beckons the theologian to enter relationship. The theologian's role is redefined in the relationship of the present. Ritual action ushers the theologian into a new and more fulfilling role as *Thou*. The goal of the theologian is to be *Thou*. The theologian is a *Thou* for the world. The present is the meeting place of the *Thou* for both the theologian and the world. They meet as *Thou* for one other. In return, they embody the *Thou* for

100. The *I-It* world is a natural fit for STEM (Science, Technology, Engineering, and Mathematics), psychology and the social sciences, and even philosophy. Theology struggles where these thrive. Whereas these should objectively, and quite correctly, stand apart from their subject, theology cannot do so.

the other. Ritual action does not just usher the theologian into the present. Ritual action ushers us into a relationship with God.

A LESSON FOR THEOLOGY

The goal cannot be to explain or even interpret the OFWB ordinance of the washing of the saints' feet. Foot washing was never the focus per se, yet paradoxically, foot washing has had everything to do with this work. Foot washing is not just something we investigate. It is something that informs and changes everything we do. Foot washing exemplifies an action that refuses objectification, as do all ritual actions. Consequently, foot washing reversed the roles between the theologian and the people. In the end, foot washing determined the course of theology.

Foot washing demonstrates the importance of allowing ritual actions to speak on its own. The OFWBs never required a theologian to tell them the meaning of their ritual actions. Their actions were already meaningful. Foot washing does not need its meaning explained or created. All that is needed is the space and opportunity to allow this practice to speak for itself. Foot washing was never silent or mute. For the meaning was already speaking and had been doing so for generations. This practice speaks through OFWBs. Foot washing speaks through the use of stories, experiences, and actions. Foot washing speaks each time it is practiced. Foot washing speaks, and the theologian listens. The theologian listens to the action through its participants and their actions.

Foot washing embraces the other, the stranger, as should the theologian. Thus, foot washing serves as a metaphor for us. It redefines our interpretation. The interpreted becomes the interpreter. Ritual action is therefore more than something we experience. It is a means of participating and entering into relationship with the people of the practice. The practice explains how theology should be.

The OFWB practice of foot washing enters into a partnership with theology. That is foot washing and theology share one and the same action. Foot washing and theology wash one another. For OFWBs this is literal whereas for theology it is metaphorical. Both are learning to serve the other. In this sense, foot washing is the physical manifestation of theology. A relational practical theology, is washing feet. Furthermore, theology washes the feet of others when theologians open themselves to the experiences and conversations of others. Theology washes the feet of others through relationship. A relational practical theology is a theology of foot washing. A theologian serves the world. We need to be the voice of the voiceless, the powerless, and the marginalized. Simply put, theologians must serve the *other*.

For the most part, the story of OFWB foot washing has remained untold. Of course, this is not to say this ritual action was silent. The impact it has had on the lives, experiences, and relationships of OFWBs has been monumental. Foot washing has changed both laypersons and pastors. In this sense foot washing has been heard, but foot washing also speaks toward the outside world. This voice speaks in a noisy world. The small size and relatively obscurity of foot washing means that unless we are listening, it is not likely to be heard. It does not mean that this voice, small as it is, is unimportant. On the contrary, volume does not equal importance. Even the smallest of voices can have powerful meanings. Their voice is a gift. The theologian is served by the people. People, with their voices and experiences, wash the theologian's feet. The theologian washes their feet in return by magnifying that voice. The theologian helps to make that voice heard. The theologian magnifies that meaning so that others can hear it. The theologian amplifies the voices of the people, making them heard far and wide.

Foot washing is remarkable in the ways it has unified and shaped the OFWB. Foot washing is their present, and thus the convergence of both the OFWB past and future. Foot washing carriers them ever forward in the continual living moment of the now. Generation after generation of OFWBs experience this ritual action. More importantly, they enter into relationship with the divine and in each other through foot washing. Foot washing is the OFWB gateway to relationship. It is their model of the *I-Thou*.

UNTIL WE MEET AGAIN

Foot washing shifts our perspective from analysis to relationship. As a work of practical theology, the purpose of this work was to enter into a relationship with the people of foot washing. Hopefully, it was a success, however marginal. Start to finish, this work was deeply influenced by the Original Free Will Baptists. This work is deeply indebted to them and their ritual action of foot washing. Each line is an attempt to give a voice to the deep meanings of foot washing. In this manner, we can only hope that the feet of the Original Free Will Baptist were also washed. This washing and being washed defines a relational practical theology. It offers a truly human path to human redemption:

> After he had washed their feet, had put on his robe, and had returned to the table, he said to them, "Do you know what I have done to you? You call me Teacher and Lord—and you

are right, for that is what I am. So if I, your Lord and Teacher, have washed your feet, you also ought to wash one another's feet. For I have set you an example, that you also should do as I have done to you. Very truly, I tell you, servants are not greater than their master, nor are messengers greater than the one who sent them. If you know these things, you are blessed if you do them.[101]

101. John 13:12–17 (NRSV).

Bibliography

Allison, Richard E. "Foot Washing." In *The Encyclopedia of Christianity*, edited by Erwin Fahlbusch et al., 322–23. Grand Rapids: Eerdmans, 2001.

Association of Religion Data Archives. "Convention of Original Free Will Baptists States (2010)." *QuickLists* (blog) *Thearda.com*, accessed June 2016, http://www.thearda.com/ql2010/QL_S_2010_2_1047c.asp.

Augustine. *Confessions*. Translated by Henry Chadwick. Oxford: Oxford University Press, 2008.

Barth, Karl. *The Doctrine of the Word of God: Second Half*. Edited by G. W. Bromiley and T. F. Torrance. Edinburgh: T. & T. Clark, 1963.

Bauman, Zygmunt. *Liquid Love*. Cambridge: Polity, 2003.

Bell, Catherine. "Ritual, Change, and Changing Rituals." In *Foundations in Ritual Studies: A Reader for Students of Christian Worship*, edited by Paul Bradshaw and John Mellow, 166–98 London: SPCK, 2007.

———. *Ritual: Perspectives and Dimensions*. New York: Oxford, 1997.

———. *Ritual Theory, Ritual Practice*. New York: Oxford, 2009.

Bonhoeffer, Dietrich. *Dietrich Bonhoeffer Works*. Vol. 6, *Ethics*. Edited by Clifford J. Green. Minneapolis: Fortress, 2005.

———. *Life Together*. Translated by John W. Doberstein. New York: Harper & Row, 1954.

———. *Sanctorum Communio: A Dogmatic Inquiry into the Sociology of the Church*. London: Collins, 1963.

Bourdieu, Pierre. *The Logic of Practice*. Translated by Richard Nice. Stanford: Stanford University Press, 1990.

———. *Outline of a Theory of Practice*. Cambridge: Cambridge University Press, 1987.

Bremborg, Anna Davidsson. "Interviewing." In *The Routledge Handbook of Research Methods in the Study of Religion*, edited by Michael Stausberg and Steven Engler, 310–22. New York: Routledge, 2011.

Buber, Martin. *I and Thou*. Translated by Ronald Gregor Smith. New York: Charles Scribner's Sons, 1958.

Butler, Judith, and Athena Athanasiou. *Disposession: The Performative in the Political*. Cambridge: Polity, 2013.

Caputo, John D. *After the Death of God*. Edited by Jeffrey W. Robbins. Columbia University Press: New York, 2007.

———. *Deconstruction in a Nutshell: A Conversation with Jacques Derrida*. New York: Fordham University Press, 1997.

———. *The Prayers and Tears of Jacques Derrida: Religion without Religion.* Bloomington: Indiana University Press, 1997.

———. *Radical Hermeneutics: Repetition, Deconstruction, and the Hermeneutic Project.* Bloomington: Indiana University Press, 1987.

———. "Spectral Hermeneutics: On the Weakness of God and the Theology of the Event." In *After the Death of God*, edited by Jeffrey W. Robbins, 47-85. New York: Columbia University Press, 2007.

———. *Truth: Philosophy in Transit.* London: Penguin, 2013.

———. *The Weakness of God: A Theology of the Event.* Bloomington: Indiana University Press, 2006.

———. *What Would Jesus Deconstruct?: The Good News of Postmodernism for the Church.* Grand Rapids: Baker, 2007.

Certeau, Michel de. *The Practice of Everyday Life.* Translated by Steven Rendall. Los Angeles: University of California Press, 1988.

Cherry, Floyd B. *An Introduction to Original Free Will Baptist.* Ayden, NC: Free Will Baptist, 1989.

———. *Original Free Will Baptist Believe: A Study of the Articles of Faith of Original Free Will Baptist.* Edited by Floyd Cherry. Pine Level, NC: Carolina Bible Institute & Seminary, 1996.

Colebrook, Claire. "Difference." In *A Companion to Derrida*, edited by Zeynep Direk and Leonard Lawlor, 57–71. Malden, MA: Blackwell, 2014.

Cupitt, Don. *The Fountain: A Secular Theology.* London: SCM, 2010.

Dastur, Francoise. "Play and Messianicity: The Question of Time and History in Derrida's Deconstruction." In *A Companion to Derrida*, edited by Zeynep Direk and Leonard Lawlor, 179–93. Malden, MA: Blackwell, 2014.

Derrida, Jacques. *The Margins of Philosophy.* Translated by Alan Bass. Chicago: University of Chicago Press, 1986.

———. *Of Grammatology.* Translated by Gayatri Chakravorty Spivak. Baltimore: Johns Hopkins University Press, 1976.

———. *Positions.* Translated by Alan Bass. Chicago: University of Chicago Press, 1981.

———. *Writing and Difference.* Translated by Alan Bass. Chicago: University of Chicago Press, 1978.

Eliade, Mircea. *The Sacred and the Profane: The Nature of Religion.* Translated by Willard R. Trask. New York: Harcourt, Brace & World, 1959.

Elden, Stuart. "Introduction." In *Rhythmanalysis: Space, Time, and Everyday Life*, by Henri Lefebvre, 1–9. London: Bloomsbury, 2013.

Fischer, J. A. "Washing of the Feet." In vol. 14 of *New Catholic Encyclopedia*, edited by W. J. O'Shea, 653. Detroit: Gale, 2003.

Franke, William. *A Philosophy of the Unsayable.* Notre Dame: University of Notre Dame Press, 2014.

Fromm, Erich. *The Art of Loving.* New York: Harper & Row, 1956.

Gadamer, Hans-Georg. "Image and Gesture." In *The Relevance of the Beautiful and Other Essays*, edited by Robert Bernasconi, 74–82. Cambridge: Cambridge University Press, 1998.

———. "The Speechless Image." In *The Relevance of the Beautiful and Other Essays*, edited by Robert Bernasconi, 83–91. Cambridge: Cambridge University Press, 1998.

———. *Truth and Method.* Translated by Joel Wensheimer and Donald G. Marshall. Continuum: London, 2004.

Geertz, Clifford. *The Interpretation of Cultures.* New York: Basic, 1973.

Gould, Glenn. "Bonus Track Glenn Gould Discusses His Performances of The *Goldberg Variations* with Tim Page, August 22, 1982." From *Glenn Gould: A State Of Wonder: The Complete Goldberg Variations 1955 & 1981.* New York: Sony Classical, 2002. Compact disc.

Griffin, J. C. *The Upper Room Ought.* Ayden, NC: Free Will Baptist, 1927.

Grimes, Ronald L. *Beginnings in Ritual Studies: Revised Edition.* Colombia: University of South Carolina Press, 1995.

Gutting, Gary. "The Obscurity of 'Différance.'" In *A Companion to Derrida*, edited by Zeynep Direk and Leonard Lawlor, 72–88. Malden, MA: Blackwell, 2014.

Hawking, Stephen. *A Brief History of Time: From the Big Bang to Black Holes.* New York: Bantam Books, 1988.

Heidegger, Martin. *Being and Time.* Translated by John Macquarrie and Edward Robinson. New York: HarperCollins, 2008.

———. *An Introduction to Metaphysics.* Translated by Gregory Fried and Richard Polt. New Haven: Yale University Press, 2000.

———. *On the Way to Language.* Translated by Peter D. Hertz. New York: Harper & Row, 1971.

Hines, David. "Tell Me the Story so that I Can Live the Story." Presentation, Mid-Year Spiritual Banquet OFWB Ministerial Association. University of Mount Olive, April 1, 2005.

Jennings, Theodore W. "On Ritual Knowledge." *The Journal of Religion* 62 (April 1982) 111–27.

Kent, H. A., Jr. "Foot Washing." In *Evangelical Dictionary of Theology*, edited by Walter A. Elwell, 419. Grand Rapids, Baker Books, 1997.

Kerr, Fergus. *Theology after Wittgenstein.* London: SPCK, 1997.

Lefebvre, Henri. *The Production of Space.* Translated by Donald Nicholson-Smith. Malden, MA: Blackwell, 1991.

———. *Rhythmanalysis: Space, Time, and Everyday Life.* London: Bloomsbury, 2013.

Lyotard, Jean-Francois. *The Postmodern Condition: A Report on Knowledge.* Translated by Geoff Bennington and Brian Massumi. Minneapolis: University of Minneapolis Press, 1997.

Marion, Jean-Luc. *God Without Being.* Chicago: The University of Chicago Press, 2012.

McBeth, H. Leon. *Four Centuries of Baptist Witness.* Nashville: Broadman, 1987.

Nancy, Jean-Luc. *Being Singular Plural.* Translated by Robert D. Richardson and Anne E. O'Byrne. Stanford: Stanford University Press, 2000.

———. *The Inoperative Community.* Translated by Peter Connor et al. Minneapolis: University of Minnesota Press, 1991.

———. "Shattered Love." Translated by Lisa Garbus and Simona Sawhney. In *The Inoperative Community*, edited by Peter Connor, 82–109. Minneapolis: University of Minnesota Press, 1991.

Navarro-Rivera, Juhem, and Barry A. Kosmin. "Surveys and Questionnaires." In *The Routledge Handbook of Research Methods in the Study of Religion*, edited by Michael Stausberg and Steven Engler, 395–420. New York: Routledge, 2011.

Norris, Christopher. *Deconstruction.* London: Routledge, 2004.

North Carolina State Convention of Original Free Will Baptists. *The Articles of Faith and Principles of Church Government for Original Free Will Baptists (Of the English General Baptist Heritage).* Ayden, NC: Free Will Baptist, 2001.

Otto, Rudolf. *The Idea of the Holy: An Inquiry Into the Non-Rational Factor in the Idea of the Divine and its Relation to the Rational.* Translated by John W. Harvey. Oxford: Oxford University Press, 1979.

Patterson, Sue. *Word, Words and World.* Bern, Switzerland: Peter Lang, 2013.

Pattison, Stephen. *The Challenge of Practical Theology: Selected Essays.* London: Jessica Kingsley Publishers, 2007.

Pelt, Michael R. *A History of Original Free Will Baptist.* Mount Olive, NC: Mount Olive College Press, 1996.

Phillips, D. Z. *Faith After Foundationalism: Critiques and Alternatives.* Boulder, CO: Westview, 1995.

Pinson, J. Matthew. *A Free Will Baptist Handbook: Heritage, Beliefs, and Ministries.* Nashville: Randall House Publications, 1998.

Merleau-Ponty, M. *Phenomenology of Perception.* Translated by Colin Smith. London: Routledge, 1999.

Power, David. *Sacrament: The Language of God's Giving.* New York: Crossroad, 1999.

Rahner, Karl. *Foundations of Christian Faith: An Introduction to the Idea of Christianity.* Translated by William V. Dych. New York: Crossroad, 2006.

———. *Theological Investigations.* Vol. 4, *More Recent Writings.* Translated by Kevin Smyth. New York: Seabury, 1974.

Rappaport, Roy A. *Ritual and Religion in the Making of Humanity.* Cambridge: Cambridge University Press, 1999.

Ricoeur, Paul. "Existence and Hermeneutics." In *The Philosophy of Paul Ricoeur: An Anthology of His Work*, edited by Charles E. Reagan and David Stewart, 97–108. Boston: Beacon, 1978.

———. "Explanation and Understanding: On Some Remarkable Connections Among the Theory of the Text, Theory of Action, and Theory of History." In *The Philosophy of Paul Ricoeur: An Anthology of His Work*, edited by Charles E. Reagan and David Steward, 149–66. Boston: Beacon, 1978.

———. "Hermeneutical Function of Distanciation." In *Hermeneutics and the Human Sciences*, edited by John B. Thompson, 131–44. Cambridge: Cambridge University Press, 1988.

———. *Interpretation Theory: Discourse and the Surplus of Meaning.* Fort Worth: Texas Christian University Press, 1976.

———. "The Model of the Text: Meaningful Action Considered as a Text." In *Paul Ricoeur: Hermeneutics and the Human Sciences*, edited by John B. Thompson, 197–221. Cambridge: Cambridge University Press, 1981.

———. "Philosophy and Religious Language." In *Figuring the Sacred: Religion, Narrative, and Imagination,* edited by Mark I. Wallace, 35–47. Fortress: Minneapolis, 1995.

———. "Structure, Word, Event." In *The Philosophy of Paul Ricoeur: An Anthology of His Work*, edited by Charles E. Reagan and David Stewart, 109–19. Boston: Beacon, 1978.

———. "The Task of Hermeneutics." In *Hermeneutics and the Human Sciences*, edited by John B. Thompson, 43–62. Cambridge: Cambridge University Press, 1988.

Rohr, Richard. *Everything Belongs: The Gift of Contemplative Prayer.* New York: Crossroad, 2003.

Rorty, Richard. *Philosophy and the Mirror of Nature*. Princeton: Princeton University Press, 1980.

Sartre, Jean-Paul. *No Exit and Three Other Plays*. New York: Vintage, 1989.

Scharen, Christian, and Aana Marie Vigen. *Ethnography as Christian Theology and Ethics*. Edited by Christian Scharen and Aana Marie Vigen. Continuum: London, 2011.

———. "What is Ethnography?" In *Ethnography as Christian Theology and Ethics*, edited by Christian Scharen and Aana Marie Vigen, 3–27. New York: Continuum, 2011.

Scheerer, Robert, dir. *Star Trek: The Next Generation*. Season 7, episode 10, "Inheritance." Aired November 20, 1993. Hollywood: Paramount Studios, 2002. DVD.

Schleiermacher, Friedrich. *Hermeneutics and Criticism: And Other Writings*. Translated by Andrew Bowie. Cambridge: Cambridge University Press, 1998.

Searle, Mark. "Ritual." In *The Study of Liturgy*, edited by Cheslyn Jones et al., 51–60. Oxford: Oxford University Press, 1992.

Shepherd, Andrew. *The Gift of the Other: Levinas, Derrida, and a Theology of Hospitality*. Eugene, OR: Pickwick, 2014.

Smith, James K. A. *Imagining the Kingdom: How Worship Works*. Grand Rapids: Baker Academic, 2013.

———. *Jacques Derrida: Live Theory*. New York: Continuum, 2005.

Smith, Jonathan Z. *To Take Place: Toward Theory in Ritual*. Chicago: University of Chicago Press, 1992.

Stevenson, George. "A Humbling Act Commanded by Christ." *The Free Will Baptist* 82 (1967) 4–5, 15.

Swinton, John, and Harriet Mowat. *Practical Theology and Qualitative Research*. London: SCM, 2006.

Taylor, Mark C. *Erring: A Postmodern A/theology*. Chicago: University of Chicago Press, 1984.

The Convention of Original Free Will Baptist Churches. "Directories/Resources," accessed November 11, 2018, http://www.ofwb.org/directories-resources/.

———. "Our Ministries," accessed November 11, 2018, http://www.ofwb.org/our-ministries/.

Tillich, Paul. *The Courage to Be*. New Haven: Yale University Press, 1980.

———. *Dynamics of Faith*. New York: Harper & Row, 1965.

———. *The Eternal Now*. New York, Charles Scribner's Sons, 1963.

———. "Knowledge Through Love." In *The Shaking of the Foundations*, by Paul Tillich, 113–17. London: Pelican Books, 1962.

———. *Love, Power, and Justice: Ontological Analyses and Ethical Applications*. London: Oxford University, 1972.

———. *Systematic Theology*. Vol. 1. Chicago: University of Chicago Press, 1961.

———. *Systematic Theology*. Vol. 3. Chicago: University of Chicago Press, 1963.

———. *Ultimate Concern: Tillich in Dialogue*. Edited by D. Mackenzie Brown. New York: Harper & Row, 1965.

———. "You Are Accepted." In *The Shaking of the Foundations*, by Paul Tillich, 155–65. London: Pelican Books, 1962.

Tracy, David. *The Analogical Imagination: Christian Theology and the Culture of Pluralism*. New York: Crossroad, 1981.

———. *Blessed Rage for Order: The New Pluralism in Theology*. Chicago: University of Chicago Press, 1996.

———. "Fragments: The Spiritual Situation of Our Times." In *God, the Gift, and Postmodernism*, edited by John D. Caputo and Michael J. Scanlon, 170–84. Bloomington: Indiana University, 1999.

———. *Plurality and Ambiguity: Hermeneutics, Religion, Hope*. Chicago: The University of Chicago Press, 1987.

Uzukwu, Elochukwu E. *Worship as Body Language: Introduction to Christian Worship: An African Orientation*. Collegeville, MN: Liturgical, 1997.

Vasquez, Manuel A. *More than Belief: A Materialist Theory of Religion*. New York: Oxford University Press, 2011.

Vattimo, Gianni. *After Christianity*. Translated by Luca D'Isanto. New York: Colombia University Press, 2002.

———. *A Farewell to Truth*. Translated by William McCuaig. New York: Columbia University Press, 2011.

Ward, Graham. "Postmodern Theology." In *The Modern Theologians: An Introduction to Christian Theology Since 1918*, edited by David F. Ford and Rachel Muers, 322–38. Malden, MA: Blackwell, 2005.

Westphal, Merold. *Whose Community? Which Interpretation? Philosophical Hermeneutics for the Church*. Grand Rapids: Baker Academic, 2009.

Wolfson, Eliot. *Language, Eros, Being: Kabbalistic Hermeneutics and Poetic Imagination*. New York: Fordham University Press, 2005.

Winfield, Nicole. "Holy Thursday: Pope Washes the Feet of 12 inmates, 1 infant." *AP NEWS* (blog) *apnews.com*, April 2, 2015, https://apnews.com/e542c492c807465eb8270fd3e7e2ebe9.

Wittgenstein, Ludwig. *The Blue and Brown Books: Preliminary Studies for the 'Philosophical Investigations.'* New York: Harper & Row, 1958.

———. *Philosophical Investigations*. Translated by G. E. M. Anscombe. New York: Macmillian, 1958.

———. *Tractatus Logico-Philosophicus*. Translated by D. F. Pears and B. F. McGuinness. New York: Routledge, 1974.

38017287R00141

Printed in Poland
by Amazon Fulfillment
Poland Sp. z o.o., Wrocław